Accessible and informative, timely and pertinent, this cultural history of Shakespeare and Indian theatre covers a vast range of styles and traditions. With a truly impressive sweep, the study introduces us to issues of translation, reception, education and performance, adjusting the conventional focus of attention showcasing continuing negotiations with cultural identity. A stellar and signature achievement.

Mark Thornton Burnett
Professor in English and Languages
School of Arts
Queen's University Belfast

Vikram Singh's book on the adaptations, translations, performances of Shakespeare's plays in some Indian languages from the late 18th century onwards is a fine addition to a long and remarkable tradition of Shakespeare scholarship in India. The book is ambitious in its scope, well-researched and written with remarkable clarity. Without the usual postcolonial kitsch, Vikram offers an illuminating analysis of how each linguistic and social group has used Shakespeare's plays to transform either its particular dramatic form or its own moral and life-shaping purpose.

Alok Bhalla
Teacher, writer, translator

The history of Shakespeare in India is long and multifaceted. Vikram Singh Thakur unlocks the mysteries that surround Indian theatre's engagement with Shakespeare, its origins and its sociopolitical contexts. This is a fascinating story of the countless native dialects and languages of India that have absorbed the work of the English playwright and have transformed the original educated Indian's Shakespeare into the popular Shakespeare practice of the 19th and 20th centuries, and the unique urban-folkish tradition in postcolonial India. *Shakespeare and Indian Theatre* is essential reading for theatre historians and those studying the stage traditions that have fed into Bollywood.

Ton Hoenselaars
Professor in Early Modern English Literature and Culture
Department of English
Utrecht University, The Netherlands

Working with issues of translation, adaptation, recension and borrowing, Vikram Singh Thakur's book takes the reader through a journey in which Shakespearean texts perform various roles at critical junctures in Indian performance and literary histories. His book is sure to be of interest to scholars and theatre practitioners alike because it seeks to engage with the imbricated histories of forms and texts and their crosscutting modifications. Thakur's research is a welcome addition to the growing study of Shakespeare in India.

Anuradha Kapur
Theatre maker and teacher

SHAKESPEARE AND INDIAN THEATRE

SHAKESPEARE AND INDIAN THEATRE

THE POLITICS OF PERFORMANCE

Vikram Singh Thakur

BLOOMSBURY
NEW DELHI • LONDON • OXFORD • NEW YORK • SYDNEY

BLOOMSBURY INDIA
Bloomsbury Publishing India Pvt. Ltd
Second Floor, LSC Building No. 4, DDA Complex, Pocket C – 6 & 7,
Vasant Kunj, New Delhi 110070

BLOOMSBURY, BLOOMSBURY ACADEMIC INDIA and the Diana logo are trademarks of Bloomsbury Publishing Plc

First published in India 2020
This edition published 2020

Bloomsbury Academic
An imprint of Bloomsbury Publishing Plc

ISBN: HB: 978-93-89351-12-5; eBook: 978-93-89351-14-9

2 4 6 8 10 9 7 5 3 1

Typeset in Minion Pro by Manipal Technologies Limited
Printed and bound in Replika Press Pvt. Ltd.

For you Papa,

who instilled in me love for literature, theatre and music

Contents

List of Images

Acknowledgements

There are many people and institutions to whom I owe a great debt and without whose support, this work would not have been possible. I express my gratitude to the following.

Bloomsbury Publishing India for publishing my work, my publisher—Mr R. Chandra Sekhar—and the entire team at Bloomsbury. Thanks Chandra for believing in me and making it happen. I will always cherish your professional acumen. I am yet to meet a publisher who is more prompt than you are in replying to all my queries. My thanks to Shreya Chakraborti too for sending me all those 'author queries' time and again. They have really been helpful in bringing the work to its present shape.

Prof. Tutun Mukherjee, Prof. B. Ananthakrishnan and Mr Rajiv Velicheti from the University of Hyderabad for their invaluable comments, suggestions and encouragement. I am especially grateful to Prof. Mukherjee and Rajiv for reading my drafts painstakingly and helping me find direction whenever I was 'lost'.

Prof. Ton Hoenselaars, former President, European Shakespeare Research Association (ESRA), and Prof. Paul Franssen from Utrecht University, The Netherlands, who made my three-month stay at Utrecht comfortable, helped me complete a research project on Shakespeare in The Netherlands and most importantly for pointing towards important questions about Shakespeare in India.

Prof. Professor Mark Thornton Burnett from Queen's University, Belfast, for providing me with an opportunity to present a paper on Shakespeare in India at the annual conference of the British Shakespeare Association held at Queen's University, Belfast, Ireland.

Mr M.K. Raina for taking out time to talk about his production *Badshah Pather* with me.

Prof. Anuradha Kapur and Prof. Alok Bhalla for reading my work and writing endorsements for this book.

I am particularly indebted to the staff of National Library (Kolkata), Natya Shodh Sansthan (Kolkata), National School of Drama (Delhi), Natrang Pratishthan (Delhi), Indira Gandhi Memorial Library (University of Hyderabad) and Ramesh Mohan Library (English and Foreign Languages University, Hyderabad).

A special thanks to Dr Shernaz Cama and the staff at Parzor (The UNESCO Parsi Zoroastrian Project) for providing invaluable archival material on Parsi theatre. Dr Cama, I must congratulate you for the mammoth work you have been doing.

My gratitude to Mr Abhijit Bhattacharya, Ms Kamalika Mukherjee and the staff at the Centre for Studies in Social Sciences Calcutta and the British Library for making available the digital archives of Endangered Archives Programme.

To all my students at Ambedkar University Delhi who have patiently listened to me over years (sometimes against their will) and helped me grow as a scholar. Special thanks to Anna Dasgupta for helping with the book cover.

Friends who are too many to name here. I am particularly grateful to friends from the University of Hyderabad, Ambedkar University Delhi and National School of Drama for all your support. A special thanks to Sayan for various conversations on archives and 'the politics of publishing houses'.

My gratitude to Achhera, my house help, for helping me read Bengali.

My parents-in-law and Aadi for all your support for so many years.

My sisters, Shelley and Mona, for always being there. Thanks Shelley, Param and Sharanya for hosting me during the conference in Belfast. Thanks Mona for believing that I could it.

Eve, thanks for being so patient with me. Thanks for being there and letting me work in solitude. I promise I would spend time with family as soon as I submit this manuscript (and before I embark on the next)!

My mother whose constant support and belief in me have been invaluable. Mummy, thanks for all the teas and breakfasts and wishes and silences for they have gone into writing this book.

Finally, my father, who has been the biggest influence on me. Papa, I can't thank you enough for your wishes and belief in me. I cherish all the discussions and 'arguments' on Shakespeare over drinks. They have helped me shape this work. I am grateful to you for introducing me to the world of literature and theatre. I so much wish that you were here to see this book. I can feel your wishes and blessings … I have missed you while writing it!

Introduction

This work titled *Shakespeare and Indian Theatre: The Politics of Performance* looks at the reception and production of Shakespeare's plays in India, that date back to the mid-18th century when the British officers in India staged Shakespeare's plays along with other English playwrights for entertainment. This was part of a larger imperialistic design that was evolving during the latter part of the 19th century to establish moral and cultural superiority over India through English education and literature. Shakespeare was a convenient ploy for achieving this aim. T.B. Macaulay, the British historian and politician, in 1835 recommended the inclusion of English language and literature in the syllabi of educational institutions in India. As a result, Shakespeare acquired a prominent place in the Indian educational curriculum. The educated Indian soon began to regard Shakespeare as the most revered writer of all ages. This compulsive love for Shakespeare, at least of young Indian students studying Bard's plays in schools and colleges, led not only to reading of his plays but also performing them, first in private and later in public as well. However, India's engagement with Shakespeare through these 250 years has not been uniform. From being 'imitative' during the first half of the 19th century to being 'popular' during the latter 19th and early 20th centuries to 'urban-folkish' in postcolonial India, the productions of Shakespeare's plays have undergone remarkable transformations.[1]

The subject of this study is the production of Shakespeare's plays in India which remains an under-researched area. Although Shakespeare has been translated, adapted and performed in India for more than two centuries, there is hardly any consolidated bibliography or cohesive history available on the subject. This is especially true for those Indian languages which have registered considerable influence of Shakespeare on their drama and theatre, let alone other languages and their theatre traditions. With so many languages and theatre traditions in India, it is quite challenging to trace Shakespeare's reception and its production throughout India. It would need several scholars from various Indian languages to compile such an encyclopaedia of Shakespeare's reception in India. This book does not attempt such a bold step. For this work, I have limited my area to a few regions with relatively higher theatre activities. There is a discussion of Shakespeare in Bengali and Parsi theatres at length. Other theatre traditions like Marathi, Kannada, Malayalam and Hindi are also equally rich and have registered considerable influence of Shakespeare. Since much of the source material on Shakespeare in India, both primary and secondary, is spread across various languages, it poses a significant challenge to a researcher in the field. However, it also renders Shakespeare a rich, nuanced and complex phenomenon in India. I am also aware that there is a new-found interest in 'Indian Shakespeare' that Bollywood has generated. There are two reasons for this love: Recognising Shakespeare's influence on Bollywood and the acceptance of Bollywood as a global phenomenon. Although Shakespeare has always 'inspired' Bollywood films, unconsciously in many cases, it is the post-Vishal Bhardwaj phenomenon that 'Bollywood Shakespeare' is now considered an important and a serious area of study. Though Shakespeare may have become more visible globally with Bhardwaj's *Maqbool* (2004) and *Omkara* (2006), there is a huge corpus of Bollywood films revolving around Shakespearean themes like star-crossed lovers, feuding families, familial infidelity and ambition overpowering duty since the 1930s.[2] However, a study of 'Bollywood Shakespeare' is beyond the scope of this work. There is some exciting work happening at the moment on Shakespeare and Indian cinema. Scholars like Craig Dionne, Parmita Kapadia, Poonam Trivedi, Paromita Chakravarti and Jyotsna Singh have been working on Shakespeare and cinema. In this book, I have restricted myself to Shakespeare in theatre only I sincerely hope that my efforts to trace Shakespeare's reception and production in India would modestly extend the existing scholarship on Shakespeare.

This work does not delve into the study of Western and Indian aesthetics of performance traditions per se yet some observations in this regard would be important for studying the fusion of the aesthetics of these two traditions in 'modern' Indian theatre. Many theatre scholars have argued that the characteristics of modern Indian theatre in its early years was an imitation of Western theatre. Girish Ghosh, a well-known Bengali director and actor, for instance, blended various traditions in his plays, taking elements from *jatra*,[3] the Sanskrit tradition, the newly emerging social drama and the Western classics.[4] Poonam Trivedi argues, 'Not just in politics and governance but in the arts too, and particularly in literature, the engagement with the West began with the imitation of Western forms.'[5] The reasons for this imitation were many. Classical Sanskrit theatre had almost disappeared by the 11th century and theatre activity in India was sustained by sparse folk and traditional performances, which too were on the decline by the 18th century due to the lack of patronage. There was a void as far as theatre activity was concerned. At this juncture, the decline of folk and traditional performances and the rise of English theatre paved the way for 'modern' Indian theatre. This was furthered by the quest of the emerging Indian middle class for a distinct cultural identity which the English theatre seemed to offer. The indigenous reform movements stemming from the colonial intervention into social practices also paved the way for the emergence of a modern sensibility and thereafter, 'modern' Indian theatre. Folk and traditional performances had already come under severe attack by the British for being 'licentious', 'immoral' and 'degraded'. The educated Indian middle class followed the colonial example and condemned these performances as degenerate that needed cleansing to become suitable for 'respectable' viewing. Indologists suggested differentiating between the 'great' and the 'little' traditions. Thus, emerged the difference between the *margi* (classical) and the desi (folk) which in turn influenced the treatment of all expressive forms. As regards the theatre, the model provided by the Western theatre was followed in terms of conventions, techniques and devices. Representing this 'imitative' theatre are the early productions of plays mostly in English by the educated Indians. School and college students especially staged Shakespeare's plays which has been discussed at length in Chapter II. However, with the 're-discovery' of Sanskrit drama, especially after William Jones's translation of Kalidasa's *Sakuntala* (1789), Indian dramatists started looking towards their classical dramatic tradition, even in the next century. This looking towards their traditions had a two-fold result. First, Indian writers started translating Sanskrit drama into other Indian languages. Before the colonial period, there were hardly any translations of Sanskrit drama in any of the Indian languages. The second and the more important result was the syncretism of Western and Indian aesthetics, dramatic and theatrical conventions, techniques and devices that characterise the later years of Indian theatre. The focus on syncretism is significant, as it generates a more nuanced way of looking at modern Indian theatre which came about as a result of a fusion between the two theatre traditions. The fusion created a new kind of theatre which while drawing upon Western aesthetics and conventions, indigenised them by incorporating aesthetics and conventions from classical and traditional performances. Trivedi rightly argues in this context that 'the imitation of Western forms in India served not so much as a model of mimetic subordination but as an intercultural interaction that created for itself 'a margin of freedom', a 'self-consciousness' of the 'possibility of the new'.[6]

Classical theatre in India had been governed by the aesthetics laid down by Bharata in the *Natyasastra* written somewhere between 2nd century BC and 2nd century AD. This is a comprehensive treatise on Sanskrit theatre, poetics, aesthetics, dance and music. Although Sanskrit theatre had lost its glory by the 11th century, various principles of the *Natyasastra* had percolated into the traditional theatres of India which sustained theatrical activity before 'modern' Indian theatre took shape. *Sutradhar*, for example, an important character in the Sanskrit theatre, retained its role in *yakshagana* as *bhagvata* and in *raslila* as swami.[7] Unlike Aristotle's *Poetics* that deals with the literary aspects of a drama, the *Natyasastra* is much wider in scope. It depicts various aspects of performance, the literary text is just one among these. A comparative study of the *Poetics* and *Natyasastra* is not the objective of this study. It is, however, necessary for the argumentative framework of this work to highlight the elements related to the dramatic text and performance in both the traditions that found a fusion in modern Indian theatre. For instance, in the Western, especially in Aristotelian aesthetics, tragedy has been regarded as the highest literary form. The preference for a tragic end in Aristotle's *Poetics* leading to catharsis or the purgation of pity and fear in the spectator is considered the ultimate end of poetry. Theoreticians like Horace and Philip Sidney endorsed that the ideal combination of *arche* and *telos* would move the audience towards ethical and moral self-realisation. All of Shakespeare's tragedies have tragic ends. Such a concept of tragedy is absent in the Sanskrit aesthetics as laid down by Bharata. The ultimate end of drama in Indian dramatic theory is the enjoyment and the realisation of rasa.[8] According to the *Natyasastra*, the play of rasa in the drama leads to *sthayibhava* after *phalprapti* that means that the protagonist attains his/her desire in the end.[9] In Kalidasa's *Sakuntala*, for instance, after the ordeals the protagonists have gone through, the drama ends with the union of Dushyanta and Sakuntala. While in Western aesthetics, there are well-defined categories of tragedy and comedy, classical Indian aesthetics does not have such definitive categories. On the contrary, the *rasa-siddhanta* (theory of rasa) in the *Natyasastra* does not subscribe to a performance that has only one rasa. This is probably the reason that one cannot find a 'pure' tragedy in the Indian dramatic tradition. Bharata insists that there be many rasas in a play (in fact, the greater number of rasas the better a play is) but one of them has to be the principle rasa. The other rasas would be merely secondary. However, as Shakespeare's plays came to be translated and performed in India in the 19th century, the tragic end gradually came to be accepted by the Indian dramatists as well as the spectators. Shakespeare's plays epitomise the inclusion of the tragic ending in the Indian dramatic tradition.

An important difference between the Western and Indian aesthetics of drama is that the Western aesthetics marks a difference between the character who represents action and articulates dialogue and the chorus which comments on the action and presents songs and dances. In Nietzschean terms, in the Western aesthetics, there is a distinction between the Apollonian and the Dionysian elements as in the classical Greek drama, while dance and drama are integrated into one and are inseparable in the Indian aesthetics of performance.[10] While in the Greek tragedies, it is generally the Apollonian element that dominates the Dionysian element, it is the Dionysian element represented by dance, music, song and stylization which is emphasized in the *Natyasastra*. Bharata's preference for *natyadharmi* (suggestive/stylised) to *lokadharmi* (ordinary/realistic) makes this clear. In Marathi theatre, Vishnudas Bhave's plays generally referred to as *akhyans* had music and songs as an essential element.[11] Songs were formally composed while the speeches and dialogues were largely improvised by the actors and were impromptu. However, one finds that the contact with English drama and theatre that was governed mainly by the Apollonian element with regard to dialogue and action, gave rise to a new kind of drama in the Indian languages in which the Apollonian element of dialogue and action became important, without completely losing the Dionysian elements of song and dance. Parsi theatre, as will be discussed in Chapter II, is a suitable example of this fusion. In Parsi theatre, dialogue and action occupy an important place, but the songs and dances are also accorded equal importance. In fact, the fusion of the two aesthetic elements of dialogue and action, song and dance, find their best manifestation in Parsi theatre.

Not only the aesthetics of playwriting but that of performance also saw a happy fusion in modern Indian theatre. Indian theatre, both classical and traditional, emphasised the capacity of the imagination of the spectators. Hence, both used empty space without décor. However, the advent of Western theatre brought the idea of representing nature on the stage. Painted scenes were hung at the back and/or rolled down for particular scenes. Although proscenium theatre became a vogue following the Western model, one finds, that even the proscenium stage was not adopted indiscriminately. Unlike the levels in the Western proscenium stage, the proscenium stage in India was mostly empty that enabled the actor to move freely either in a realistic manner or in a stylised way. The empty stage also helped the actors, particularly for the dance sequences that demanded free movement. Again, a good example to prove this is to look at the performances of Parsi theatre in the proscenium theatre. While they employed box sets, painted curtains and transformation scenes, they also incorporated folk forms like *bhavai*, *yaksagana* or *lavani* and Urdu, Gujarati or Persian ghazals and thumris. The mixing of these conventions becomes clearer in the following account provided by R.K. Yajnik:

> In the midst of the noise and bustle of the Urdu theatre, opened an hour before the performance, one hears three bells at short intervals and with the third bell a thundering gunshot is heard as the drop-curtain, gorgeously painted with mythological legends, goes up. The chorus girls sing a prayer or a 'welcome' to the accompaniment of the harmonium and rhythmic drum beats. This song ends with an offering of flowers to the distinguished patrons and with garlanding the portraits of the pioneers of the respective company or of deities. Then the action commences.[12]

The account detailed previously clearly shows that even if Parsi theatre drew upon Western stage conventions, they were adapted to suit the sensibility of the target culture. Rustom Bharucha refers to this fusion of the theatrical conventions of the two performance traditions in Parsi theatre which were,

> mediated by the colonial machinery of the nineteenth-century theatre, the conventions and stage tricks derived from the pantomimes and

> historical extravaganzas of the English Victorian stage. However, it should be emphasized that these derivations had been thoroughly 'Indianized' through music, song, colour, pathos, melodrama and the histrionic delivery of lines that are intrinsically a part of the popular theatrical tradition in India.[13]

It is this fusion of aesthetics exemplified by performances of Shakespeare's plays in India that this study hopes to illustrate.

The last two decades have seen a shift of focus from text to performance in Shakespeare studies as evident from the number of studies on Shakespeare's performance published over the last two decades. Although the domain of Shakespeare studies has always accommodated new perspectives, Western scholarship has tended to ignore Shakespeare productions in non-Western countries. If non-Western Shakespeare appears at all in Western scholarship, it is mostly the 'intercultural' performances using non-Western traditional forms of performance. Productions like that of Annette Leday and David McRuvie's *Kathakali King Lear* (1989), Tim Supple's multilingual production of *A Midsummer Night's Dream* (2006) or productions of Ariane Mnouchkine and Peter Brook that appropriate non-Western forms of performance have been noticed in the Western world. Non-Western Shakespeare productions, however, have largely been ignored in the West especially in the recent discourse on the performance of Shakespeare at a time when postcolonial theory has made significant contributions and even changed the critical paradigms in understanding Shakespeare's text.

Recently some attempts have been made in the West to include non-English Shakespeare productions in Shakespeare studies. Some of these works include Dennis Kennedy's edited volume *Foreign Shakespeare: Contemporary Performance* (1993), James C. Bulamn's edited book *Shakespeare, Theory and Performance* (1996), Pascale Aebischer et al. also published an edited volume in 2003, *Remaking Shakespeare: Performance across Media, Genres and Culture*, the 2005 Barbara Hodgdon and W.B. Worthen's edited *A Companion to*

Shakespeare and Performance and Sonia Massai's edited book *World-wide Shakespeares: Local Appropriations in Film and Performance* published in 2005. However, the number of essays related to the performance of Shakespeare in Asia, particularly in India that probably has the longest history of Shakespearean performances outside England, is quite scant in all these volumes. The major portions are dedicated to the study of Western productions. Kennedy's *Foreign Shakespeare*, no doubt, tries to broaden the scope of the scholarship on Shakespeare by taking into account non-English Shakespearean productions. Unfortunately, the work only accommodates Shakespearean productions from Germany, France and Central Europe. By leaving out Shakespearean productions from non-European countries, except one essay discussing Shakespearean performances in Japan, the work too remains largely Euro-centric. There is no mention of Shakespearean productions in India. Bulman's *Shakespeare, Theory and Performance* discusses various issues involved in Shakespearean performance ranging from actor's body, gender, stagecraft and performance editions. Here too, postcolonial Shakespeare finds a place in only an essay by Dennis Salter 'Acting Shakespeare in Postcolonial Space' that discusses the problems faced by actors in enacting a colonial text in a postcolonial society. However, his analysis is limited to Shakespeare's performances in Quebec. Aebischer's *Remaking Shakespeare* expands the range of Shakespeare studies by including performances across media like biography, sign language and novel, in addition to films and theatre. There is, however, only one essay in the volume by Poonam Trivedi titled 'Reading "Other Shakespeares"' on non-Western Shakespeare. Hodgdon's *A Companion to Shakespeare and Performance* is the most comprehensive of all the works on Shakespeare performance containing 34 essays out of which only Ania Loomba's 'Shakespeare and the Possibilities of Postcolonial Performance' and Yong Li Lan's 'Shakespeare and the Fiction of the Intercultural' discuss Shakespearean performances in Asia. The rest of the volume is about Shakespearean performances in the West. Massai's *World-wide Shakespeares: Local Appropriations in Film and Performance* is a welcome attempt, as it includes Shakespeare 'world-wide'. As Massai herself admits, the book has 'a genuinely international scope', and includes various Shakespearean performances across the world including an essay on Shakespearean productions in India by Poonam Trivedi titled '"It is the bloody business which informs thus ...": Local Politics and Performative Praxis'.

Realising this Eurocentrism in Shakespearean studies, scholars from postcolonial societies that still show a considerable influence of Shakespeare in their literatures and theatres, have attempted to represent non-Western Shakespearean studies. Two attempts on Shakespearean performances in India are notable. The first is an unpublished PhD dissertation by Parmita Kapadia (University of Massachusetts, 1999) titled *Bastardizing the Bard: Appropriations of Shakespeare's Plays in Post-Colonial India*. Although the dissertation takes into account the postcolonial appropriations of Shakespeare in India, it discusses only the English productions. The second is an edited anthology by Poonam Trivedi and Dennis Bartholomeusz titled *India's Shakespeare: Translation, Interpretation, and Performance* (2005). The work is commendable for its scope and includes the translation, interpretation and performance of Shakespeare's plays in India. However, the analyses of performances like Dutt's *Macbeth*, Tanveer's *Kamdeo ka Apna Vasant Ritu ka Sapna* or Karanth's *Barnam Van* finds just a page each of discussion. Understandably, some important productions like Lokendra Arambam's *Macbeth: Stage of Blood* which fuses the original text with the troubled history of Manipur is absent. Trivedi, however, published an essay later on the same in Massai's aforementioned work. Arambam's production using elements from Meitei mythology, rituals, culture and performance traditions like *thang ta* is probably the best example of using Shakespeare to subvert specific agenda and express the political concerns and aspirations of contemporary society.[14]

Two more recent works *Re-playing Shakespeare in Asia* (2010) edited by Poonam Trivedi and Minami Ryuta and *Performing Shakespeare in India: Exploring Indianness, Literatures and Cultures* (2016) edited by Shormishtha Panja and Babli Moitra Saraf are welcome attempts. Another interesting work that has come out exploring the relationship between Shakespeare and India is *Bollywood Shakespeares* (2014) edited by Craig Dionne and Parmita Kapadia. As the title suggests the work deals with Shakespeare and Indian cinema with two chapters on Vikram Singh Thakur's 'Parsi Shakespeare: The Precursor to "Bollywood Shakespeare"' and Parmita Kapadia's 'Bollywood Battles the Bard: The Evolving Relationship between Film and Theater in *Shakespeare Wallah*' linking theatre and cinema in India. The most recent work that has appeared in the field of Shakespeare Studies in India is Jonathan Gil Harris's *Masala Shakespeare: How a Firangi Writer Became Indian* (2018). It is quite different from all the other works mentioned earlier. Written in a style that follows the structure of Shakespearean drama, the book is divided into five acts and several scenes. Most of the scenes are titled after well-known Bollywood songs. The book in fact in a curious and a personal way establishes the relationship between Shakespeare's art and the Indian *masala* film. It is heartening to see a wide range of recent work in contemporary Shakespeare studies. However, there is much more in the area that needs to be explored.

This work is divided into four chapters, an 'Introduction' and a 'Conclusion' along with an appendix of translations and adaptations of Shakespeare available in various Indian languages. Following the 'Introduction', Chapter I is titled 'The Beginnings: Shakespeare in Calcutta' that in turn is divided into three sections. Section I on 'English Theatre in the 18th and Early 19th Centuries in Calcutta' discusses English theatres in Calcutta opened by the British colonists that staged Shakespeare's plays along with those of other English eminent playwrights for entertainment. It also discusses the role played by the English in the opening of play-houses in Calcutta.

Section II, 'Spread of English Education in India', discusses the role of English education through the introduction of Shakespeare into the curriculum to promote the colonial project. Section III, 'Shakespeare Productions in Calcutta', discusses Shakespeare's adaptations and translations in Calcutta starting with various school and college productions that were staged in Calcutta. It also looks at the shift from English to Bengali productions with time.

An important point that one might miss when dealing with these early Shakespeare productions is that even during the colonial period, the reception of Shakespeare's plays in India did face some resistance which is not usually acknowledged by scholars. Dennis Kennedy observes,

> [W]hereas in Europe the Shakespeare project embraced the translation and outright appropriation of the texts, in Asia the imperial mode tended to bring them in the original language as a demonstration of the linguistic and the cultural superiority of the conqueror. This was most notable in India, of course, where the insertion of the Shakespearean text into native life paralleled the insertion of the power of the master's race.[15]

Such an argument assumes that Shakespeare was received passively in colonial societies like India. However, this was not always the case. Resistance to Shakespeare was registered in various ways. Scholars like Samarjit Dutta whose *Shakespeare's Macbeth: An Oriental Study* (1921), *Shakespeare's Othello: An Oriental Study* (1923) and *Shakespeare's Hamlet: An Oriental Study* (1928) and Ranjee Shahni whose *Shakespeare Through Eastern Eyes* (1932) were trying to evoke Indian responses to Shakespeare's work, taking into account various factors like race, ethnicity and culture. Another form of resistance was seen in the comparisons made between Shakespeare and Kalidasa. Parmita Kapadia argues, 'in their comparisons, Indian scholars seeking to promote Indian nationalism and pride would universalise Kalidasa and argue that Shakespeare was the more provincial writer'.[16] Yet, another instance is Jai Vijay Narain Singh Sharma's 'Introduction' to *Shakespeare Katha-gatha (Shakespeare's Tales and*

Stories, 1912) where he turns the table on colonist condescension and writes that, 'Shakespeare is regarded as supreme in English literature and is described as the *Kalidasa of English*.'[17]

Chapter II titled 'Shakespeare in Parsi Theatre' studies Shakespeare's plays as adapted by Parsi theatre, one of the major theatre movements in the history of modern Indian theatre. The most important factor, probably, in popularising Shakespeare in India was Parsi theatre. Adapting Shakespeare's plays was a common feature, especially during the early years of its inception. Shakespeare and Parsi theatre worked well for each other. While Shakespeare helped Parsi theatre to establish itself, Parsi theatre helped in popularising Shakespeare in India by taking theatre away from the confines of the educated elite to the masses of the mofussil. This chapter is divided into five sections. Section I, 'Parsis and the Public Sphere', discusses the emergence of the public sphere in Bombay and the role played by the Parsis. It is my contention that Parsi theatre emerged as a part of Parsi philanthropy that regarded the theatre as a civic and cultured activity. The failure to locate Parsi theatre in this context has led theatre scholars to argue that Parsi theatre from its very inception was 'commercial' with profit as its sole motive. I argue that this aspect holds true for the later Parsi theatre but not for the early times. Only in the 1870s did Parsi theatre become thoroughly professional and commercial. Section II, 'The Beginnings of Parsi Theatre', defines Parsi theatre and provides a short history of its emergence and development. Section III, 'Shakespeare in Parsi Theatre', deals with various productions of Shakespeare in Parsi theatre which were largely free adaptations. While adapting Shakespeare's plays, plots, characters and locales the situations were sometimes Indianised to such an extent that the productions hardly resembled the originals. Section IV, '"Hybridity" in Parsi Theatre', discusses the problems involved in locating Parsi theatre within the discourse of postcolonial hybridity. The eclectic nature of Parsi theatre and its free borrowings from various sources, might make it appear hybrid in the sense of

Bhabha's notion of 'hybridity'; but a close study of Parsi theatre reveals that there was no desire to 'mimic' European theatre in order to 'become like that' which is so central to Bhabha's definition of the term. It was more, as Rajiva Verma argues, a case of 'one professional playwright borrowing plots and situations and other tricks of the trade from another'.[18] Parsi theatre enjoyed its heyday from the 1870s to the 1920s. By the 1930s, in the wake of high nationalism, performances of Shakespeare started declining and gave way to the social and political theatre that Indian People's Theatre Association (IPTA) promoted. Another factor that led to the decline of Parsi theatre was the advent of the talkies. Parsi theatre might have disappeared now, but its legacy of song and dance continues in the Indian film industry.

Chapter III titled 'Shakespeare in Marathi, Kannada, Malayalam and Hindi Theatres' is divided into four sections—Shakespeare in Marathi, Kannada, Malayalam and Hindi theatre traditions. Marathi and Kannada theatres exhibit a comparable response to Shakespeare. Since both these traditions had professional theatre companies, Shakespeare was a popular choice for adaptation. Marathi playwrights had two models in front of them: Shakespearean and the Sanskrit model. The first gave rise to 'prose' plays unfamiliar to Marathi theatre which had hitherto been dominated by the musicals. The second gave rise to *sangeet natak* (musical drama). Shakespeare, however, was common to both kinds. While the educated English adapters tried to remain close to Shakespeare's text and either wrote prose plays or translated Shakespeare in prose, *sangeet natak* moulded Shakespeare into musicals and took liberties with their plot and structure, following Parsi theatre. Similarly, Shakespearean reception in Kannada represents two sensibilities as T.S. Satyanath suggests: the literary and the stage tradition. One is led by love for Shakespeare and the other by love for the stage. While the first translated Shakespeare 'faithfully', the second, the company theatre, like the Parsi theatres of Bombay, freely adapted Shakespeare. Malayalam and Hindi theatres registered lesser influence of Shakespeare as far as theatrical performances were concerned. The absence of play-houses modelled on the English theatres, the presence of already available strong performance traditions like *teyyam*, *tullal* and kathakali, and more emphasis on prose farce during the first decade of the 20th century might have prevented the staging of Shakespeare's plays in Kerala.[19] This is not to say that there were no translations or adaptations of Shakespeare's plays in Malayalam. Although there were translations or adaptations of Bard's plays, these early adaptations, unlike those in Karnataka and Maharashtra, were not done with an eye on the stage. It is in the post-Independence Malayalam theatre that Shakespeare's plays received more attention by various theatre groups of Kerala. There have been attempts at producing at least three plays of Shakespeare in kathakali viz. *King Lear*, *Othello* and *Julius Caesar*. Among other notable Malayalam productions are *Othello* in *Kathaprasangam*[20] by V. Sambasivam, K.N. Panikkar's *Kodumkattu* (*The Tempest*, 2000), Chandradasan's *Chatthankattu* (*The Tempest*, 1995) and *Macbeth* (2002) and M.G. Jyothish's *Macbeth* (2009). Unlike Marathi, Bengali and Kannada theatres, Hindi did not have professional theatres. Hindustani was employed by Parsi theatre for its performances, but Hindi theatre right from the beginning distanced itself from Parsi theatre for its 'vulgarity', 'crudity' and 'commercialism'. In the absence of such theatres, most of the Shakespearean translations in Hindi before Independence were done as literary exercises rather than for the stage. This is probably the reason that many of these translations were 'faithful' to the original unlike in Parsi theatre. Some of the Hindi translators of various plays of Shakespeare during this period were Lala Sitaram, Ganga Prasad, Kashinath Khattri, Jai Vijay Narain Singh Sharma, Seth Govind Das, Mathura Prasad Chaudhari and Govind Prasad Ghidiyal. It is only in post-Independence India that one finds Hindi translations of Shakespeare done for the stage, though translations by Rangeya Raghav, who translated 15 plays of Shakespeare during the 1957–1958, *Mano na Mano* (*As You Like It*, 1960) and *Athens ka Raja Timon* (*Timon of Athens*, 1960) by Dharam

Pal Shastri, *Barehvin Raat* (*Twelfth Night*, 1961) by Kuldeep Kapoor, *Barehvin Raat* (*Twelfth Night*, 1962) by Shyam Sunder Suman, *Othello* (1962) by Vidyarthi Diwakar Prasad and *Hamlet* (1988) by Amrit Rai, are mainly literary exercises that have not found favour on the Hindi stage. Two translators stand out during this period—Harivansh Rai Bachchan and Raghuvir Sahay. Both being poets in Hindi were able to translate Shakespeare's plays into verse, a rare feat achieved in Hindi translations of Shakespeare. The success of the translations by them is evident from the fact that they have been successfully staged.

Chapter IV titled 'Performing Shakespeare in Post-Independence India' is divided into two sections. Section I, 'Decolonising Indian Theatre', discusses the issues involved in the postcolonial Indian theatre and the subsequent rise of 'theatre of roots' movement. Ania Loomba and Martin Orkin in *Post-Colonial Shakespeares* observe, 'history does not just provide a background to the study of texts, but forms an essential part of thes textual meaning; conversely, texts or representations are seen as fundamental to the creation of history and culture'.[21] Thus, I have located Shakespearean productions in post-Independence India in the discourse of decolonisation vis-à-vis Indian theatre which gained significance during the first three decades after Independence. The discourse on postcolonial Indian theatre does not only present a context for these productions but also a 'co'-text that has to be read along with the productions. Only then can one understand the complex Shakespeare productions in post-Independence Indian theatre. Section II, 'Shakespeare Performances in "Urban-Folk" Theatre', discusses several Shakespeare productions that incorporate elements from folk and traditional performances in post-Independence Indian theatre. Christy Desmet in *Shakespeare and Appropriation* describes the process of adapting Shakespeare by postcolonial societies as one 'in which post-colonial societies take over those aspects of imperial culture … that may be of use to them in articulating their own social and cultural identities'.[22] In the post-Independence Indian theatre, Shakespeare productions like Utpal

Dutt's *Macbeth* (1954) and *Bhuli Nai Priya* (*Romeo Juliet*, 1970), B.V. Karanth's *Barnam Van* (*Macbeth*, 1989), Habib Tanvir's *Kamdev ka Apna Vasantritu ka Sapna* (*A Mid-Summer Night's Dream*, 1993), Lokendra Arambam's *Macbeth: Stage of Blood* (1997) and M.K. Raina's *Badshah Pather* (*King Lear*, 2010) illustrate the practical application of this process. Although these productions cannot claim to be truly 'folk', they represent the use of indigenous elements from traditional forms typical to Indian performance traditions. This chapter is followed by the 'Conclusion'. Lastly, I have tried to gather details of Shakespeare adaptations/translations in various Indian languages in a tabular form as Appendix at the end. I hope that this should be useful to researchers who want to pursue further research in the area of Shakespeare studies in India.

Notes

1. I use the term 'urban-folk' theatre as used by Aparna Bhargava Dharwadker in *Theatres of Independence: Drama, Theory, and Urban Performance in India since 1947*. She makes the distinction between folk and urban folk drama as follows:

    > in radical distinction from folk theatre itself, urban folk drama is a transportable entity: while folk theatre always belongs to a specific region, language, ecological cycle, and participating community, the urban folk drama can be detached from all these particularities and performed (in the original language or translation) anywhere an audience is available. (322)

2. One of the earliest Bollywood talkies to be based on a Shakespearean play was Modi's *Khoon ka Khoon (Hamlet)* in 1935 which was followed by *Said-e-Havas (King John)* in 1936.
3. *Jatra* means journey, it is a popular folk form of performance in Eastern India especially in the states of West Bengal, Odisha and Assam.
4. Sudipto Chatterjee, *The Colonial Staged: Theatre in Colonial Calcutta* (Calcutta: Seagull, 2007), 13.

5. Poonam Trivedi, '"Bananas on a Mango Tree": Colonial Mimesis, Hybridity and Modern Indian Theatre', *Refiguring Mimesis: Representation in Early Modern Literature*, eds. Jonathan Holmes and Adrian Streete (Hatfield: University of Hertfordshire Press, 2005), 100.
6. Ibid.
7. *Sutradhar* means 'one who holds the strings' *sutradhar* refers to the principal actor who conducts a performance in Sanskrit and various folk theatres; Yakshagana means song of the yaksha (spirit), is a traditional form of performance performed in the coastal areas of Karnataka, India; *Ras-lila* is a dance-drama form which celebrates Lord Krishna's seduction of *gopis* (cow herding girls) of Mathura.
8. Rasa means juice. In Sanskrit aesthetics, it refers to the emotional and aesthetic impact that a literary or performative work has on the audience.
9. *Sthayibhava* has been defined variously ranging from strong sentiment to dominant emotion, permanent mental condition to principal mood by scholars J.L. Masson and M.V. Patwardhan define *sthayibhava* as 'a state of mind which because it is more deeply felt dominates all other emotions. It belongs to both the character and the spectator. The difference is this: Once the character experiences the *sthayibhava*, he has reached the height of emotion. But the spectator can go further, and is a sense deeper' in J.L. Masson and M.V. Patwardhan, *Aesthetic Rupture: The Rasadhyaya of the Natyasastra*, Vol. 1 (Poona: Deccan College, 1970), 23.
10. For Nietzsche's discussion of these two concepts, see Friedrich Nietzsche, *The Birth of Tragedy*, tr. Douglas Smith (New York: Oxford University Press, 2000).
11. *Akhyan* means 'to narrate' an akhyan is a long narrative poem based on Puranas and epics.
12. R.K. Yajnik, *The Indian Theatre: Its Origins and its Later Developments under European Influence* (London: George Allen & Unwin Ltd., 1933), 112.
13. Rustom Bharucha, Theatre and the World: Essays on Performance and Politics of Culture (New Delhi: Manohar, 1992), 251.
14. *Thang ta* is a traditional Manipuri martial arts form.
15. Dennis Kennedy, ed., *Foreign Shakespeare: Contemporary Performance* (Cambridge: Cambridge University Press, 1993), 291.

16. Parmita Kapadia, 'Bastardizing the Bard: Appropriations of Shakespeare's Plays in Post-Colonial India', PhD Diss. (University of Massachusetts, 1997), 4.
17. Quoted in Harish Trivedi, *Colonial Transactions: English Literature and India* (Manchester: Manchester University Press, 1995), 18 (emphasis mine).
18. Rajiva Verma, 'Shakespeare in Hindi Cinema', in *India's Shakespeare: Translation, Interpretation and Performance,* eds. Poonam Trivedi and Dennis Bartholomeusz (New Delhi: Pearson Longman, 2005), 243.
19. *Teyyam* means 'Dance of Gods'. It is a ritual art form of North Malabar, Kerala; *tullal* means 'to jump or leap'. It is a traditional performance of Kerala in which a tale is explicated through dance; kathakali means 'story play'. It is a classical Indian dance form of Kerala.
20. *Kathaprasangam* is a form of story-telling from Kerala that combines acting, speaking and singing.
21. Ania Loomba and Martin Orkin, eds., *Post-Colonial Shakespeares* (London: Routledge, 1998), 3.
22. Christy Desmet and Robert Sawyer, eds., *Shakespeare and Appropriation* (London: Routledge, 1999), 19.

I

The Beginnings: Shakespeare in Calcutta

This chapter looks at the English theatre as it was introduced in India, primarily in Calcutta (now Kolkata) in the mid-18th century and the development of 'modern' Indian theatre. The focus of the chapter is the use of English education, especially the introduction of Shakespeare into the curriculum, to assert the English moral and cultural superiority over the natives. It would, however, be incorrect to maintain that Shakespeare's plays made their way into India through English education. Much before English education was institutionalised in India, educated Indians, especially in cities like Calcutta and Bombay (now Mumbai), had become familiar with the Bard through the playhouses set up by the Englishmen. As Sushil Kumar Mukherjee notes, the 'names of David Garrick (1717-79) the great 18th century Shakespearean actor and Garrick's Drury Lane Theatre, built in 1662, were familiar in Calcutta among the readers of Shakespeare and the lovers of theatre.'[1] The first Bengali theatre might have been set up in Calcutta in 1831 but there had been ample theatrical activity in Calcutta by the British for about eighty years or so before that that it created a need for Indians to set up their own theatres on the English lines. S.K. Bhattacharya, for instance, corroborates the argument that 'the English playhouses by their production of English, especially Shakespeare's plays, created an appetite for theatrical performances'.[2] The chapter is divided into three sections. Section I, 'English Theatre in the 18th and Early 19th Centuries in Calcutta', discusses English theatres in Calcutta opened by the British colonists that staged Shakespeare's plays along with those of other English eminent playwrights for entertainment. Section II, 'Spread of English Education in India', discusses the role of English education through the introduction of Shakespeare into the curriculum to promote the colonial project. Section III, 'Shakespeare Productions in Calcutta', discusses Shakespeare adaptations and translations in Calcutta. This section traces the transformation from the phase of 'imitation' to that of 'indigenisation', whereby Shakespeare's plays were translated, adapted and sometimes appropriated into a familiar Bengali context for Calcutta audiences, which helped in popularising Shakespeare among the masses of the city.

English Theatre in the 18th and Early 19th Centuries in Calcutta

Shakespeare productions in India date back to the mid-18th century when British officers in India staged the Bard's plays along with those of other English eminent playwrights for entertainment. The sources of entertainment were limited for the British officials and so English theatre was imported to Calcutta. Many playhouses came into existence as a consequence. While Nandi Bhatia notes that theatres formed an important part of the English social life in India as early as 1757, Poonam Trivedi notes that the earliest modern theatre to be established in India was the Calcutta Theatre (1775).[3] However, theatre scholars like Sushil Kumar Mukherjee and Kironmoy Raha state that much before the Calcutta Theatre, the first English theatre to be set up in Calcutta was the Playhouse in 1753 that received help from David Garrick, one of the most celebrated actors of London.[4] The Playhouse shut down soon with Nawab Siraj-ud-Daula's attack on Calcutta in 1756. It was 19 years later in 1775, during the Governor Generalship of Warren Hastings (1772–1785), that the New Playhouse or the Calcutta Theatre was built at the expense of one lakh rupees. The Calcutta Theatre ran for 33 years and was closed due to financial strain. David Garrick, who had earlier helped to set up the Playhouse, supplied several painted scenes from London and an artist named Bernard Messink. In a letter dated 26 March 1781, Eliza

Fay, an English letter-writer who had spent time in India between the 1780s and 1790s, noted that the Calcutta Theatre was well-equipped. She also noted:

> [it was] very neatly fitted up and the scenery and decoration quite equal to what could be expected here. The parts are entirely represented by amateurs in the drama: no hired persons being allowed to act. I assure you I have seen characters supported in a manner that would not disgrace any European stage.[5]

The Calcutta Theatre staged plays of Shakespeare, Massinger, Congreve, Sheridan and others. Among various plays staged here, some eight plays were by Shakespeare and were performed more than once. The Calcutta Theatre was known for its performances and got a special mention in the reviews of the newspapers. For example, the following is a review of *The Merchant of Venice* published in the *Calcutta Gazette.*

> **THURSDAY, OCTOBER 21st, 1784.**
> ***Calcutta.***
> On Monday evening the Comedy of the "Merchant of Venice" was Performed here to a very full theatre. Shylock never appeared to greater Advantage, and the other characters were, in general, well supported.

On 11 November 1784, a production of *Hamlet* was advertised as follows in the *Calcutta Gazette.*

> **THURSDAY, NOVEMBER 11th, 1784**
> ***Calcutta.***
> We hear the Tragedy of "Hamlet" will be performed in the course of Next week; but the managers have thought proper to omit the farce of the "Mock Doctor." For the better accommodation of the Ladies and Gentlemen of the Settlement, the Gallery is to be converted into Boxes.

The *Calcutta Gazette* dated 28 February 1788 reports on the production of *Henry IV* at the Calcutta Theatre as follows:

> The representation of such a character as Falstaff requires very uncommon and eccentric powers. It is only one of all Shakespeare's, never (we believe) even attempted by Garrick who certainly thus

tacitly acknowledges his want of the requisite talents to do it justice. The gentleman who performed the part on Friday Night though he gave it almost entirely after a manner of his own, conveyed the humour of his author very irresistibly to the audience.[6]

Another performance of *Richard III* on 25 January 1788 at the Calcutta Theatre was also praised in the *Calcutta Gazette*.

THURSDAY, JANUARY 31st, 1788.

Theatre.

So much has been already said on the performance of *Richard the Third*, exhibited on the Theatre on Friday evening, that there scarce remains anything to be added on the subject. We agree in the general opinion that the whole performance went off with well merited éclat.

The part of Richard was given in that masterly style which characterizes our Roscius, and though this character requires all the exertions of a first-rate performer in the full possession of every faculty, it was impossible for the most critical eye to observe the smallest want of activity, even in the most bustling scenes, notwithstanding the late severe illness under which the gentleman who represented it has so long laboured, and from the effects of which he is yet but imperfectly recovered.

The character of Buckingham is a very important one in this performance, and it was well supported.

The eldest of the Princes spoke distinctly and collectedly, but the youngest was rather too young to be heard. The scenery in general was excellent, particularly the Camp Scene, in which Richard's Pavillion was very ingeniously contrived.

We understand the favorite musical piece of the "Poor Soldier" and Footers Comedy of "the Author" are in rehearsal, and will be performed on Tuesday next.

A review of *The Merchant of Venice* was published in the *Calcutta Gazette* on 20 November 1788 as follows.

THURSDAY, NOVEMBER 20th, 1788.

Calcutta.

Last night the Comedy of the 'Merchant of Venice' was performed before a respectable audience. Shylock was accurate and spirited, and Portia elegant and interesting; her dress was much remarked and admired. Antonio displayed dignity and feeling, and Gratiano spoke his "infinite deal of nothing" with great pleasantry.

In the meanwhile, several other playhouses were established like Mrs Bristow's Private Theatre (1789–1790), Wheler Place Theatre (1797–1798), Atheneum Theatre (1812–1814), Chowringhee Theatre (1813–1839), Dum Dum Theatre (1817–1824), Baitaconah Theatre (1824) and Sans Souci Theatre (1839–1849). The number of such English playhouses shows the growing status of theatre in the social life of the English. Besides the repertoire of their local actors, the play-houses also invited actors from London, for instance, Mrs Atkinson who came from Drury Lane Theatre and Mrs Chester from London's Royal Theatre, James and Mrs Barry, Mrs Deacle, Miss Cowley and James Vining of Covent Garden and Drury Lane Theatres. It is, therefore, clear that Shakespeare was one of the major dramatists to be produced in India in the colonial times. Jyotsna Singh argues that Shakespeare was readily imported to India

> since productions of Shakespeare's works enjoyed great popularity in Britain from the late eighteenth to the end of the nineteenth centuries. And by the mid-Victorian period, the grand-scale pictorial realism of the London productions, combined with the trend of canonizing individual characters, had left strong impression on the popular imagination. Shakespeare's characters and plots had become both commonplace and source of inspiration for artists and writers. Thus, the Victorian colonists in India, while apishly promoting Shakespeare's works in colonial Calcutta, were, in effect, reproducing the metropolitan culture as a part of the 'civilizing mission' of the British Raj. And not only were the Calcutta productions popular, but visiting troupes from overseas increased the local exposure to dramatic 'classics' such as Shakespeare [...].[7]

Among the previously mentioned theatres, the Chowringhee and the Sans Souci were especially known for their Shakespearean performances such as *Henry IV*, *Richard III*, *The Merry Wives of Windsor*, *The Merchant of Venice* and *Othello*. The Chowringhee which opened on 25 November 1813 was to have the most considerable influence on the educated Bengalis. The Chowringhee could boast of the best talents of the times like D.L. Richardson, Horace Haymen,

Esther Leach, J.H. Stokler and Henry Meredith Parker. Stokler was especially famous for enacting powerful characters like Iago, Cassius and Falstaff at the Chowringhee. Following is a review of *Merry Wives of Windsor* performed at the Chowringhee.[8]

> Last Friday, *Merry Wives of Windsor* gratified expectations. The quarrel was sustained with infinite drollery. Governor General was present. The house was crowded to excess and reminded us of the lines in the rejected address:-
>
> "Now the full benches, to late comers, doom
> No room for standing, miscalled standing room."

The Chowringhee continued till 31 May 1839 when a tragic fire destroyed it completely.

In August of the same year when the Chowringhee was gutted, Mrs Leach, previously associated with this theatre, opened the Sans Souci at Waterloo Street. The Sans Souci continued to stage plays here for a year when a bigger theatre was built by raising a subscription at the Park Street. Dwarkanath Tagore and Lord Auckland contributed Rs. 1,000 each for the new theatre. The new Sans Souci opened on 8 March 1841 with a production of Sheridan Knowles's *The Wife*.[9] The theatre's fortunes dwindled when in 1843, during a performance, Mrs Leach's costume caught fire. She was fatally burnt and succumbed to her injuries in a few days. Nandi Bhatia notes, '[D]uring the performance of *The Merchant of Venice* in 1843, Mrs Leach died as a result of her gown catching fire from the footlights. After facing financial and administrative difficulties, the Sans Souci closed down in 1849.'[10] However, the accident mentioned did not happen during *The Merchant of Venice*'s performance as Bhatia observes. The accident took place during the performance of *The Handsome Husband*, which followed *The Merchant of Venice*, in which Mrs Leach was performing the role of Mrs Wyindham. Regarding the closure of the Sans Souci there seems to be a disagreement among scholars. Most scholars mention its use in 1849. Dasgupta explains that the Sans Souci was leased out to a French Company and in 1846 the building was sold to Archbishop, Rt. Hon'ble Dr Carew.[11] However, James Barry, a friend of Mrs Leach continued to give occasional performances under the name of the Sans Souci at his private residence at 14 Wellington Square.[12] It is thus a debatable issue as to where the famous performance of *Othello* in 1848 took place. Dasgupta quotes from *Sambad Pravakar* that Baishnav Charan Addy played the role of Othello twice at Barry's residence in 1848.[13] Sudipto Chatterjee and Jyotsna Singh, on the other hand, quote from a letter by one Mr Cheeks in the *Calcutta Star* (12 August 1848) that the performance took place at the Sans Souci in Park Street.[14] Wherever the performance may have been staged, it is significant in the annals of Indian theatre because a native played the lead role for the first time in an otherwise all-English cast. The play was directed by James Barry and had Mrs Leach's daughter playing Desdemona with Basihnav Charan Addy, a Bengali, as Othello. It may be argued that the Indian actor was probably not cast for his histrionic talents, but his colour, which made him suitable for the role. This seems to be endorsed by a report in an English newspaper which called him a 'real unpainted nigger Othello' setting 'the whole world of Calcutta agog'.[15] The novelty of a 'native' playing Othello was advertised in the *Calcutta Star* thus

> On Thursday Evening, August 10th, 1848, will be acted Shakespeare's Tragedy of 'Othello'. Othello … the Moor of Venice … By a Native Gentleman….[16]

Although the play was advertised well, it could not be staged as scheduled. A report from the *Bengal Hurkaru and India Gazette* provides information regarding the reason.

> The friends of Young Bengal mustered in considerable numbers at the place of recreation, on Thursday night, to witness the long looked for *debut* of a native amateur in the character of Othello. Unfortunately, they were doomed to disappointment—not indeed owing to any defection on the part of the *debutant* or the Calcutta amateurs, but, solely because the parties who were severally to have played Iago, Brabantio and

> Emilia, were prohibited from doing so by the peremptory military order of the Brigadier of Dum Dum. A letter to that effect, we understand, was forwarded to the stage manager by half past 6; moreover, the police were in attendance, having received military notice to arrest the well-known amateurs should they have attempted to make their appearance. Many appeared to be greatly cut up at this untoward event, but none more so than poor Mr. Barry who promised to use his every effort to produce the play on Thursday next, and thus far solace those who might surmise— 'Othello's occupation's gone'.[17]

The play was successfully staged on 17 August 1848 and later on 12 September 1848. The *Bengal Hurkaru*'s review of 19 August 1848 praised Addy's confidence and pronunciation.

> Othello's entry was greeted with a hearty welcome, and the first speech, 'Let him do his spite', evidenced considerable study and the absence of that timidity so constantly the concomitant of a first appearance. Slim, but symmetrical in person, his delivery was somewhat cramped, but, under all circumstances, his pronunciation of English was for a native remarkably good.[18]

Another review in *The Englishman* criticised Addy's speech and pronunciation but lauded him for attempting the role:

> In the delivery, however, the effects of imperfect pronunciation were but too manifest. This was to be expected, but not to the extent it occurred. Scarcely a line was intelligible, and this did not arise from the low tone of voice; Othello spoke quite loud enough, but he 'mouthed' too much. Had he spoken in his natural tone, he would have succeeded far better. His action was remarkably good in some parts, and once or twice when he delivered himself in a modulated tone, we were much pleased with the effect produced. Taking it as a whole, we consider the performance wonderful for a Native. It reflects great credit on his industry and performance.[19]

Jyotsna Singh, following Bhabha's concept of mimicry, sees Addy's entry into the colonial world as disrupting the simple coloniser-colonised binary whereby the Bengali actor by putting on the 'white mask' also 'enacted his difference from the white world, both in fictional Venice and in colonial Calcutta'.[20] She elaborates that instead of being appropriated by 'the colonial sahib's play-text, the Indian actor revealed the ambivalence of its cultural authority through a native strategy perhaps best described by Homi Bhabha as "camouflage, mimicry, black skin/white masks."'[21]

Thus, it is clear that prior to 1831, before the establishment of the first Bengali theatre, the Hindu Theatre in 1831, there was enough theatrical activity by the English.[22] This played an important role in establishing modern Indian theatre. Whether the Indian elite had access to these theatres prior to 1813 is not easy to ascertain, but in all probability, the audience was exclusively English.[23] Even the ushers and doorkeepers of such theatres were Englishmen. Even if the Indian elite did not have direct access to these theatres, they might have been influenced by extensive newspaper coverage of these theatres and their productions. One can find that the English newspapers like the *Calcutta Gazette*, the *Bengal Hurkaru*, the *Bengal Courier* and the *Asiatic Journal* regularly published notices and reviews of the performances held at the Chowringhee Theatre. The *Calcutta Gazette*, one of the earliest English language newspapers in India founded in 1784, described Mrs Emma Bristow's residential theatre at the Chowringhee in its issue of 7 May 1789:

> It was not merely an apartment in a house temporarily fitted up for a single representation, but a distinct edifice completely furnished with every usual convenience and decorated with every ornament customary in familiar places of exhibition—in short, a perfect theatre differing only from a public one in its dimension.

The *Calcutta Gazette* dated 31 August 1815 wrote about a performance of *Richard III* held on 25 August 1815: 'We have not known there of any representation for some time past with more success.'

Gradually, these theatres opened their doors to the Indian elite, which furthered the cause of establishing theatres by Indians. The reason for this selective inclusion of the native elites into the English society was the realisation on the part of the British that they could not rule over the natives if they exercised the policy of segregation. Having understood the need to co-opt the native elite as a 'conduit of Western thought and ideas', the British employed the strategy of—what Homi Bhabha calls—'mimicry' whereby the native elite was encouraged to 'mimic' English culture, values, habits and assumptions.[24] This inclusion of the Indian elite can be perceived as a strategic move to expose them to the Western culture and values and to create 'a class of persons Indian in blood and colour, but English in tastes, opinions, in morals, and in intellect'.[25] Theatre was a vital instrument that could provide the elite Indians access to English culture. The first prominent member of the Bengali aristocracy to enter the English theatre circuit was Dwarkanath Tagore who was also one of the founding members of the Chowringhee Theatre (1813) along with D.L. Richardson, H.N. Wilson and Henry Meredith Parker. Subsequently, the English colonial authorities encouraged the natives to establish their own theatres. (This will be discussed in the following section of the chapter.) The strong urge to have theatres of their own came not only from the English-educated Indian elite but also from the orthodox nationalists. One such project of 'imitation' can be found in the following editorial of the *Samachar Chandrika*, a 19th century Bengali newspaper, as quoted in the *Asiatic Journal and Monthly Miscellany*.

> In the extensive city public institutions of various kinds and moral descriptions have lately sprung up for the improvement and gratification of its inhabitants; but their amusement has not yet been consulted and they have not, like the English community, any place of public entertainment.... It is therefore very desirable that men of wealth and rank should associate and establish a theatre on the principle of shares, as the English gentlemen have done, and retaining qualified persons on fixed salaries, exhibit a performance of song and poetry once a month conformably to the written natakas or plays ... such a plan will promote the pleasure of all classes of society.[26]

The point to note is that such a plea to set up theatres for Indians based on Western models was published in an orthodox Hindu newspaper like the *Samachar Chandrika*. The newspaper had earned its reputation by using orthodox arguments in the religious and social controversies of the day. It was, for example, against *sati* abolition and had campaigned against it. This shows that the need to imitate the colonial master was, at least on part of the nationalists, a sort of retort to stress that they were in no way inferior to them. A committee was formed to establish a theatre based on the English model. The members comprised Prasanna Kumar Tagore, Srikrishna Sinha, Krishna Chandra Dutt, Ganganarayan Sen, Madhab Chandra Mullick, Tarakchand Chakravorty and Hara Chandra Ghosh. As a result, the Hindu Theatre opened on 28 December 1831 in the garden-house of Prasanna Kumar Tagore. This was the first Bengali theatre that was owned by an Indian. In fact, three decades before Hindu Theatre came into existence Gerasim Lebedeff, a Russian adventurer, had established the first Bengali theatre in Calcutta in 1795. The Bengally Theatre, as it was called, staged a Bengali translation of *The Disguise* with a Bengali cast. The *Calcutta Gazette* of 5 November 1795 advertised it thus (see Image 1.1).

Image 1.1: An advertisement of Herasim Lebedeff's the Bengalee Theatre[27]

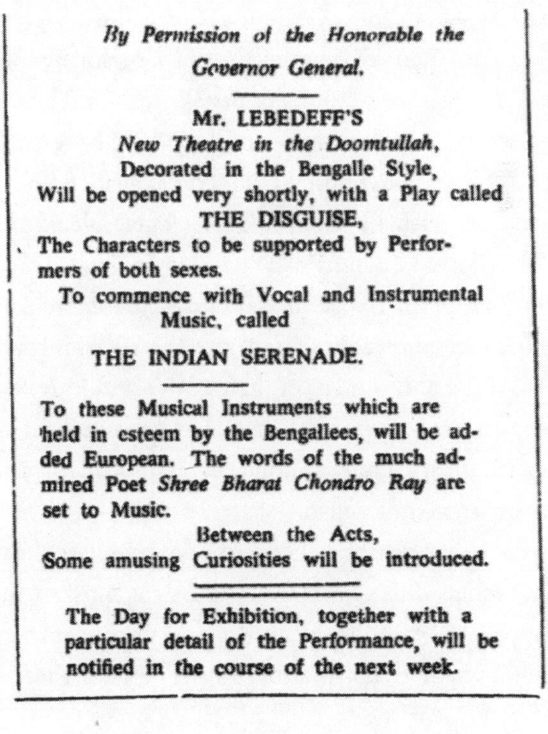

By Permission of the Honorable the Governor General.

Mr. LEBEDEFF'S
New Theatre in the Doomtullah,
Decorated in the Bengalle Style,
Will be opened very shortly, with a Play called
THE DISGUISE,
The Characters to be supported by Performers of both sexes.
To commence with Vocal and Instrumental Music, called
THE INDIAN SERENADE.

To these Musical Instruments which are held in esteem by the Bengallees, will be added European. The words of the much admired Poet *Shree Bharat Chondro Ray* are set to Music.

Between the Acts,
Some amusing Curiosities will be introduced.

The Day for Exhibition, together with a particular detail of the Performance, will be notified in the course of the next week.

The reason that Lebedeff gives for translating the plays *The Disguise* and *Love is the Best Doctor* (staged on 21 March 1786) needs some attention as it throws light on the contemporary taste of the Calcutta society. Lebedeff in the 'Introduction' to his *A Grammar of the Pure and Mixed East Indian Dialects* writes

> I translated two English dramatic pieces, namely, The Disguise, and Love is the Best Doctor, into Bengal [sic.] language; and having observed that the Indians preferred mimicry and drollery to plain grave solid sense, however purely expressed—I therefore fixed on those plays, and which were most pleasantly filled up with a groupe [sic.] of watchmen, *chokeydars*; savo-yards, *canera*; thieves, *ghoonia*; lawyers, *gumosta*; and amongst the rest a crops [sic.] of petty plunderers.[28]

Despite these plays being successful, the life of the native theatre, however, was cut short in its infancy as Lebedeff's fortunes dwindled and he left India in 1797. It was only with the opening of Hindu Theatre that native theatrical activity resumed in Calcutta. Although this theatre was set up for a Bengali audience and was established in a predominantly Bengali quarter, the plays performed were either in English or English translations of Sanskrit plays. The theatre was inaugurated with the performances of Act V of Shakespeare's *Julius Caesar* and Act I of Bhavbhuti's *Uttar Ramcharit* (Ram's Last Act) translated into English by H.H. Wilson. The *Calcutta Courier* of 4 April 1832 reported, 'Babu Prasanna Kumar Tagore has fitted up a neat little stage in his house in Narkeldangah where some young Hindoo gentlemen admirably schooled in the Histrionic art exercise their talents for the amusement of their native and European friends *who are admitted by invitation.*'[29] The theatre was not really a public one as it catered to an exclusive audience. It closed down after staging another performance in English.

There were other reasons that promoted Indian theatre based on Western models during this time. Classical Sanskrit theatre had almost disappeared by the 11th century and theatre activity in India was sustained by sparse folk and traditional performances which too were on the decline by the 18th century due to lack of patronage. There was a void as far as theatre was concerned. At this juncture, the decline of folk and traditional performances and the rise of English theatre paved the way for modern Indian theatre. This was furthered by the quest of the middle-class Bengali men for a distinct cultural identity which the English theatre seemed to impart. Otherwise, why would a Bengali theatre—especially, the Hindu Theatre—meant for Bengali audience in a Bengali quarter of Calcutta choose to perform either English plays or Sanskrit plays in English translation? Sudipto Chatterjee describes this Bengali quest for a distinct cultural identity in the following words.

> The Bengal Renaissance was the outgrowth of the grafting of a foreign culture onto a more-than-willing native culture. For the Bengalis their response to what was imposed by the British was a search for a cultural identity that could, at some level, set them on a par with their European overlords. It is in the wake of this endeavour to assume/regain a respectful self-identity that, in 1840s, several theatres [among other institutions] were spawned in the native quarters of Calcutta.[30]

Moreover, the indigenous reform movements stemming from the colonial intervention into social practices also paved the way for the emergence of modern Indian theatre. Folk and traditional performances had already come under severe attack for being 'licentious', 'immoral' and 'degraded' by the British. The *Asiatic Journal* (1837), for instance, notes that '[T]he songs, tales, histories, in fact everything connected with Asiatic amusements and literature, are, with few exceptions, more or less licentious'.[31] Following the British perception of the native amusements, the educated Bengali middle class too condemned these performances as 'degenerate' that needed cleansing to become a 'respectable' viewing. English theatre also seemed to provide access to power and a cultural 'respectability' for the middle-class. That is why, as Kathryn Hansen observes in connection with *jatra* in Bengal, the *bhadralok* tried to consolidate their position and exerted 'increasing pressure on their womenfolk to conform to British standards of ideal womanly conduct. They considered women's popular songs with their robust sense of humour and frank sensuality threatening to the new ideal of domestic order and heavily restricted elite women's association with female performers.'[32] Sharmishtha Saha points out the role of Brahmo Samaj, during the second half of the 19th century Bengal, in religious reforms, particularly stressing its resistance to theatre.

> The existing performance genres like *kathakatha* and *khemta* came to be seen as crude and vulgar, informed by notions of morality of the time.... The Brahmo Samaj, the forebear of religious reforms in India, had its own problems with the theatre. When female performers were introduced onto the Bengali stage, there were huge protests from the Brahmo Samaj and going to the theatre came to be understood as a sin. Therefore, the 'house of assembly' that the theatre was, on the one hand, was a potential site of visible evil..., but on the other hand, this potentiality was often used to confront existing social norms.[33]

In north India Bhartendu Harishchandra too, had launched an attack on the popular theatres and tried to create a theatre based on the English models provided by the British playwrights and theatre. Modern Indian theatre could define itself against the 'crude' and 'degenerate' indigenous theatre by adopting Western theatre which was taken to be 'high' culture by the Indian elite. Following the lead of the Hindu Theatre, Calcutta soon witnessed a flood of playhouses.

Spread of English Education in India

The interest of the Indian elite in Western culture and theatre coincided with the British colonial policy of institutionalising English education in India which played an important role in promoting Shakespeare and helped the growth of modern Indian theatre. The aim of imparting English education in India was from the very beginning a political strategy to consolidate British control over the subcontinent.

In the words of Macaulay, English education was necessary to 'form a class who may be interpreters between us and the millions whom we govern.'[34] The middle-class Indian, accepting the colonial master as his 'saviour', was more than willing to adopt Western education. An example of such reverence towards the Western education is manifested in a letter written to one Revd Henry Ware of Cambridge on 2 February 1824 by Ram Mohun Roy who wrote, 'I may be fully justified in stating that two-thirds of the native population of Bengal would be exceedingly glad to see their children educated in English learning.'[35] This aim of the British, manifest in Macaulay's words, could not be realised unless they could convince the natives of their socio-cultural 'inferiority'. This also provided the necessary justification for the British 'civilising mission' in India. Ngugi wa Thiong'O has convincingly argued in his polemic *Decolonising the Mind* the colonial strategy to achieve dominance over its colonised subjects:

> For colonialism this involved two aspects of the same process: the destruction or the deliberate undervaluing of a people's culture, their art, dances, religions, history, geography, education, orature and literature, and the conscious elevation of the language of the colonizer. The domination of a people's language by the languages of the colonizing nations was crucial to the domination of the mental universe of the colonized.[36]

This was true not just for Africa but for India too. The deliberate denigration of Indian culture, languages and education helped the British appear as a superior race and culture. Edward Said in his influential work *Orientalism* describes the Orient as quoted further.

> as the corporate institution for dealing with the Orient—dealing with it by making statements about it, authorizing views of it, describing it, by teaching it, settling it, ruling over it: in short, Orientalism as a Western style for dominating, restructuring, and having authority over the Orient.[37]

As this knowledge about the Orient was created, the Occident could define itself against the Orient by making comparative evaluations and, thereby, emerging as the 'superior' and 'civilized' culture. However, the knowledge thus created is not objective but, as Said argues, 'it is at once controlled, selected, organized and redistributed according to a certain number of procedures'.[38] Following Foucault's notion of discourse, Said understands Orientalism as a discourse which joins power and knowledge—power produces knowledge and knowledge, thus produced, produces power. Once such knowledge is produced and is taken to be 'objective knowledge,' it gives the 'Occident' the authority to rule over the subjects about whom such knowledge has been produced. Gauri Viswanathan notes, '[T]hrough its government-supported research and scholarly investigations, Orientalism had produced a vast body of knowledge about the native subjects which the Anglicists subsequently drew upon to mount their attack on the culture as a whole'.[39]

Once the 'superiority' of the British was established, it turned to 'educate' the 'uncivilized' and 'morally depraved' natives. However, under the guise of education were the political and economic interests of the British. The educated Indian would provide the British with cheap labour in the form of baboos for administrative jobs and also, as Charles Trevelyan—a civil servant and brother-in-law of Macaulay—in 1838 noted, '[T]hey will then cease to desire and aim at independence on the old Indian footing ... and a long continuance of our present connection with India will even be assured to us.'[40] There was, however, a clash as to what should form the subject of study. The missionaries wanted to educate the natives through religious morals and values of Christianity as was the case in England where the Church exerted influence on educational institutions. Along with the Bible, R. Nelson's *The Whole Duty of a Christian Designed for the Charity Schools in and about London* (1704), T. Green's *Principles of Religion for Charity Children*, Ellesby's *A Caution against Ill-company: The Dignity and Duty of a Christian and the Great Duty of Submission to the Will of God* and White Kennett's *The Christian Scholar; or, Rules and Directions for Children and Youths sent to English Schools, more especially designed for the Poor Boys Taught and Cloathed by Charity in the Parish of St. Botolph's, Aldgate* (1710), among others, were taught in schools in England while 'works of imagination' were kept out of the mainstream curriculum.[41] However, the colonial authority feared violent reactions from the natives, especially the educated ones if such a religious education were to be imposed upon them. An education that was secular was favoured for the 'moral upliftment' of the natives. English literature and language were the best possible alternative for the British, although it had still not been established as a discipline in England itself, rather than religious studies or military control. Thus, literature was appropriated to inculcate European values, beliefs, assumptions and tastes among the natives. An ideological and a humanistic function was assigned to literature and language which was, as Viswanathan argues, 'essential to the process of sociopolitical control'.[42] The desired role that literature was to play is clearly manifested in Horace Wilson's words where he emphasised the need to 'initiate them [Indians] into our literature, particularly at an early age, and get them to adopt feelings and sentiments from our standard writers, can we make an impression on them, and effect any considerable alteration in their feelings and notions.'[43]

There were, however, two thoughts as to how the natives should be educated. While the Orientalists wanted to impart education in the European knowledge system through native languages along with indigenous forms of knowledge, the Anglicists favoured imparting European knowledge in the medium of the English language. The Orientalist view is well articulated in the words of the British orientalist H.H. Wilson.

> Upon its [Sanskrit's] cultivation depends the means of native dialects to embody European learning and science. It is a visionary absurdity to think of making English the language of India. It should be extensively studied, no doubt, but the improvement of native dialects enriching them with Sanskrit terms for English ideas must be continued and to effect this, Sanskrit must be cultivated as well as English.[44]

The Oriental philosophy was based on the assumption that India had a 'glorious past' which was lost and that it was the 'white man's burden' to 're'-cover the 'riches of Indian heritage' and thus to 're'-present the Indian (read: Hindu) identity. Thus, there were '"re"-discoveries' of the 'glorious' Sanskrit literature and languages by Orientalists. William Jones's 1789 translation of Kalidasa's *Sakuntalam* is an example. Jones in his 'Preface' to the play calls Kalidasa the 'Shakespeare of India' and the play 'a most pleasing and authentick picture of old Hindu manners and one of the greatest curiosities that the literature of Asia has yet brought to light'.[45] Frantz Fanon in *The Wretched of the Earth* describes the polarisation of a colonial culture into two categories—those who 'threw themselves in a frenzied fashion into the frantic acquisition of the culture of the occupying power and (took) every opportunity of unfavourably criticizing their own national culture' and those who sought refuge in 'setting out and substantiating the claims of their indigenous culture in a way which rapidly becomes unproductive'.[46] In India, however, there seems to be a convergence of the two, thus making the English literary text, 'not a site of conflict, but an accommodative ideal where the humanistic assumptions of that discipline could include both a Westernised consciousness and a revivalist one'.[47] Such an approach had the support of middle-class Indians who felt that western education would usher the revival of their own literature. The Hindu College founded in Calcutta (1817) represented such thinking. Sir Edward Hyde East writes of his reminiscences of a meeting held on 14 May 1816 with the founders of the Hindu College as follows.

> the head pundit, in the name of himself and the others, said that they rejoiced in having lived to see the day when literature (many parts of which had formerly been cultivated in this country with considerable success, but which were now extinct) was about to be revived with great lusture and prospect of success than ever.[48]

There was a palliating effect on the coloniser-colonised relationship but this proximity did not augur well for the Hindu-Muslim amity. As Sudipto Chatterjee notes, the 'otherness' of the British was 'transferred to the Muslims who were now looked upon as invaders of the land (*jaban*) and corrupters of Hindu heritage (*mleccha*)'.[49] The Muslims were thus disconnected from the mainstream Bengali culture. The policy of creating nostalgia among the Hindu Indians and the British duty to '"re"-cover' for them provided a kind of authority to the British to '"re"-present' the natives. This glorification of historical past was a colonial strategy 'deliberately posited at the heart of the coloniser's historiography to justify and consequently solidify the colonial enterprise'.[50]

Anglicists like Macaulay and Charles Trevelyan, on the other hand, dismissed Indian literature and languages and promoted English education among the natives. Macaulay's *Minute on Indian Education* (1835) arrogantly declared that 'a single shelf of a good European library was worth the whole native literature of India and Arabia' and that he had never 'met with any Orientalist who ventured to maintain that the Arabic and Sanscrit poetry could be compared to that of the great European nations'.[51] Trevelyan justified the 'civilising mission' and supported the need to educate the Indian middle and upper classes in the 'superior' European literature so that the natives would be able to produce their own 'worthy' literature. He writes,

> The cases in which the most lasting impressions have been made upon national character, in which the *superior civilization* of one country has taken deepest root and fructified most abundantly in other countries, have a *strong general resemblance* to the case before us [in India]. In those cases, the foreign systems of learning were first studied in the original tongue by the *upper and middle classes*, who alone possessed the necessary leisure. From this followed a diffusion of the knowledge contained in the foreign literature, a general inclination of the national taste towards it, and an assimilation of the vernacular language, by the introduction into it of numerous scientific and other terms. Last

> of all, the vernacular tongue began to be cultivated in its improved state; translations and imitations sprang up in abundance, and creative genius occasionally caught the impulse, and struck out a masterpiece of its own.[52]

The Anglicists finally won the debate between them and the Orientalists regarding the subject and medium of study. Consequently, English education and English language as the medium were institutionalised in 1835.

Whether it was introducing the natives to English knowledge and language or providing them access to English theatres and later encouraging them to imitate the Western theatre, both were, in effect, manifestations of what Gramsci would later call 'hegemony' whereby

> Domination is [thus] exerted not by force, nor even necessarily by active persuasion, but by a more subtle and inclusive power over the economy, and over state apparatuses such as education and the media, by which the ruling class's interest is presented as the common interest and thus comes to be taken for granted.[53]

Ania Loomba argues that English education offered 'a programme of building a new man who would feel himself to be a citizen of the world while the very face of the world was being constructed in the mirror of the dominant culture of the West'.[54] In this way, English education and culture proved to be an effective tool of domination for the British as the Indian elite welcomed the advent of English education as a window to the new world which was 'rational' and culturally and morally 'superior' than their own.

Shakespeare Productions in Calcutta

Shakespeare who was considered the greatest achievement of his race and culture and the repository of Christian beliefs formed the core of the curriculum of English education introduced by the British to inculcate in the natives, codes of proper moral behaviour, culture and values. Even the missionaries who had earlier resisted the British policy of secular education in favour of a religious one found in Shakespeare, along with Goldsmith, a champion of their agenda. Revd William Keane found Shakespeare useful for imparting Christian values to the natives. He comments,

> Shakespeare, though by no means a good standard, is full of religion; it is full of the commonsense principles which none but Christian men can recognize. Sound Protestant Bible principles, though not actually told in words, are there set out to advantage, and the opposite often condemned. So with Goldsmith … and many other books … which are taught in the schools; though the natives hear they are not to be proselytized, yet such books have undoubtedly sometimes a favourable effect in actually bringing them to us missionaries.[55]

Hence, from the beginning, Shakespeare was made to bear the burden of the civilising mission of the British. It was necessary, therefore, to valorise Shakespeare and represent his plays as 'universal', 'timeless' and 'transcendental'. This proved quite successful as the native elite took to Shakespeare and made him synonymous with 'universal humanism'. In fact, such reverence for the Bard has continued even in the postcolonial India where his quotes are invoked left, right and centre by India's who's who.[56] Ngugi wa Thiong'O, albeit in the context of colonial Kenya, expresses a similar sentiment: 'How many seminars we spent on detecting this moral significance in every paragraph, in every word, even in Shakespeare's full stops and commas?'[57]

In addition to the formal introduction of Shakespeare, there were other reasons that helped strengthen Shakespeare's position. For instance, Shakespeare was taught by Henry Derozio and D.L. Richardson who created among their students an unfading admiration for the dramatist. They were taught to recite lines from Shakespeare and enact them. Richardson advised his students to watch Shakespeare productions. Macaulay noted of Richardson: 'I may forget everything else about India, but your reading of Shakespeare never.'[58] The 1853 Act which introduced competitive examination for civil services included English literature and language as optional subjects which included Shakespeare's plays. Also, the travelling companies that frequently visited India performed Shakespeare's plays and helped in popularising them among the educated Indians. Soon it became a rage among the educated Bengalis to stage Shakespeare. As late as 1926, the English professor C.J. Sisson observed this fad for performing Shakespeare among Indian students who 'busy[ied] themselves almost exclusively with Shakespeare in English'.[59]

The early 19th-century Shakespearean productions in Calcutta which were mostly the student productions seem to have been 'faithful' to English culture and language. Emily Eden, who spent some years in India with her brother in the early 19th century, gives one such account of Calcutta College in her letters to her sister:

> Yesterday we had an examination at Government House of the Hindu College, and the great banqueting-hall was completely filled with natives of the higher class. Some of the boys in their gorgeous dresses looked very well, reciting and acting scenes from Shakespeare. It is one of the prettiest sights I have seen in Calcutta.[60]

Most notable student performances were the performances and recitations by the students of Hindu College and Sanskrit College. In 1837, the students performed *The Merchant of Venice* at the Government White House under the supervision of Dr Wilson. The period from 1837 to 1853 was quite dull for Bengali theatre. *The Merchant of Venice* was staged twice by the David Hare Academy students in 1853. The *Bengal Hurkaru* of 28 February 1853 observes,

> Mr. Clunger, Headmaster of the English Department of the Calcutta Madrassa gave instruction on Shakespeare's dramatic plays to the alumni of the David Hare Academy and succeeded in training some boys to the competent performance of the plays taught [to] them and accordingly the play took place on two *nights* in the hall of the Institution. The part of Shylock was pronounced the best and the Merchant of Venice etc. was rather defective which it was hoped, diligence and performance would perfect in time.[61]

The play was attended by some six or seven hundred Indians and Englishmen who were quite pleased with the performance. Other Shakespeare enthusiasts were to be found in the Oriental Seminary. The *Bengal Hurkaru*, 7 April 1853, informs us that a subscription of eight hundred rupees was raised by the students and ex-students of the Oriental Seminary with which the stage was built. The new theatre which was called the Oriental Theatre was situated in the school premises. The theatre was established mainly for staging Shakespeare plays and opened on 26 September 1853 with a production of *Othello* with a repeat performance on 5 October 1853. The production received rave reviews from newspapers. The *Bengal Hurkaru* on 28 September 1853 appreciated the production for helping to 'improve' the native intellect:

> The performers were, all of them, young men ... and the character which we feared would be the worst represented, was the best represented—Iago by Babu Prianath Dey [Dutt] was acted with an evident knowledge of the character ... the mode in which they acquitted themselves must have given much satisfaction to every member of the audience who cares for the intellectual improvement of his native fellow-citizens.

Another performance at the Oriental Theatre was advertised in *The Citizen* on 2 March 1854 thus:[62]

The Oriental Theatre
No. 268, Gurranhatta, Chitpore Road,
The Merchant of Venice
Will be performed at the above Theatre
On Thursday, the 2nd March 1854
By Hindu Amateurs
Doors open at 8 P.M.
Performance to commence at 8½ P.M.
Tickets to be had of Messers F.W. Brown & Co. and Baboo
Woomesh Chunder Banerjee, Cashier, Spences Hotel.
Price of Tickets Rs. 2/- each.
The Tickets distributed will avail on the above evening

The *Morning Chronicle* of the same day appealed to

> [T]hose who are desirous of seeing how young native gentlemen can wear the buskin, should attend the Oriental Theatre this evening and we promise them that they will come away with a higher impression of native tragic talent than that which they may possibly, at present, be improved. We recollect some months ago witnessing at the same Theatre a performance of Othello and we presume the same company will appear tonight, we have no doubt that they will be well worth-hearing.[63]

Not only the performance reviews but also the twenty-fourth annual examination conducted at the Oriental Seminary on 6 March 1854 was thus recorded in *The Citizen*, 7 March 1854.

> ***The Citizen, March 7, 1854.***
> The proceedings commenced precisely at half past ten o'clock, when the first class was called up and examined in their readings from Shakespeare. The portion first selected for examination was "Othello's Apology," which was gone through very creditably. Dr. Nash then desired the class to read the "Soliloquy" in Hamlet, as well as several other passages in that play. He questioned them very closely on the meaning of the absolute words and phrases, and the answers elicited were such as to make a favourable impression on the minds of the audience with reference to the intelligence and quickness displayed by the students composing that class.[64]

The productions of the Oriental Theatre are significant because the performances were open to the public who could buy a ticket to watch them unlike the private theatres of Calcutta. But the Oriental Theatre had a short life and their last production was that of *Henry IV (Part I)* on 15 February 1855.

Apart from the student productions, there were other productions held in private and public theatres in Calcutta. Pyari (Parry) Mohan Bose's Jorsanko Natyasala staged the much-acclaimed performance of *Julius Caesar* in English on 3 May 1854. The *Sambad Pravakar* of 5 May 1854 showered praises on the production and compared it with the Oriental Theatre.

> Pyari Babu's house was illumined and decorated in the nicest way. The audience numbered around 400, and would have been more but for rain and storm. Babu Mohendra Nath Bose acted in the role of Caesar, Kistoodhan Dutt of Brutus and Jadu Nath Chatterjee of Cassius and the artists were thus all of culture. Even the performance by the amateurs of the Oriental Theatre stood inferior in comparison, and they were astonished at the excellent way the performance of such a play was rendered.[65]

However, *The Hindoo Patriot*, a nationalist English Weekly, of 11 May 1854 was quite critical of the production and condemned it for bastardising the Bard.

> We ourselves are the most steadfast admirers of the Drama. Nothing will give us greater pleasure than to behold Shakespeare springing into new life under the histrionic talent of our educated countrymen, but we cannot calmly look on while the old gentleman is being murdered and mangled.

From the earlier discussion, it is clear that early Bengali theatre and its Shakespearean productions in the 1850s were driven by a desire to 'imitate' the Western canons of drama and theatre. A change occurred in the post-1850s when the Bengali audience craved for Bengali plays. Newspapers started voicing the need to stage Bengali plays in Bengali theatres. The same review of *The Hindoo Patriot* mentioned previously further suggested that 'the Joranskowallahs [to] take in hand a couple of good Bengallee plays and [we] will promise them success'. In the same vein, the review of the Oriental Theatre's *Henry IV* in *The Hindoo Patriot*, 21 February 1855 lamented the lack of public response and advised the staging of Bengali plays. It was probably due to this reason that there was a decline in the number of Shakespearean productions from 1857 onwards. Bengali drama, on the other hand, was on the rise. The first original Bengali play to be written was Ram Narayan Tarkaratna's *Kulin Kulasarvasa* in 1854 that focuses on the evils of polygamy. The next 20 years saw the emergence of Bengali social drama when plays like Tarkaratna's *Kulin Kulasarvasa* and *Naba-Natak* (1867), Umesh Chandra Mitra's *Bidhba Bibaha* (1856), Michael Madhusudan Dutt's

Sarmistha (1859) and Dinabandhu Mitra's *Nildarpan* (1860), were staged. The year 1872 witnessed the establishment of first Bengali public theatre—National Theatre—though housed in a private residence. Soon more public theatres were opened in Calcutta like Hindu National Theatre (1873), Oriental Theatre (1873), Bengal Theatre (1873), Star Theatre (1883), Minerva Theatre (1893), Emerald Theatre (1887) and Unique Theatre (1903) and they advertised their plays extensively in newspapers (see Images 1.2 to 1.6).

Image 1.2: An advertisement of Girish Ghosh's *Sita Haran* (1898) in the *Amrita Bazar Patrika*, 2 April 1898

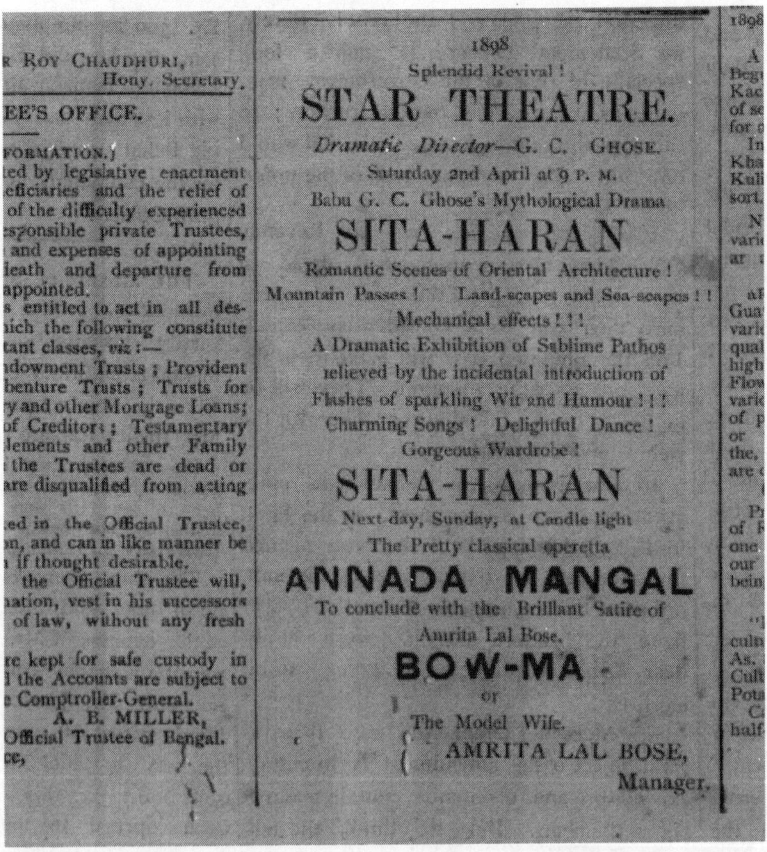

1898
Splendid Revival !
STAR THEATRE.
Dramatic Director—G. C. GHOSE.
Saturday 2nd April at 9 P. M.
Babu G. C. Ghose's Mythological Drama
SITA-HARAN
Romantic Scenes of Oriental Architecture !
Mountain Passes ! Land-scapes and Sea-scapes ! !
Mechanical effects ! ! !
A Dramatic Exhibition of Sublime Pathos
relieved by the incidental introduction of
Flashes of sparkling Wit and Humour ! ! !
Charming Songs ! Delightful Dance !
Gorgeous Wardrobe !
SITA-HARAN
Next day, Sunday, at Candle light
The Pretty classical operetta
ANNADA MANGAL
To conclude with the Brillant Satire of
Amrita Lal Bose,
BOW-MA
or
The Model Wife.
AMRITA LAL BOSE,
Manager.

Courtesy: The Archives of the Centre for Studies in Social Sciences, Calcutta and the Endangered Archives Programme of the British Library.

Image 1.3: An advertisement of *D'arc's Marionettes* or *Living Dolls* (1898) in the *Amrita Bazar Patrika*, 4 April 1898

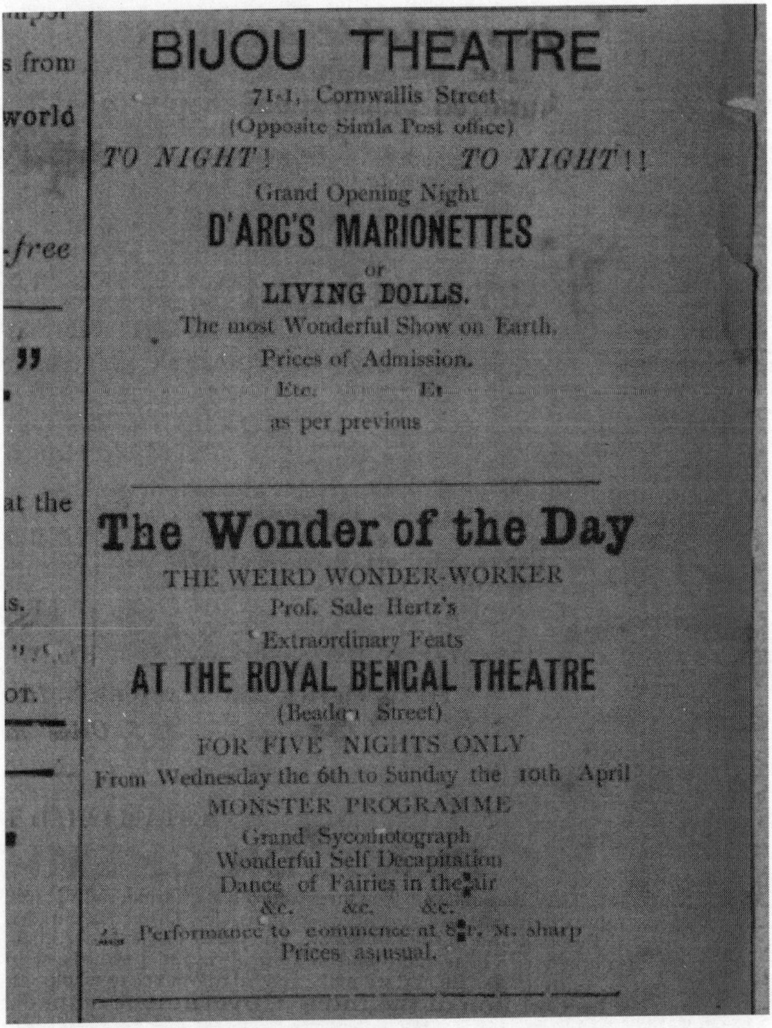
BIJOU THEATRE
71-1, Cornwallis Street
(Opposite Simla Post office)
TO NIGHT! *TO NIGHT!!*
Grand Opening Night
D'ARC'S MARIONETTES
or
LIVING DOLLS.
The most Wonderful Show on Earth.
Prices of Admission.
Etc. Et
as per previous

The Wonder of the Day
THE WEIRD WONDER-WORKER
Prof. Sale Hertz's
Extraordinary Feats
AT THE ROYAL BENGAL THEATRE
(Beadon Street)
FOR FIVE NIGHTS ONLY
From Wednesday the 6th to Sunday the 10th April
MONSTER PROGRAMME
Grand Sycoliotograph
Wonderful Self Decapitation
Dance of Fairies in the air
&c. &c. &c.
Performance to commence at 8 P. M. sharp
Prices as usual.

Courtesy: The Archives of the Centre for Studies in Social Sciences, Calcutta and the Endangered Archives Programme of the British Library.

Image 1.4: An advertisement of *Raja Basant Roy* in the *Amrita Bazar Patrika*, 4 June 1898

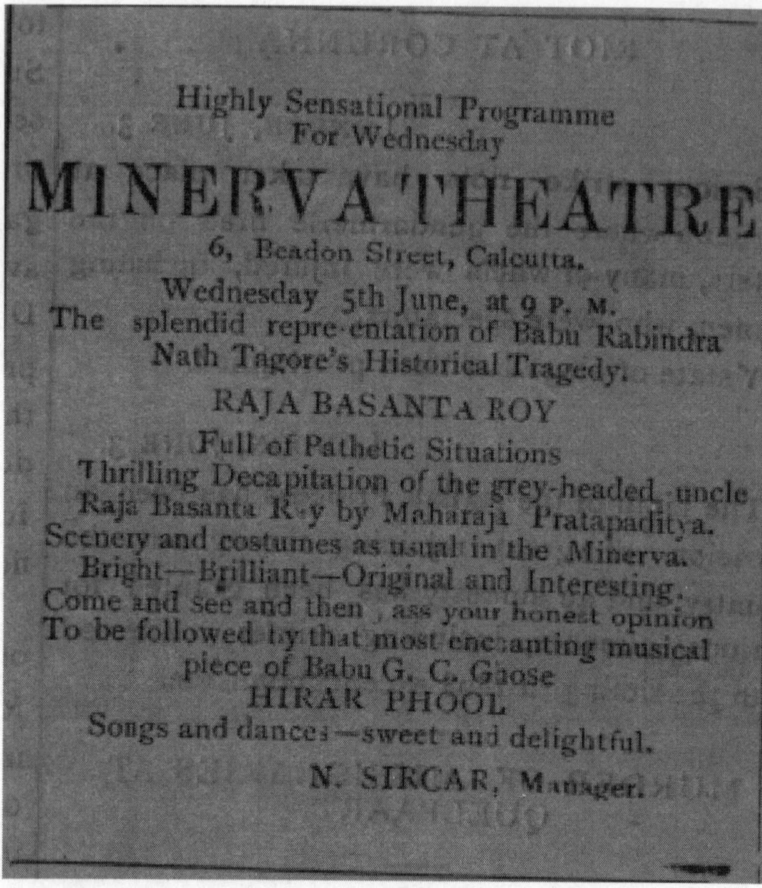

Courtesy: The Archives of the Centre for Studies in Social Sciences, Calcutta and the Endangered Archives Programme of the British Library.

Image 1.5: An advertisement of *The Flower of Persia* and *Sarala* in the *Amrita Bazar Patrika*, 9 September 1897

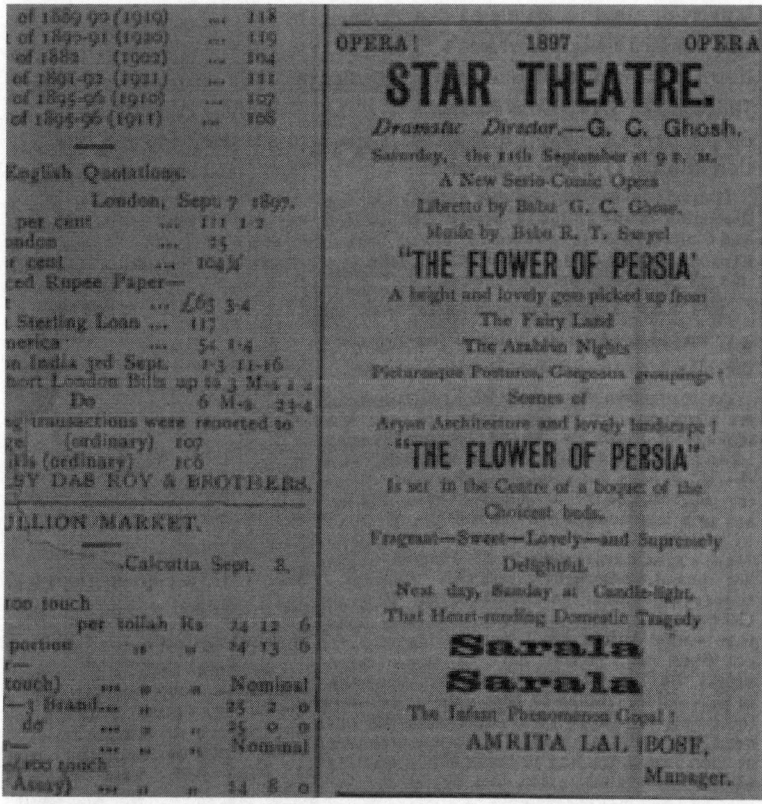

Courtesy: The Archives of the Centre for Studies in Social Sciences, Calcutta and the Endangered Archives Programme of the British Library.

Image 1.6: An advertisement of *Annoda Mangal* and *Sarat-Sarojini* in the *Amrita Bazar Patrika*, 3 August 1899

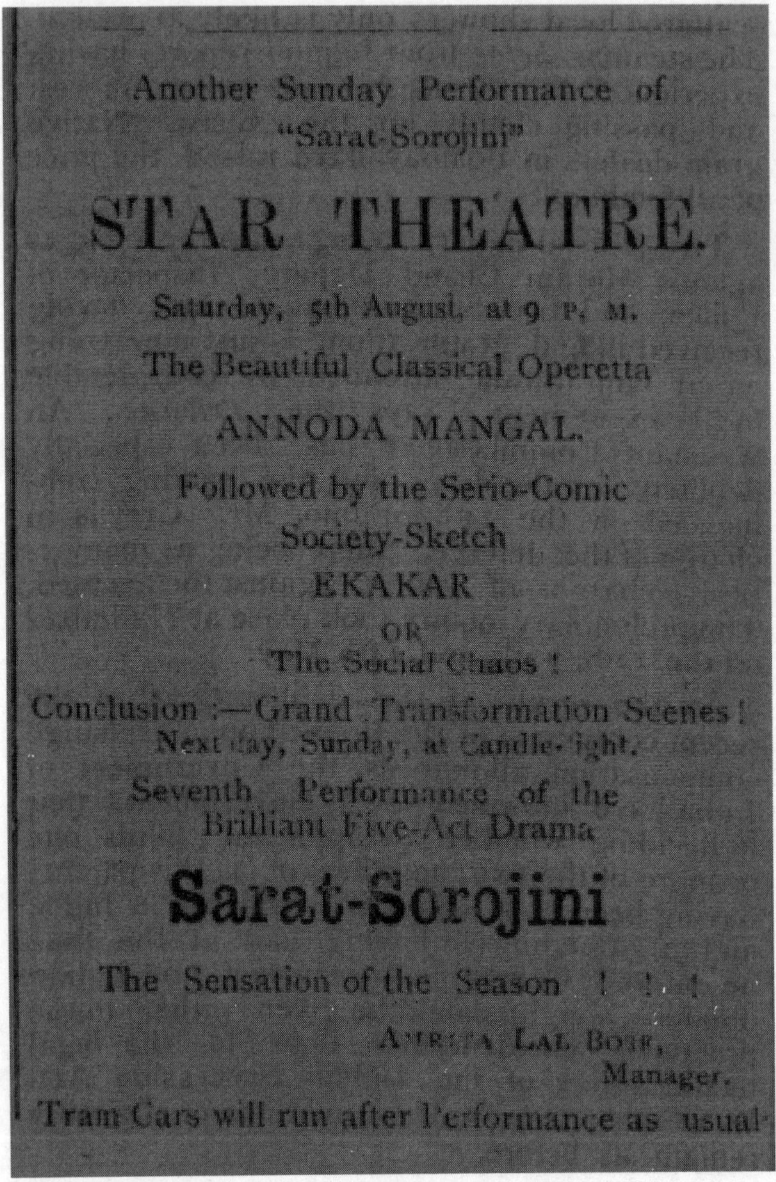

Courtesy: The Archives of the Centre for Studies in Social Sciences, Calcutta and the Endangered Archives Programme of the British Library.

It is interesting to note in most of these advertisements the way technology, costumes, songs and dance were advertised: 'Romantic scenes of Oriental architecture', 'mechanical effects', 'charming songs', 'delightful dances', 'gorgeous wardrobe', 'pathetic situations', 'thrilling decapitation'. This seems to be the influence of Parsi theatre which will be discussed in the next chapter. While professional theatres emerged in Calcutta, it also saw the decline of the newly born Bengali social drama. Perhaps a reason for this was the institution of Dramatic Performances Control Act of 1876. Rustom Bharucha says that professional Bengali theatre of the time 'was not equipped to deal with the rigours of censorship on a theatrical level'.[66] He adds,

> For the most part, the plays of the Bengali theatre between 1872 and 1912 included musicals, domestic comedies, sensationalized versions of mythological stories, and religious melodramas based on the lives of saints and devotees. Even historical subjects were pretexts for escapist entertainments that specialized in songs, dances, theatrical tricks, spectacular devices, and melodrama.[67]

Bengali theatre of the last quarter of the 19th century thus seems to follow the footsteps of Parsi theatre. This was possible due to the Parsi theatre companies travelling not only across India but also to Rangoon and Jaffna. It was around this time that Shakespeare's plays began to be staged again with vigour albeit with a difference. His plays were performed in Bengali by professional Bengali theatres. The trend was to indigenise and assimilate his plays. Hemchandra Bandopadhyay, for instance, in his 'Introduction' to the translation of *Romeo and Juliet* which first appeared as *Charumukh Chittahara Natak* in 1864 and then as *Romeo-Juliet* in 1881, defends his indigenisation of the play in the following words:

> I have tried to present the story of the play of Shakespeare and the essential features of the characters in a native mould to suit the taste of the readers of my country. I cannot say how successful I have been. But I believe that without adopting such a method no foreign play will ever find a place in Bengali literature, which will be denied

> nourishment and advancement. After a period of such exercises, faithful translations of foreign plays and poems will find acceptance in Bengali literature. But now, for some time to come, I believe, this method is indispensable.[68]

Another translation that appeared in 1894 and then in 1918 was Ashutosh Ghose's *Macbeth.* The book cover of Ghose's translation referred to it as 'Literally translated in Bengali Blank Verse'. In the 'Introduction' to the play, T.N. Mukherjee writes,

> In the year 1883 the translator conceived the idea of issuing literal translations of the principal dramas of Shakespeare. The metrical translation of Macbeth was accordingly undertaken and finished. But certain circumstances prevented the author from publishing the work. About three years ago in the year 1891 ... the translator showed me the translation of Macbeth. I was so struck with the beautiful metrical translation of Macbeth that to make English dramas popular in Bengal, immediately the well-known Manager of a distinguished Indian theatre was written to for its production on the stage, but somehow the scheme fell through. However I insisted the translator to publish the translation one by one. The reader will see the accuracy of translation line by line, as well as the beauty of its rendering in Bengalee blank verse. I hope the reading public will appreciate the translation of the tragedy and encourage the translator to publish the translations of hamlet and other works of the Immortal Bard of the Avon.[69]

The Englishman of 11 January 1919 praised the translation for being 'verbatim' and mentioned it as 'unique in Bengali literature'. One cannot miss the reverence of the Bengali translator writers towards Shakespeare. The reason for the translation not seeing the light of day could be attributed to it being too 'literal' which might not have gone well with the Calcutta audience.

The earliest Bengali production of Shakespeare on the public stage was probably *The Comedy of Errors* in 1873. Nothing much is known about the performance. The following year saw the productions of *Cymbeline* (*Kusum Kumari*) and *Macbeth* (*Rudrapal*). *Kusum Kumari*, an adaptation of *Cymbeline* by Chandrakali Ghosh, was staged at the National Theatre. *Macbeth* was adapted by Haralal Ray as *Rudrapal* for The Great National Theatre and performed in 1874. R.K. Yajnik notes that the adaptation was too literal to impress the ordinary playgoers.[70] Ray had only changed the English names to Hindu ones. Sarottama Majumdar observes, 'contemporary accounts report an unruly and abusive audience who actually managed at one performance to have the play abandoned halfway through'.[71] Perhaps one of the most significant, though not commercially successful Shakespeare performances on the 19th-century Bengali stage was Girish Chandra Ghosh's *Macbeth.* It was staged on the opening night of Minerva Theatre in 1893. The event was reported by the newspapers as an important one in the history of Bengali theatre. Ghosh considered Shakespeare to be his model and had wanted to familiarise the masses with Shakespeare's plays. His reverence towards the Bard can be noticed in the *nandi,* the invocation, he had introduced in his production.

To my learned audience, I have come to the stage
To manifest a trifle poetic gift of mine…
Shakespeare is my role model…
I am only an actor, follower of the Bard.
Hence, criticism of his creation is not within my purview.
I know not what inspires me
Yet, with all humility I desire
To offer my token of regard to the great poet.[72]

Ghosh's *Macbeth* was advertised in the *Amrita Bazar Patrika* on 28 January 1893 as follows:

OPENING NIGHT
THE
MINERVA THEATRE
6, BEADON STREET
Saturday, the 28th January, 9 P. M.
Shakespeare in Bengali
MACBETH
I have got the piece mounted
by European Artists and Dressed
it under European supervision

and "make up" by Mr. J. Pimm.
For particulars see play-bills.
Next Day Sunday at candle light.
MACBETH

G. C. Ghosh
Manager

Image 1.7: Cover page of Girish Ghosh's *Macbeth* in Bengali

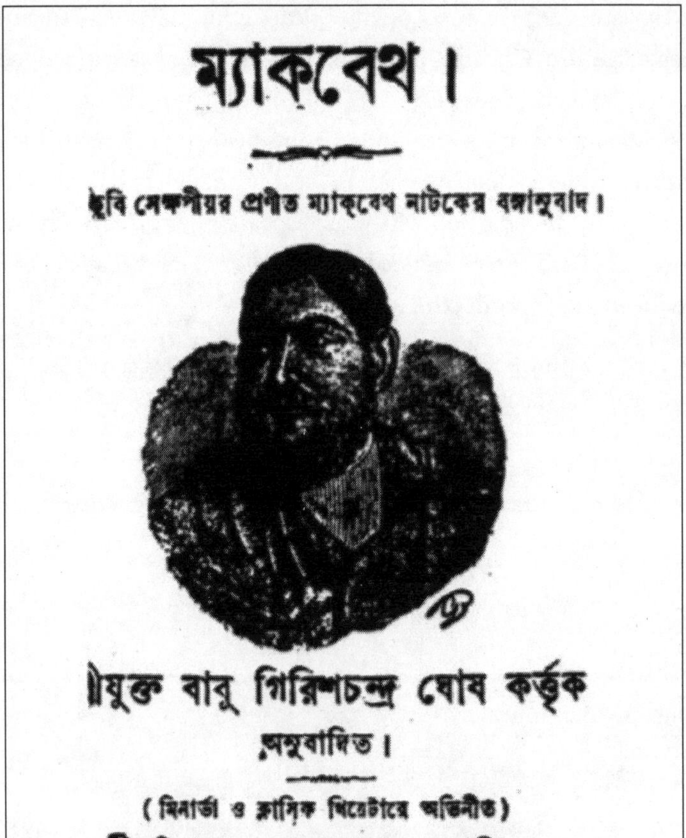

ম্যাকবেথ।

কবি সেক্সপীয়র প্রণীত ম্যাক্‌বেথ নাটকের বঙ্গানুবাদ।

শ্রীযুক্ত বাবু গিরিশচন্দ্র ঘোষ কর্ত্তৃক
অনুবাদিত।

(মিনার্ভা ও ক্লাসিক থিয়েটারে অভিনীত)
শ্রীঅবিনাশচন্দ্র গঙ্গোপাধ্যায় প্রকাশিত।

কলিকাতা,

সন ১৩০৬ সাল।

The play was appreciated by a reviewer in the *Amrita Bazar Patrika* on 30 January 1893

> **SHAKESPEARE ON BENGALI STAGE**
> The Minerva Theatre Company, under the management of Babu G.C. Ghosh, gave their first appearance on Saturday. As announced, the tragedy of Macbeth was the entertainment of the night, and the house was literally full, many having had to go away disappointed. Shakespeare's matter and manner are all singularly his own; yet it must be said that Babu G.C. Ghosh's translation of the immortal tragedy has been a rich contribution to Bengali Dramatic Literature. Indeed, many among the audience were at once [sic.] put in mind of several well-known passages in Shakespeare's Macbeth while listening to their Bengali versions. There were flashes of histrionic talent in the display of Macbeth's character; while Lady Macbeth must have made an impression on the assembly. The stage-effect of the play was heightened by the grandeur of painting and dresses.

The set was mounted by one Mr Weelard. Ghosh himself played the part of Macbeth with Teenkouri as Lady Macbeth. The production proved to be a boon for Teenkouri's career as she left an impression on the minds of the audience. The *Indian Nation* of 20 February 1893 praised Teenkouri's histrionics and commented,

> [I]t is impossible to say of a Shakespearean play that it has been acted to perfection, but we can say of this play that it was acted very well at the Minerva. The parts that were especially well done were those of Macbeth and Lady Macbeth, who had a Mrs. Siddons-like appearance.[73]

Despite the positive reviews it received the play could not prove to be a commercial success. The failure of this production is significant as it throws light on the Bengali taste of the time. While it was well-received by the elite Indians and the Anglo-Indian newspapers, the masses rejected it. *The Englishman* on 8 February 1893 commented,

> The Second performance of *Macbeth* was shown before a large audience including several European gentlemen. Babu Girish Chandra Ghosh, the manager, played the part of Macbeth and the play as a whole was

> well rendered. A Bengali Thane of Cawdor is a living suggestion of incongruity, but the reality is an astonishing reproduction of the standard convention of the English stage.[74]

The *Hindoo Patriot* published a lengthy review of the production:

> The representation of *Macbeth* in the Minerva Theatre on Saturday last as the opening piece, marks a new departure in the dramatic history of Bengal. The novelty of the representation, as well as the excellence of the general get-up, had attracted a large audience which turned out to be an appreciative one. Babu Girish Chandra Ghosh, the father of the modern stage of Bengal, as he may be rightly called, had the whole work under his personal supervision, commencing with the translation of the masterpiece and including the scenery and dresses which were as correct and effective as might be desired. The success became, therefore, a foregone conclusion, when Babu Girish Chandra took the leading character. The part of Lady Macbeth is always one of great difficulty, even in the hands of accomplished actresses, and it is not much of surprise if it was not so well done as might have been desired. But as time wears on, better results may be expected. The other actors sustained their parts very well and the witch-scene was full of mystic terrors that impressed themselves deeply upon the audience. It is difficult to predict whether translations of Shakespearean masterpieces will be favourably received as a rule. If this does not turn out to be the case, Macbeth bids fair to prove an exception. The pavilion has been built and fitted up at enormous cost and the best dramatic talent of the city has been engaged.[75]

However, the play had to be withdrawn from the boards after ten productions. The reason for the failure of the production on the box-office might have been many. However, the most important among the many reasons, which Ghosh himself admitted, was the lack of songs and dances. In a letter addressed to a friend of his, he wrote, 'most go to see songs and dances, few for drama. The public are too uneducated to appreciate Shakespeare'.[76] Although Ghosh had translated the play from English to Bengali, he did not take away the 'foreignness' from the text. The stage was English, the costumes were English, the make-up was English, the locale was Scotland, in fact, the whole context was foreign. Ghosh had failed to notice that the Bengali desire of imitating the Western canon of drama and theatre by the late 19th century, had given way to more local aesthetics. The Bengali audiences of public theatres did not want mere substitution of names or locales in Bengali but wanted a genuine Bengali play steeped in Bengali culture. In fact, during the late 19th century there was a debate regarding how Bengali theatre should develop. *Madhyastha*, a literary journal, published an article by Nripendra Saha emphasising the need to include songs in Bengali theatre:

> Some members of our modern educated community believe that theatre does not require songs at all. They have subjected themselves to such a belief having noted the lack of songs in the European theatre. However, they have failed to contemplate that India is not Europe, European society and our own society are very different, European tastes and our tastes are credibly independent of each other.[77]

There was only one way for foreign playwrights to be accepted by the general public. As Chatterjee argues:

> when the principles of Shakespearean drama were applied unannounced to indigenous dramas, the plays were well received. In other words, the Bengali audience did not object to hybridity, but disliked direct imports. The blind respect for everything Sanskrit and/or Shakespearean had given way to a firm basis for an indigenous aesthetics that fed on both the foreign and the native.[78]

This brings me to another production of Shakespeare by Amrendranath Datta on 21 June 1897 which was a huge success with the audience. The production was *Hariraj*, an adaptation of *Hamlet* by Nagendranath Chaudhuri for Classic Theatre (1897–1906). The play ran for almost three years in Calcutta theatres. Amrendranath played Hariraj while Tarasundari acted as Aruna and in later productions as Srilekha. The play had a huge success unlike Ghosh's *Macbeth* and many others that met the same fate. The *Indian Mirror* of 22 May 1900 praised Amrendranath extravagantly and wrote, '[W]e must confess that Babu Amrendranath, rightly called by the theatre going public the Garrick of the Bengal stage, absolutely surpassed himself in it (*Hariraj*).'[79] Another review in *The Hindoo Patriot* of 20 June 1899 praised the performance:

> The popular and evergreen tragedy *Hariraj* was put on the stage of the Classic Theatre on Sunday last.... The management of the Theatre is excellent and it has spared no expense in the direction either of dress or scenery to make the play attractive.... The parts played by Hariraj (Amrendranath Dutta) and Aroona (Sreemutty Tara Soondary) are undoubtedly praiseworthy.

Amrendranath succeeded where Ghosh had failed—in 'indigenising' Shakespeare. Raha notes Amrendranath's anticipation, 'Dutta foresaw that unless served as Bengali plays with names, locales, characters and situations metamorphosed into native equivalents—unless, that is, they were free adaptations—Shakespeare or, for that matter, any foreign playwright had little chance with the audience.'[80] Another reason for the easy acceptance of *Hariraj* with the audience was that it did not acknowledge any relation with Shakespeare's *Hamlet*. Thus, for the Bengali masses, *Hariraj* was a genuine Bengali play without any foreign air about it. Moreover, catering to the demands of the audience, Datta had incorporated several songs and dances. Shormishta Panja notes,

> Bengali theatre historians revere Ghosh as a giant of 19th century Bengali theatre and have mostly uncharitable things to say about Dutta, criticizing him for trivializing the dignity of the theatre. Still, Dutta's efforts to attract the average Bengali to the theatre presented an alternative to colonial staging practices and brought the theatre much closer to the relatively informal and interactive staging of Shakespeare's plays in Elizabethan England.[81]

The period from 1912 to 1922 in Bengali theatre is generally regarded as the period of decline. With the death of Girish Ghosh in 1912, the Bengali theatre seems to decline. By 1912, the well-known dramatists and actors of the Bengali public stage had gone. The decade did not produce many plays of merit. It was probably due to the absence of worthy plays in Bengali that one finds some adaptations of Shakespeare during this period. However, these adaptations did not go very well with the audiences. In 1913, Minerva Theatre staged *Cleopatra*, an adaptation of the original by Pramathanath Bhattacharya. The play had Tarasundari in the title role and Dani Babu as Antony. The *Amrita Bazar Patrika* of 5 September 1913 advertised the play having, 'new princely costumes and superb sceneries made by following Western ideals, which with a very rich cast and loved songs and dances will certainly prove to be a unique display'. Nothing much is known about the performance. However, a guess can be made by looking at the title which suggests it to be a 'faithful' translation of the original. It might not have succeeded much as there is hardly anything documented about the performance. Another performance of Shakespeare entitled *Saudagar* featured Amrendranath again in 1915 at the Star Theatre. *Saudagar* was an adaptation of *The Merchant of Venice* by Bhupendranath Banerjee. The performance, unfortunately, turned out to be the last performance of Amrendranath. While performing the role of Kuliraka, Amrendranath vomited blood and later on died. After Amrendranath's death, it was only in 1919 that a Shakespeare play was staged at the Star Theatre. The play was a Bengali translation of *Othello* by Devendranath Basu. *The Bengalee* on 15 March 1919 praised Tarasundari: 'We were assured by more than one critic that the acting of Desdemona approached perfection and the heroine had shown a remarkable power of adaptability which extorted unstinted praise from the audience.'[82] However, except Tarasundari and Dani Babu, the production could not capture the attention of the audience. Dasgupta notes, '[T]he sales in the first night were good, but fell down from the second. None of the parts except that of Tarasundari was done to the spirit of the dramatist'.[83] *Othello* shared the same reason which was responsible for the failure of Ghosh's *Macbeth*. The translator had tried to be 'faithful' to the original which did not match the expectations of the audience.

The 1920s witnessed a sea change in the Bengali theatre. Mukherjee informs that this change was especially evident in 'scenes and lighting arrangements, dress and properties, as well as in external arrangements and administrative matters'.[84] As far as the content of the drama is concerned the focus once again shifted to the social and the political instead of mythological or supernatural which later found manifestation in Indian People's Theatre Association (IPTA). It was the availability of Bengali dramas now that might have pushed Shakespeare to the margins as there were not many Shakespeare plays staged in Bengali theatre after the 1920s. Another reason might have been the growing fervour of nationalism when a foreign playwright would need to struggle to find a place. With the growing momentum of the freedom movement, Shakespeare's plays lost ground to more obvert and fervent nationalistic articulations. Majumdar argues that 'the public stage and Bengali playwrights consciously attempted to free themselves from his [Shakespeare's] influence in order to find an individual voice and identity in keeping with the growing flavour of nationalism in the country'.[85] It was only after the Independence that Shakespeare was taken up by the Bengali stage for production with a new zeal, evident in Utpal Dutt's productions of Shakespeare.

Notes

1. Sushil Kumar Mukherjee, *The Story of the Calcutta Theatres: 1753–1980* (Calcutta and New Delhi: K.P. Bagchi & Company, 1982), 1.
2. S.K. Bhattacharya, 'Shakespeare and Bengali Theatre,' *Indian Literature* 7, no. 1 (1964): 29.
3. Nandi Bhatia, *Acts of Authority/Acts of Resistance* (New Delhi: Oxford University Press, 2004), 12; Poonam Trivedi, '"Folk Shakespeare": The Performance of Shakespeare in Traditional Indian Theater Forms,' in *India's Shakespeare: Translation, Interpretation, and Performance*, eds. Poonam Trivedi and Dennis Bartholomeusz (New Delhi: Pearson Longman, 2005), 13.
4. Mukherjee, *The Story of the Calcutta Theatres*, 2.
5. Fay, Eliza. *The Original Letters from India of Mrs. Eliza Fay* (Calcutta: Thacker, Spink and Co., 1908), 153.
6. Quoted in Hemendranath Dasgupta, *The Indian Stage* (Calcutta: Metropolitan Printing & Publishing House, 1934), 195.

7. Jyotsna, Singh, *Colonial Narratives/Cultural Dialogues: 'Discoveries' of India in the Language of Colonialism* (London: Routledge, 1996), 103.
8. Quoted in Dasgupta, *The Indian Stage*, 262.
9. Ibid., 269.
10. Nandi Bhatia, '*Different Othello(s) and Contentious Spectators: Changing Responses in India*', *GRAMMA: Special Issues: Shakespeare Worldwide and the Idea of an Audience* 15 (2007): 160.
11. Dasgupta, *The Indian Stage*, 274.
12. Ibid., 274–275.
13. Ibid., 275.
14. Quoted in Sudipto Chatterjee and Jyotsna Singh, 'Moor or Less? The Surveillance of Othello, Calcutta 1848', in *Shakespeare and Appropriation*, eds. Christy Desmet and Robert Sawyer (London: Routledge, 1999), 76.
15. Quoted in Kironmoy Raha, *Bengali Theatre* (New Delhi: National Book Trust, 1978), 13.
16. Quoted in Sudipto Chatterjee, *The Colonial Staged: Theatre in Colonial Calcutta* (Calcutta: Seagull, 2007), 59.
17. Quoted in Christine Mangala Frost, '30 Rupees for Shakespeare: A Consideration of Imperial Theatre in India,' *Modern Drama* 35, no. 1 (1992): 97.
18. Quoted in Chatterjee, *The Colonial Staged*, 61.
19. Ibid., 64.
20. Jyotsna Singh, 'Different Shakespeares: The Bard in Colonial/Postcolonial India,' *Theatre Journal* 41, no. 4 (1989): 446.
21. Ibid.
22. While most theatre scholars consider 1831 to be the year in which the Hindu Theatre was establsished, P. Guha-Thakurta dates it to 1832 in *The Bengali Drama: Its Origin and Development*.
23. It was in the year 1813 that the Chowringhee Theatre was opened and was the first to have an Indian, Dwarkanath Tagore as one of its founders.
24. Gauri Viswanathan, 'The Beginnings of English Literary Studies in India,' *Oxford Literary Review* 9 (1987): 10.
25. T.B. Macaulay, 'Minute on Indian Education,' in *Selected Writings*, eds. J. Clive and T. Pinney (Chicago: University of Chicago Press, 1972), 249.
26. 'Asiatic Intelligence,' *The Asiatic Journal and Monthly Miscellany*, 22 (1826): 214.

27. As produced in P. Thankappan Nair, 'Lebedeff's Life in Calcutta', in Herasim Lebedeff, *A Grammar of the Pure and Mixed East Indian Dialects*, ed. Mahadev Prasad Saha, 2nd ed. (1960), vii. This was the first advertisement for a Bengali theatre in a newspaper.
28. Ibid., 5.
29. Quoted in Mukherjee, *The Story of the Calcutta Theatres*, 14; emphasis mine.
30. Sudipto Chatterjee, 'Mise-en-(Colonial-) Scene: The Theatre of the Bengal Renaissance,' in *Imperialism and Theatre: Essays on World Theatre, rama, and Performance 1795–1995*, ed. J. Ellen Gainor (London: Routledge, 1995), 20.
31. 'Dramatic Amusements of the Natives of India,' *The Asiatic Journal* 22 (1837), 28.
32. Kathryn Hansen, *Grounds for Play: The Nautanki Theatre of North India* (New Delhi: Manohar, 1992), 255.
33. Sharmishtha Saha, *Theatre and National Identity in Colonial India: Formation of a Community through Cultural Practice* (Delhi: Aakar Books, 2018), 96–97.
34. Macaulay, 'Minute on Indian Education,' 249.
35. Quoted in Dilip Kumar Biswas and Prabhat Chandra Ganguli, eds., *The Life and Letters of Raja Rammohun Roy*, 3rd ed. (Calcutta: Sadharan Brahmo Samaj, 1962), 153.
36. Ngugi wa Thiong'O, *Decolonizing the Mind: The Politics of Language in African Literature* (London: Currey, 1986), 16.
37. Edward Said, *Orientalism: Western Conceptions of the Orient* (NY: Vintage Books, 1979), 3.
38. Edward Said, '"The Text, the World, the Critic", *Textual Strategies: Perspectives in Post-Structuralist Criticism*,' ed. Josue V. Harari (London: Metheun & Co., 1980), 181.
39. Viswanathan, 'The Beginnings,' 7.
40. Charles E. Trevelyan, *On the Education of the People of India* (London: Orient Longman, 1838), 93.
41. Viswanathan, 'The Beginnings,' 16.
42. Ibid., 2.
43. Quoted in ibid., 14.
44. Quoted in David Kopf, *British Orientalism and the Bengal Renaissance* (Calcutta: Firma K.L. Mukhopadhyaya, 1969), 505.

45. William Jones, 'Preface,' in *Sacontala or the Fatal Ring: An Indian Drama by Calidas*, tr. William Jones (1792), accessed 2 July 2019, http://www.columbia.edu/itc/mealac/pritchett/00litlinks/shakuntala_jones/00_preface.htm.
46. Frantz Fanon, The *Wretched of the Earth*, tr. Constance Farrington (NY: Grove Press, 1963), 237.
47. Ania Loomba, *Gender, Race, Renaissance Drama* (Manchester: Manchester University Press, 1989), 15–16.
48. Quoted in Kopf, *British Orientalism*, 182.
49. Sudipto Chatterjee, 'The Nation Staged: Nationalist Discourse in Late Nineteenth Century Bengali Theatre,' in *Modern Indian Theatre: A Reader*, ed. Nandi Bhatia (New Delhi: Oxford University Press, 2009), 100.
50. Ibid., 102.
51. Macaulay, 'Minute on Indian Education,' 241.
52. Trevelyan, *On the Education*, 36–37; emphasis mine.
53. Bill Ashcroft, Gareth Griffiths and Helen Tiffin, *Post-Colonial Studies: The Key Concepts* (London: Routledge, 2009), 116.
54. Loomba, *Gender, Race, Renaissance Drama*, 21.
55. William Keane, 'On the Government of Indian Territories,' in *The Sessional Papers*, In the Session of 1852–53 Vol. XXIX, 302.
56. See Vikram Singh Thakur, 'Where art thou, Shakespeare?', *The Hindu*, 2 July 2019.
57. Ngugi wa Thiong'O, *Decolonizing the* Mind, 90.
58. Quoted in Subodhchandra Sengupta, 'Part One: History of the College,' in *Centenary Volume* (Presidency College: West Bengal Government Press, 1955), 4.
59. C.J. Sisson, *Shakespeare in India: Popular Adaptations on the Bombay Stage* (London: The Shakespearean Association, 1926), 15.
60. Emily Eden, '"Miss Eden to Mrs. Lister," Letter from Barrackpore, March 24, 1836,' in *Miss Eden's Letters*, ed. Violet Dickinson (London: Macmillan, 1919), 265.
61. Quoted in Dasgupta, *The Indian Stage*, 298–299.
62. Quoted in Mukherjee, *The Story of the Calcutta Theatres*, 16.
63. Quoted in Dasgupta, *The Indian Stage*, 301–302.
64. Quoted in *Report of the Oriental Seminary and its Branch Schools for the Year 1853–54* (Calcutta: Poornochundrodoy Press, n.d.), 21.

65. Quoted in ibid., 305–306.
66. Rustom Bharucha, *Rehearsals of Revolution: The Political Theater of Bengal* (Calcutta: Seagull, 1983), 23.
67. Ibid.
68. Quoted in S.K. Das, 'Shakespeare in Indian Languages,' in *India's Shakespeare,* eds. Trivedi and Bartholomeusz, 58.
69. T.N. Mukherjee, 'Introduction,' *Shakespeare's Macbeth*, tr. Ashutosh Ghose, 2nd ed. (Calcutta: M.I. Press, 1918).
70. R.K. Yajnik, *The Indian Theatre: Its Origins and its Later Developments Under European Influence* (London: George Allen & Unwin Ltd., 1933), 176.
71. Sarottama Majumdar, 'That Sublime "Old Gentleman": Shakespeare's plays in Calcutta, 1775–1930,' in *India's Shakespeare*, eds. Trivedi and Bartholomeusz, 237.
72. Quoted in Sarbani Putatunda, 'Shakespeare Infused into Indian Culture,' *The Statesman*, 3 July 2019.
73. Quoted in Mukherjee, *The Story of the Calcutta Theatres*, 82.
74. Quoted in Hemendranath Dasgupta, *The Indian Stage, Vol. III*: *Girish Centenary Edition* (Calcutta: Metropolitan Printing & Publishing House, 1944), 115.
75. Ibid., 115–116.
76. Quoted in Raha, *Bengali Theatre*, 41.
77. Quoted in Chatterjee, *The Colonial Staged*, 160–161.
78. Ibid., p. 159.
79. Quoted in Majumdar, 'That Sublime "Old Gentleman,"' 268.
80. Raha, *Bengali Theatre*, 76–77.
81. Shormishtha Panja, 'Shakespeare on the Indian Stage: Resistance, Recalcitrance, Recuperation,' in *Transnational Exchange in Early Modern Theater*, eds. Robert Henke and Eric Nicholsan (Hampshire: Ashgate, 2008), 219.
82. Quoted in Debjani Sengupta, 'Playing the Canon: Shakespeare and the Bengali Actress on the Calcutta Stage,' in *India's Shakespeare*, eds. Trivedi and Bartholomeusz, 254.
83. Hemendranath Dasgupta, *The Indian Stage, Vol. IV*: *Girish Natya Sansad Series* (Calcutta: Truth Press, 1944), 177.
84. Mukherjee, *The Story of the Calcutta Theatres*, 152.
85. Majumdar, 'That Sublime "Old Gentleman,"' 237.

II

Shakespeare in Parsi Theatre

There is but one country in the world, to the best of my knowledge, except possibly Germany, where the plays of Shakespeare have of recent times formed the safest and surest attraction to the indiscriminate masses who attend popular theatres, where the proprietor of a theatre could count on a profit on a Shakespeare production. That country is India, and the theatres in question are a group of theatres in the city of Bombay, clustered together in the heart of a poor Indian population.

C.J. Sisson, *Shakespeare in India*[1]

This chapter looks at the way Shakespeare's plays were appropriated in Parsi theatre—one of the major constituents in the history of modern Indian theatre. Parsi theatre has played a significant role among various factors that assisted the birth of modern Indian theatre. Although Parsi theatre, like its predecessors, looked at the Western theatre, especially Shakespeare, for inspiration and its development, but it appropriated both. The young English-educated Parsis of Bombay (now Mumbai) were already familiar with Shakespeare and led by their British teachers had been performing his plays during their school and college days as an amateur activity. Hence, once Parsi theatre began its activities, it was no surprise that Shakespeare would be one of the major playwrights in its repertoire. Shakespeare and Parsi theatre worked well for each other. While Shakespeare helped Parsi theatre to establish itself as an important theatre movement, Parsi theatre helped popularise Shakespeare in India by taking theatre beyond the educated elite circuit of the metropolis to the masses of the mofussil. Shakespeare provided the necessary material to cater to the needs of the audience—action, spectacle, rhetoric, declamation and thrill. In short, Shakespearean melodrama helped Parsi theatre find a potential and secure industry.

Parsi theatre, however, was quite a complex phenomenon and to comprehend it, it would be necessary to have an understanding of the socioeconomic and cultural developments that were taking place in 19th-century Bombay. The beginnings of Parsi theatre lie in the emerging discourses in the public sphere, civic activities, cultural philanthropy and social reforms that 19th-century Bombay was witnessing. The failure to locate Parsi theatre in this context has led many theatre scholars to argue that from its inception, Parsi theatre was commercial with profit as its sole motive. I argue that this aspect holds true for the later Parsi theatre. The early Parsi theatre in the 1850s was promoted by the Parsis as a civic and cultural activity. Only in the 1870s did it become thoroughly professional and commercial. Therefore, it is important to situate Parsi theatre in these emerging discourses of the 19th century.[2]

Parsis and the Public Sphere

The early history of Bombay shows it to be a cluster of seven separate islands ruled by different rulers.[3] In the 16th century, the Portuguese arrived in Bombay and controlled it till the mid-17th century. In 1661, Bombay ceded to the British consequent to the marriage treaty between Charles II and the Infanta Catherine of Portugal. In the year 1668, the British Crown transferred the control of Bombay to the East India Company. After the Portuguese pullout, the British started developing Bombay as a commercial centre. Thus, began the history of Bombay's 'capitalisation' and 'imperialisation'.[4] It was at this point in time that many Parsis migrated from Surat to Bombay. In fact, Dorabji Nanabhai, the first Parsi merchant, had already migrated to Bombay from Surat in 1640 to transact business on behalf of the

Portuguese. By the end of the 17th century, there were several Parsi families in Bombay, as it appeared from an account given by Sir Streynsham Master, a prominent East India Company official—'Here is allsoe some Parsees, but they are lately come since the English had the Island, and most of them are weavers, and have not yet any place to doe their Devotion in or to Bury their Dead.'[5] As a result of the British imperial project, Bombay underwent significant number of social, economic and cultural changes. Parsis in Bombay played a major role in ushering these changes. From the beginning, the British relied on the Parsis for trade and commerce. An important reason for this may be their recognition of the enterprising nature of the Parsis and readiness to accept English language and culture. Parsi merchants worked in close conjunction with the British, which led to mutual prosperity. The material prosperity of the Parsis can be estimated from the information published in the *Gazetteer of Bombay (1900–1910)* that by 1805, 'Bombay had 16 leading Parsi firms and two Parsi China agencies, as against three Portuguese, four Armenian, 15 Hindu and four Bohra firms.'[6] The commercial partnership with the British also helped the wealthy Parsi merchants to forge socio-political links with the latter that helped them to create a cultural and public space for themselves in the colonial society of Bombay. Jesse S. Palsetia explains that under the colonial regime the wealthy Indians in proximity to the British 'drew upon a set of new words and phrases … the public good, good governance, humanitarianism and loyalty'.[7] However, the meanings of these words and models were appropriated that created 'a colonial civic culture receptive and sensitive to Indian requirement'.[8] I contend that Parsi theatre too was an outcome of this civic culture as discussed later in the chapter. To create a public space for themselves, the wealthy Parsi merchants engaged in public welfare. Such civic activities undertaken by various Parsi merchants like Jamsetji Jeejeebhoy, Dadabhai Naoroji and others have already been documented at length.[9]

An important reason for the Parsis to gain power in the public sphere of Bombay was the cosmopolitan nature of the city itself. In other words, the absence of any dominating tradition encouraged a minority group like the Parsi community to gain a prominent position at the centre of the social, economic, cultural and public life of Bombay. David Willmer notes:

> Unlike older Indian cities, such as Delhi with its Mughal culture or Benares with its Sanskritic tradition, or other imperial cities, such as Calcutta and Madras, which were distinctly Bengali or Tamil in character, Bombay was characterized by an ecumene that was markedly more cosmopolitan or 'ethnically diverse' in nature. Although Bombay was situated in the province of Maharashtra, the Marathi tradition was by no means the only influence on the city's public formation. Gujarati (Hindu, Muslim and Jain as well as Parsi) traditions were at the very least equally as prominent at all stages in Bombay's history. Furthermore, this absence of a single dominant cultural tradition meant that other, numerically smaller communities (such as Goan Christians and Baghdadi Jews) had greater access to public space.[10]

Thus, the role of Parsis in developing a public space in Bombay is an immensely significant one. An appropriate example here would be that of Sir Jamsetji Jeejeebhoy who besides being a wealthy merchant played a crucial role in the development of public culture in the early colonial society of Bombay. He was also one of the earliest patrons of modern theatre in Bombay. Having made fortune in various business ventures in collaboration with the British, Jeejeebhoy was able to carve out a space for himself in the British society of Bombay. His proximity to the British allowed him to use British contacts to 'shape his image as a great philanthropist and eminent citizen and to enhance the potentialities of Indians in the public culture of colonial urban Bombay'.[11] He engaged in welfare activities and collaborated with the colonial government on various public projects like establishing western India's first civil hospital, educational institutions for the native students, and various public charities. Recognising his role in the public welfare of India, the British government conferred upon him for the first time on an Indian the title of baronet in 1842.

Theatre too was part of this public discourse as it was seen 'as the public manifestation of the respectable, 'gentlemanly' civic culture of the mercantile and administrative elite in that city, and not merely as a source of popular entertainment for the masses'.[12] This is evident from the fact that the English and Gujarati newspapers of Bombay supported the cause of Parsi theatre and played an important role in its establishment and consolidation. There was extensive coverage of Parsi performances in the form of advertisements, reviews and previews. Kathryn Hansen maintains, '[T]his coverage established a bourgeois, public space for theatre, linking it to adjacent discourses of respectability, civic order and moral reform.'[13] There is ample evidence of equating theatre with civic-mindedness. For instance, the *Rast Goftar* of 15 December 1867 informs its readers about a performance of Shakespeare's *Comedy of Errors* emphasising that the proceeds would go a public gymnasium. It is clear that the rich Parsi merchants promoted theatre as cultural philanthropy. Due to the efforts of Jeejeebhoy and a fellow Parsi Framji Cowasji, the Grant Road Theatre was opened in 1846, the first public theatre of Bombay, with the help of one Shankarseth. It was due to such acts that 'Indian financial and civic leaders embraced theatre as an object of cultural philanthropy and demonstrated their status and taste, laying the foundation for much broader participation by the Bombay populace in years to come'.[14] The contribution of wealthy merchants like Jeejeebhoy also presents an example of colonial agency. Colonial subjects like Jeejeebhoy were able to create a space within the colonial society where they could choose to act as agents of social, economic and cultural change, if not political. Moreover, their 'resistance' to imperial power can be located not in the outright rejection of colonialism but in the appropriation of Western beliefs, values and models to suit their own requirements. An example of this appropriation as resistance is the way Parsi theatre appropriated

Western theatre and drama, especially Shakespeare, to suit the audience sensibility. It was this appropriation of the Western theatre conventions that inverted the colonial 'hybridisation' of Parsi theatre which many postcolonial critics would not agree with. For such scholars, Parsi theatre was essentially 'hybrid', in the sense of Homi Bhabha's notion of 'hybridity', which I refute in the later section of this chapter. It is in recognition of the 'agency' exerted by the Parsis that Eckehard Kulke in the title of his work refers to the Parsi community as 'A Minority as Agent of Social Change'.[15]

The Beginnings of Parsi Theatre

Parsi theatre came into being with the opening of Grant Road Theatre in 1846. The location of Grant Road Theatre played an important role in determining the nature of Parsi theatre. The neighbourhood of Grant Road area had become an important commercial centre for Indians which provided impetus to the growth of population in this area. Its neighbourhoods like Kamathipura had already been populous with the working classes. Such availability of the native audience proved helpful for the growth and development of Parsi theatre. As Kathryn Hansen writes

> Grant Road was shortly populated by a number of other theatre houses including the Elphinstone, the Victoria Theatre, the Hindi Natyashala, the Grand Theatre, the Ripon and others. This district, separate from the better neighbourhoods of South Bombay, suited theatre managers intent on attracting a larger, more heterogeneous audience. Proximity to Khetwadi, Mazagaon and Girgaum ensured that the Hindu middle class would have ready access, just as the location of Market, Umarkhadi and Mandvi nearby invited Muslims. As textile mills mushroomed in Tardeo adjoining Grant Road to the west, workers availed of the chance to amuse themselves after long hours of employment.[16]

The Grant Road Theatre succeeded in thus broadening the audience base by including the working classes. It is here, in the Grant Road

Theatre that Parsi theatre's origins lie. The 'new' audience and its 'horizon of expectations' shaped the nature of the later Parsi theatre when it became thoroughly professional.[17] The first theatrical company to be launched was Parsi Theatrical Company in 1853. There were newspaper advertisements that referred to this company by many names such as Parsi Dramatic Corps, Parsi Theatrical Committee and Parsi Theatre. The performances of the company within the very first year are generally regarded as the beginning of Parsi theatre. However, S.K. Das opines that Parsi theatre, the way it came to be known later, came into existence in the 1870s as a commercial venture with Pestanji Framji's company.[18] Although Das does not mention the name of the company, Gupta refers to this company as Persian Zoroastrian Club.[19] Das ignores the contribution of companies like Parsi Theatrical Company (1853) and Zoroastrian Theatrical Club (1866).

It is a challenging proposition to define Parsi theatre because the process of which Parsi theatre was the result is itself quite complex. There are two main problems in defining Parsi theatre. First, there are scholars who do not focus on the Parsi origins of Parsi theatre. Some scholars define Parsi theatre etymologically as belonging solely to the Parsi community even though Parsi theatre flourished with Gujarati, Urdu and Hindi playwrights and actors. Such scholars, whether in Urdu literature or in Gujarati and Hindi literatures, either neglect Parsi playwrights or subsume them under their respective literary traditions. For instance, R.K. Yajnik equates Parsi theatre with Urdu theatre. Somnath Gupt finds fault with Abdul Ali Nami who includes Parsi theatre under 'Urdu theatre' in his volume on *Urdu Theatre*.[20] Willmer calls this tendency to define Parsi theatre without even acknowledging the Parsi origins as 'dehistoricizing the whole context of the term, ignoring as it does the actuality of an originative moment for the concept of "Parsi theatre."'[21] Second, some scholars define Parsi theatre etymologically as belonging solely to the Parsi community even though Parsi theatre flourished with Gujarati, Urdu and Hindi playwrights and actors. Thus any attempt at defining Parsi theatre must take these considerations into account. Willmer argues,

> to comprehend properly the meaning of the term "Parsi theatre" it is necessary to seek out its origins within the specific social and historical context which produced it. Without necessarily adopting an "ethnographic" approach to the subject, we must nevertheless recover those particular factors that were internal to the social context of the original Parsi theatre and which led to its transcending its originative moment.[22]

Gupt's attempt at defining Parsi theatre is probably the most comprehensive one. He defines Parsi theatre as follows.

> The phrase 'Parsi theatre' signifies the playhouses built and operated by the Parsi community, along with Parsi playwrights, Parsi dramas, Parsi stages, Parsi theatrical companies, Parsi actors, Parsi directors, and so on. Also included are those playwrights and actors who were not Parsis, but who worked on a salaried basis for the Parsi theatrical companies. Further, those companies, owners, and actors are counted who, while not being from the Parsi community and not being residents of Bombay, added the words 'of Bombay' to their theatre companies in order to show their connections to the Parsi theatre.[23]

Thus, Gupt helps one understand Parsi as a genre rather than an etymologically-defined community-specific affair.

Several Parsi theatrical companies mushroomed after 1877 like Amateurs Dramatic Club, Elphinstone Dramatic Club, Parsi Theatrical Company, Elphinstone Amateurs, Persian Theatrical Company, Parsi Stage Players Gentlemen Amateurs, Zoroastrian Theatrical Company, Zoroastrian Dramatic Society, Persian Zoroastrian Theatrical Company, Victoria Theatrical Company, Oriental Theatrical Company, Baronet Theatrical Company, Albert Theatrical Company, Shakespeare Theatrical Company, The Volunteers Club, Original Victoria Club, Hindi Theatrical Company and Parsi Victoria Opera Troupe. The companies were different, yet all of them shared some characteristics in their choice of subject and production style like melodramatic and sensational plots, song and dance sequences, spectacle, display of technology. Most of them followed the repertory system and painted curtain. Professional rivalry was common and there are many instances where a successful play by a company was copied with minor alterations by another company and staged. The managers would lure the good actors of other companies. On some occasions, a company manager would hire a band of claques to applaud his play to gain publicity. At other times, these claques were used to jeer the performance of another company to create the impression of the production as a failure.[24] Such fierce competition among these companies led their owners to spend huge amounts of money on making their productions attractive.

Parsi theatre survived on melodramatic plots and their emotional appeal, expansive sets and costumes, songs and dances and wonderful stage effects. Gupt observes,

> If the taste of the Bombay audiences can be guessed from the dramas performed, then it seems they preferred melodramas and farces. This was the influence of the contemporary English theatre. In London in the mid-nineteenth century, these were the kinds of drama that were most frequently performed. [...] This influence had come to England from Germany. The plays of Lessing, Goethe, and Schiller were influential throughout the European world. Their dramas contained an excess of sentiment in lieu of logic and thought.[25]

Shakespeare seemed to provide the necessary material to cater to the needs of the audience. However, a production cannot survive on indiscriminate borrowing of material from another culture. Adaptation scholars like Hannah Scolnicov, Peter Holland, Linda Hutcheon and Margaret Jane Kidnie in their theorisation of adaptation have stressed the need to look for appropriate cultural and gestural parallels in addition to linguistic ones.[26] Here lies the success of Parsi theatre in making Shakespeare relevant and popular among the Indian masses. Unlike the English performances of the Bard's plays staged by the educated elite, Parsi theatre indigenised them. Although the Parsi theatre playwrights borrowed a great deal from Shakespeare, they aimed not only at linguistic translation or adaptation but also cultural adaptation. The characters, locales, stories, costumes and forms were all indigenised. Even while performing in the proscenium, Indian folk forms like *bhavai* or *lavani* were used. This is well acknowledged by C.J. Sisson in his 1926 lecture at King's College, London when he says, 'Shakespeare is here [in India], not translated formally, not imitated, but transplanted as a living organism.'[27]

Parsi theatre used English, Gujarati, Urdu and Hindi in its productions. English was largely confined to the Shakespeare productions by college students. The Parsi Elphinstone Dramatic Club, for instance, which was a Parsi student club founded by Kunvarji Sohrabji Nazir in 1858, performed English plays in the college as well as at the Grant Road Theatre on Saturday nights.[28] These students were trained by European professionals and performed Shakespeare and other English playwrights. Willmer quotes a review published in the *Rast Goftar*, 25 February 1866 of a production of *Twelfth Night* by the Elphinstone Club 'in the presence of a "private" audience (the college governor and other ladies and gentlemen)' to praise the students' efforts in trying to put up the original English version of the play.[29] Another student group called the Shakespeare Society also performed Shakespeare plays annually in their college. It is not very difficult to assume the reason for the young English-educated Parsis for imitating the English theatre. They had already welcomed and taken to the English culture and theatre was no exception. The amateur student productions, however, continued to perform scenes from Shakespeare's plays even into the first half of the 20th century. Following is a 'Programme Note' of a social gathering of the New High School, 1915–1916 (see Images 2.1 and 2.2).

Image 2.1: 'Programme Note' of a *Social Gathering* of the New High School, 1915–1916

Courtesy: Parzor (The UNESCO Parsi Zoroastrian Project).

Image 2.2: 'Programme Note' of a *Social Gathering* of the New High School, 1915–1916 with a note on the performances of scenes from Shakespeare's *Romeo and Juliet* and *Julius Caesar*

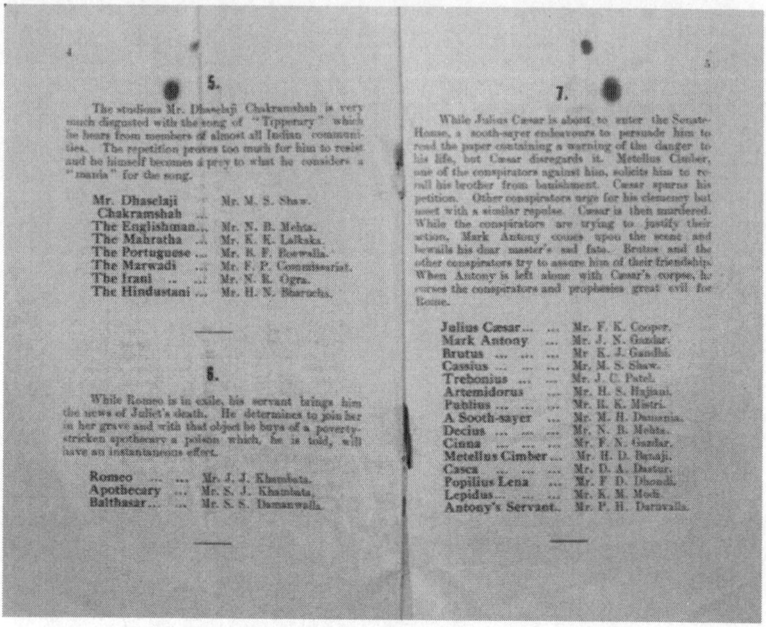

4

5.

The studious Mr. Dhaselaji Chakramshah is very much disgusted with the song of "Tipperary" which he hears from members of almost all Indian communities. The repetition proves too much for him to resist and he himself becomes a prey to what he considers a "mania" for the song.

Mr. Dhaselaji Chakramshah ... Mr. M. S. Shaw.
The Englishman... Mr. N. B. Mehta.
The Mahratha ... Mr. K. K. Lalkaka.
The Portuguese ... Mr. R. F. Rowalla.
The Marwadi ... Mr. F. P. Commissariat.
The Irani .. ... Mr. N. K. Ogra.
The Hindustani ... Mr. H. N. Bharucha.

6.

While Romeo is in exile, his servant brings him the news of Juliet's death. He determines to join her in her grave and with that object he buys of a poverty-stricken apothecary a poison which, he is told, will have an instantaneous effect.

Romeo ... ... Mr. J. J. Khambata.
Apothecary ... Mr. S. J. Khambata.
Balthasar... ... Mr. S. S. Damanwalla.

5

7.

While Julius Caesar is about to enter the Senate-House, a sooth-sayer endeavours to persuade him to read the paper containing a warning of the danger to his life, but Cæsar disregards it. Metellus Cimber, one of the conspirators against him, solicits him to recall his brother from banishment. Cæsar spurns his petition. Other conspirators urge for his clemency but meet with a similar repulse. Cæsar is then murdered. While the conspirators are trying to justify their action, Mark Antony comes upon the scene and bewails his dear master's sad fate. Brutus and the other conspirators try to assure him of their friendship. When Antony is left alone with Cæsar's corpse, he curses the conspirators and prophesies great evil for Rome.

Julius Cæsar... ... Mr. F. K. Cooper.
Mark Antony ... Mr. J. N. Gandar.
Brutus ... ... Mr K. J. Gandhi.
Cassius ... ... Mr. M. S. Shaw.
Trebonius ... ... Mr. J. C. Patel.
Artemidorus ... Mr. H. S. Hajiani.
Publius ... ... Mr. R. K. Mistri.
A Sooth-sayer ... Mr. M. H. Damania.
Decius ... ... Mr. N. B. Mehta.
Cinna ... ... Mr. F. N. Gandar.
Metellus Cimber ... Mr. H. D. Banaji.
Casca ... ... Mr. D. A. Dastur.
Popilius Lena ... Mr. F. D. Dhondi.
Lepidus... ... ... Mr. K. M. Modi.
Antony's Servant.. Mr. P. H. Daruvalla.

Courtesy: Parzor (The UNESCO Parsi Zoroastrian Project).

Another 'Programme Note' for an event (22 January 1922) by the Parsi students of St. Xavier's College featuring scenes from various Shakespeare plays is shown in Images 2.3 to 2.6.

Image 2.3: 'Programme Note' of a performance by the Parsi students of St. Xavier's College, Bombay (in the aid of The Parsi Sankat Nivaran Fund) on 22 January 1922

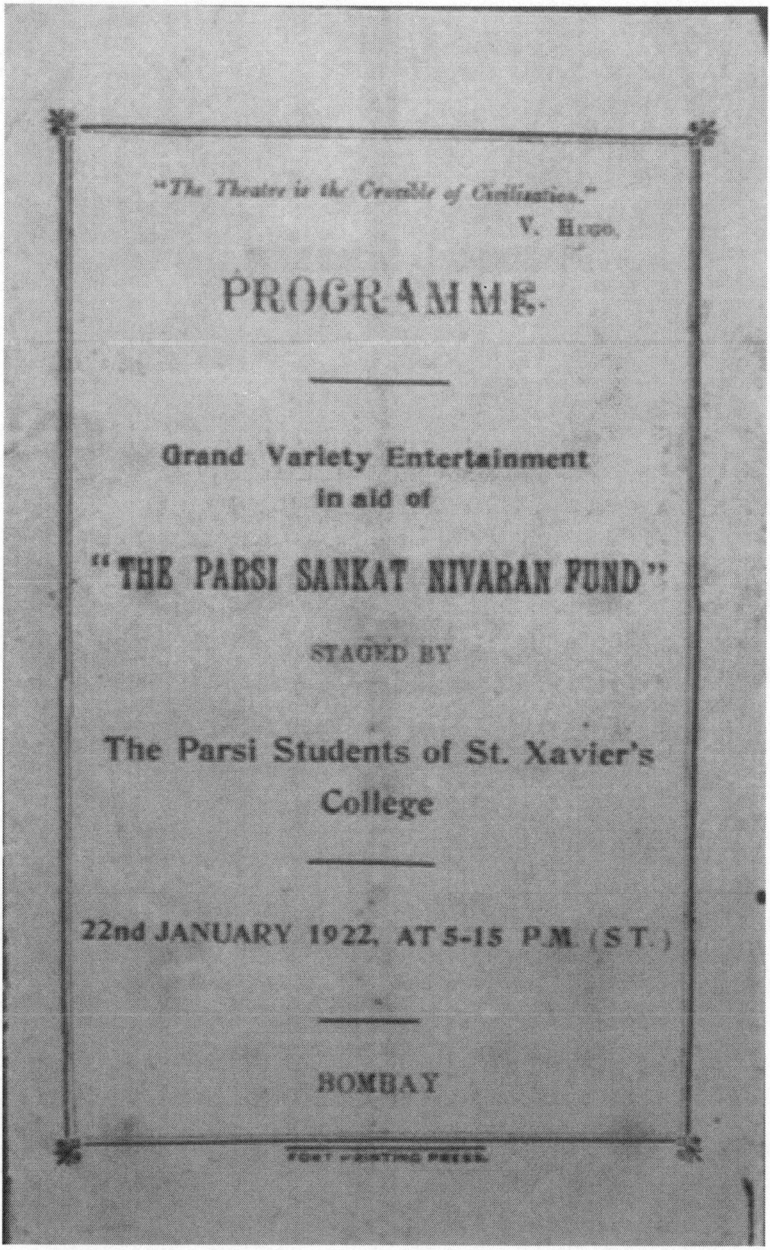
"The Theatre is the Crucible of Civilisation."
V. Hugo.

PROGRAMME.

Grand Variety Entertainment
in aid of

"THE PARSI SANKAT NIVARAN FUND"

STAGED BY

The Parsi Students of St. Xavier's
College

22nd JANUARY 1922, AT 5-15 P.M. (S.T.)

BOMBAY

FORT PRINTING PRESS.

Courtesy: Parzor (The UNESCO Parsi Zoroastrian Project).

Image 2.4: 'Programme Note' of a performance by the Parsi students of St. Xavier's College, Bombay on 22 January 1922 depicting the cast of *Romeo and Juliet* and synopsis of Act 111, scene 1

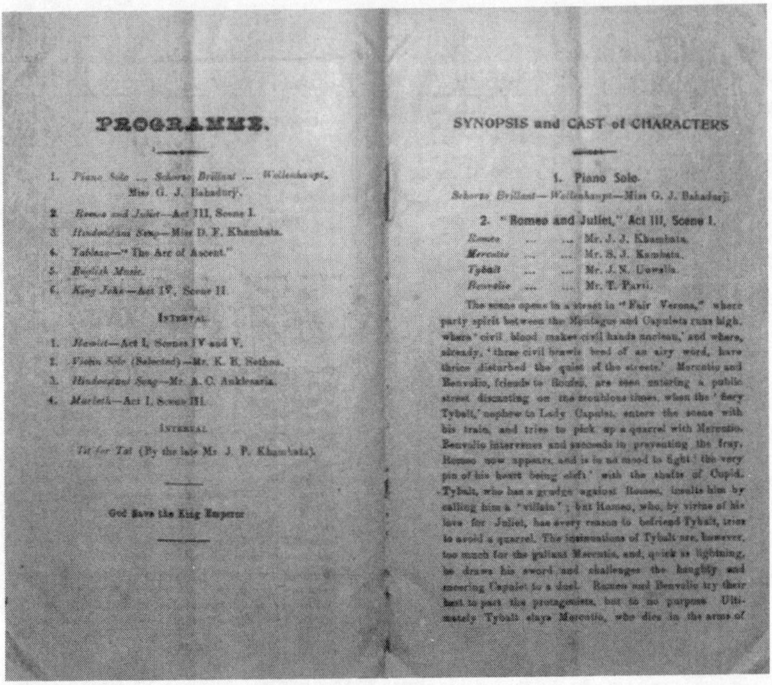

PROGRAMME.

1. *Piano Solo* ... *Scherzo Brillant* ... Wollenhaupt. Miss G. J. Bahadurji.
2. *Romeo and Juliet*—Act III, Scene I.
3. *Hindustani Song*—Miss D. F. Khambata.
4. Tableau—"The Arc of Ascent."
5. *English Music.*
6. *King John*—Act IV, Scene II.

INTERVAL.

1. *Hamlet*—Act I, Scenes IV and V.
2. *Violin Solo (Selected)*—Mr. K. R. Sethna.
3. *Hindustani Song*—Mr. A. C. Anklesaria.
4. *Macbeth*—Act I, Scene III.

INTERVAL.

Tit for Tat (By the late Mr. J. P. Khambata).

God Save the King Emperor

SYNOPSIS and CAST of CHARACTERS

1. Piano Solo.

Scherzo Brillant—Wollenhaupt—Miss G. J. Bahadurji.

2. "Romeo and Juliet," Act III, Scene I.

Romeo ... ... Mr. J. J. Khambata.
Mercutio ... ... Mr. S. J. Kambata.
Tybalt ... ... Mr. J. N. Unwalla.
Benvolio ... ... Mr. T. Parsi.

The scene opens in a street in "Fair Verona," where party spirit between the Montagues and Capulets runs high, where 'civil blood makes civil hands unclean,' and where, already, 'three civil brawls bred of an airy word, have thrice disturbed the quiet of the streets.' Mercutio and Benvolio, friends to Romeo, are seen entering a public street discanting on the troublous times, when the 'fiery Tybalt,' nephew to Lady Capulet, enters the scene with his train, and tries to pick up a quarrel with Mercutio. Benvolio intervenes and succeeds in preventing the fray. Romeo now appears, and is in no mood to fight: 'the very pin of his heart being cleft' with the shafts of Cupid. Tybalt, who has a grudge against Romeo, insults him by calling him a 'villain'; but Romeo, who, by virtue of his love for Juliet, has every reason to befriend Tybalt, tries to avoid a quarrel. The insinuations of Tybalt are, however, too much for the gallant Mercutio, and, quick as lightning, he draws his sword and challenges the haughty and sneering Capulet to a duel. Romeo and Benvolio try their best to part the protagonists, but to no purpose. Ultimately Tybalt slays Mercutio, who dies in the arms of

Courtesy: Parzor (The UNESCO Parsi Zoroastrian Project).

Image 2.5: 'Programme Note' of a performance by the Parsi students of St. Xavier's College, Bombay (in the aid of The Parsi Sankat Nivaran Fund) on 22 January 1922 depicting the programme schedule and synopsis and cast in Act IV, scene II of Shakespeare's *King John* and Act I, scenes IV and V of *Hamlet*

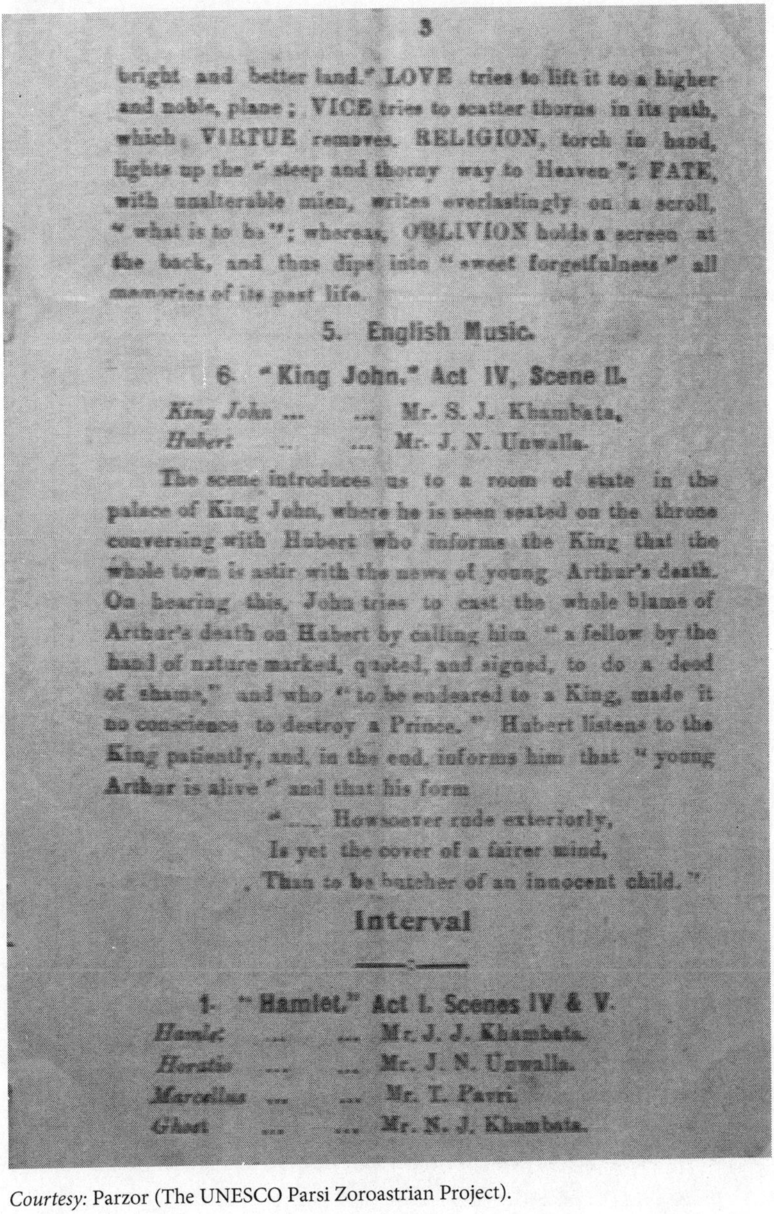

3

bright and better land." LOVE tries to lift it to a higher and noble, plane ; VICE tries to scatter thorns in its path, which VIRTUE removes. RELIGION, torch in hand, lights up the "steep and thorny way to Heaven"; FATE, with unalterable mien, writes everlastingly on a scroll, "what is to be"; whereas, OBLIVION holds a screen at the back, and thus dips into "sweet forgetfulness" all memories of its past life.

5. English Music.

6. "King John." Act IV, Scene II.

King John ... ... Mr. S. J. Khambata,
Hubert ... ... Mr. J. N. Unwalla.

The scene introduces us to a room of state in the palace of King John, where he is seen seated on the throne conversing with Hubert who informs the King that the whole town is astir with the news of young Arthur's death. On hearing this, John tries to cast the whole blame of Arthur's death on Hubert by calling him "a fellow by the hand of nature marked, quoted, and signed, to do a deed of shame," and who "to be endeared to a King, made it no conscience to destroy a Prince." Hubert listens to the King patiently, and, in the end, informs him that "young Arthur is alive" and that his form

"...... Howsoever rude exteriorly,
Is yet the cover of a fairer mind,
Than to be butcher of an innocent child."

Interval

1. "Hamlet," Act I, Scenes IV & V.

Hamlet ... ... Mr. J. J. Khambata.
Horatio ... ... Mr. J. N. Unwalla.
Marcellus ... ... Mr. T. Pavri.
Ghost ... ... Mr. N. J. Khambata.

Courtesy: Parzor (The UNESCO Parsi Zoroastrian Project).

Image 2.6: 'Programme Note' of a performance by the Parsi students of St. Xavier's College, Bombay (in the aid of The Parsi Sankat Nivaran Fund) on 22 January 1922 depicting the synopsis and cast in Act I, scene III of Shakespeare's *Macbeth*

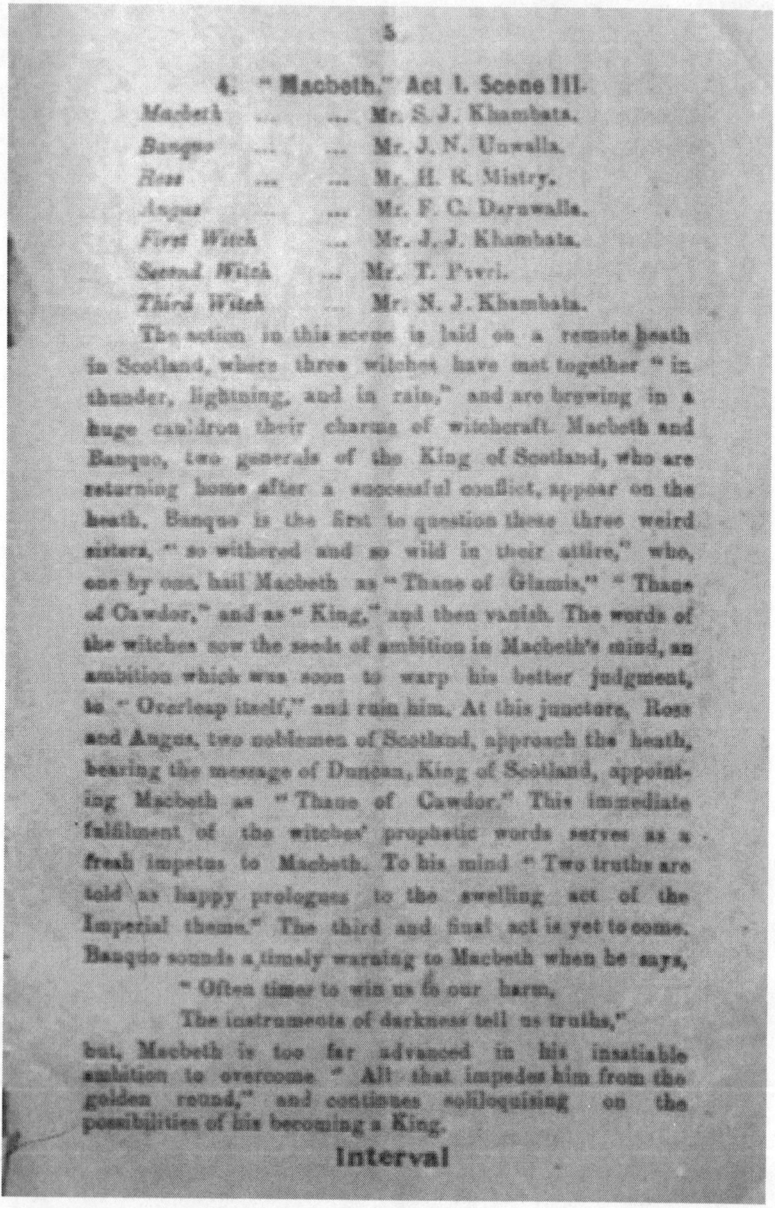

5

4. "Macbeth." Act 1. Scene III.

Macbeth	Mr. S. J. Khambata.
Banquo	Mr. J. N. Unwalla.
Ross	Mr. H. K. Mistry.
Angus	Mr. F. C. Daruwalla.
First Witch ...	Mr. J. J. Khambata.
Second Witch ...	Mr. T. P[illegible].
Third Witch ...	Mr. N. J. Khambata.

The action in this scene is laid on a remote heath in Scotland, where three witches have met together "in thunder, lightning, and in rain," and are brewing in a huge cauldron their charms of witchcraft. Macbeth and Banquo, two generals of the King of Scotland, who are returning home after a successful conflict, appear on the heath. Banquo is the first to question these three weird sisters, "so withered and so wild in their attire," who, one by one, hail Macbeth as "Thane of Glamis," "Thane of Cawdor," and as "King," and then vanish. The words of the witches sow the seeds of ambition in Macbeth's mind, an ambition which was soon to warp his better judgment, to "Overleap itself," and ruin him. At this juncture, Ross and Angus, two noblemen of Scotland, approach the heath, bearing the message of Duncan, King of Scotland, appointing Macbeth as "Thane of Cawdor." This immediate fulfilment of the witches' prophetic words serves as a fresh impetus to Macbeth. To his mind "Two truths are told as happy prologues to the swelling act of the Imperial theme." The third and final act is yet to come. Banquo sounds a timely warning to Macbeth when he says,

"Often times to win us to our harm,
The instruments of darkness tell us truths,"

but, Macbeth is too far advanced in his insatiable ambition to overcome "All that impedes him from the golden round," and continues soliloquising on the possibilities of his becoming a King.

Interval

Courtesy: Parzor (The UNESCO Parsi Zoroastrian Project).

However, the professional Parsi theatre being a public enterprise had to cater to the demands of the audience that largely comprised the working class from the neighbouring areas of the Grant Road Theatre who did not know English. Thus, the earlier vogue for English productions gradually gave way to Gujarati and Urdu/Hindustani productions. Hansen provides the following account that reflects upon the shift from English to Urdu/Hindustani productions.

> Although a contest might have developed between English and the Indian languages, English was quickly sidelined. The central rivalry that emerged was between Gujarati and Urdu, and this is well documented by the body of play texts published between 1865 and 1890. Out of a total of 80 printed plays identified in The British Library and newspaper notices, 35 are in Gujarati and 45 are in Urdu/Hindustani. However, the 'Urdu' category includes 17 plays published in Urdu language written in the Gujarati script. This sample undoubtedly under-represents the number of published plays. Nonetheless, of the 80 play texts, 44% were published in Gujarati, 21% in Urdu printed in Gujarati script and 35% in Urdu in Arabic script.[30]

Even the Parsi Elphinstone Dramatic Club was later transformed into a commercial company called the Elphinstone Theatrical Company and started performing plays in Gujarati and later on in Urdu. Their most favoured playwright Shakespeare too was adapted in Gujarati and Urdu/Hindustani in the 1870s. Image 2.7 depicts a Gujarati playbill of the 'Opening Night', 31 July 1913 of *Dhartikamp* (The Earthquake) directed by Jahangir Pestoni Khambatta.

Image 2.7: Playbill of a Gujarati play *Dhartikamp* (The Earthquake) directed by Jahangir Pestonji Khambatta and performed on 31 July 1913

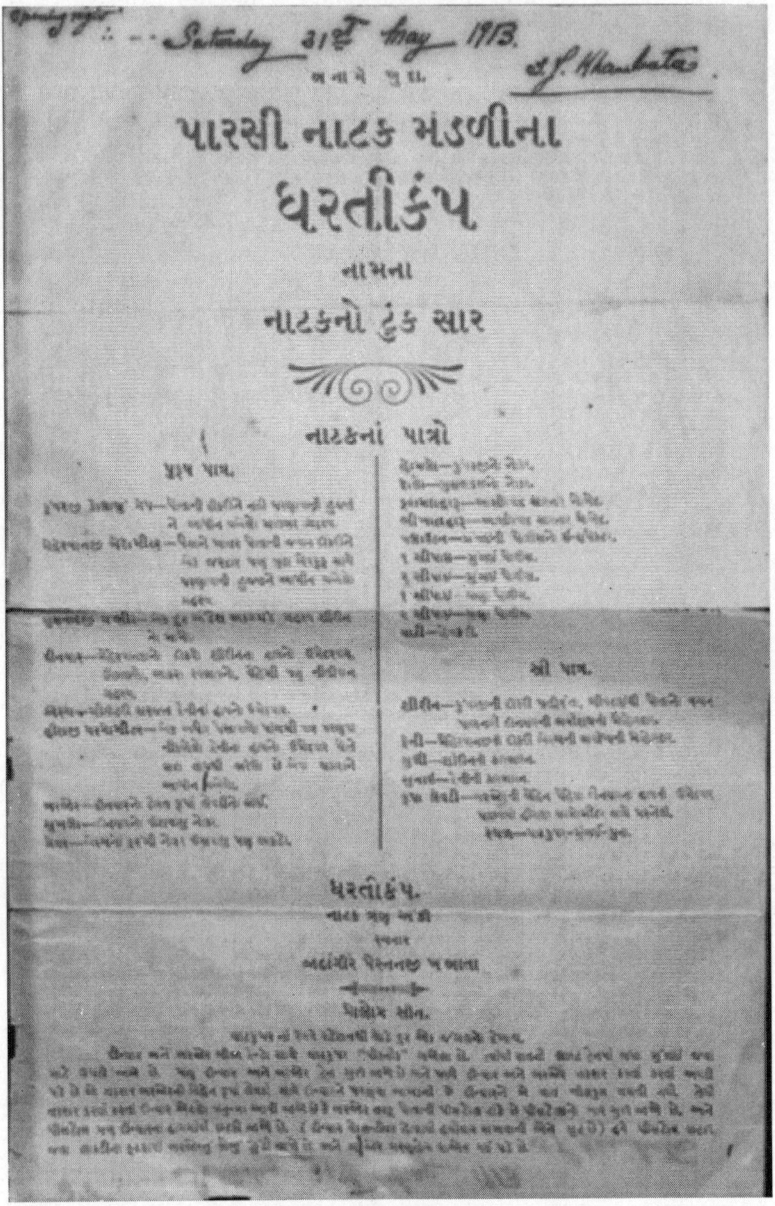

પારસી નાટક મંડળીના

ધરતીકંપ

નામના

નાટકનો ટુંક સાર

નાટકનાં પાત્રો

ધરતીકંપ.

Courtesy: Parzor (The UNESCO Parsi Zoroastrian Project).

Willmer refers to the early Gujarati-Parsi theatre as 'Janus-faced, looking back to the semi-mythological Persian history of the Parsi community and, at the same time, looking forward to the Parsis' role as mediators of the process of modernization in the new India'.[31] It is noteworthy that the Parsi-Gujarati playwrights wanted to present Parsi culture to their audience and also 'recover' the lost Parsi past. This pursuit of recovering the past is evident in the prefaces to the plays written during this period. Gupt cites the preface written by Kaikhushro Navrojji Kabra, the well-known journalist, for his play *Faredun* where he stresses his objective for writing the play.

> My main objective is only now, when Parsis have begun to forget their land, their power, their glory, and their feelings towards their people, to freshen the memory of previous glory by presenting before them a picture of that previous rule mingled with amusement and knowledge. And if my feeble efforts are of any help in increasing an enthusiasm for these matters among Parsis, I will consider myself amply repaid.[32]

Similarly, other early Parsi playwrights like Edalji Jamshedji Khori, Nanabhai Rustamji Ranina, Nasharvanji Mehrvanji Khansahab Aram, Bahmanji Navrojji Kabra, Khurshedji Mehrvanji Balivala, Dadabhai Edalji Ponchkhanevala Bandekhuda, Jahangir Khambata and Khurshedji Bahmanji Framroz drew inspiration from Parsi history, culture and works like *Shahnama*. Some of the Parsi playwrights not familiar with the Persian language turned to the English translations. Hansen mentions Edalji Khori who drew upon Mathew Arnold's and Atkinson's translations of *Rustam-o-Sohrab* (*Rustom and Sohrab*).[33] Shakespeare was also an important influence as his plays were quite popular from the inception of Parsi theatre. They were translated and published in Gujarati. Willmer mentions Gujarati translations of *Comedy of Errors* as *Jedia Bhai—Adhle Beheru Kutavu* (The Twins—The Blind and the Deaf) and *Othello* as *Kasrivajna Karstan* (Scheming Kasrivaj) by Nanabhai Rustamji Ranina published in 24 December 1865 in the *Rast Goftar* describing the translator as 'the foremost Gujarati translator of *mahaguru* Shakespeare's plays'.[34] Plays such as

The Taming of the Shrew, *The Merchant of Venice*, *Two Gentlemen of Verona* and *Timon of Athens* were produced in the early years of Parsi theatre, between 1857 and 1859 in Gujarati.[35]

The trend started changing after the 1860s when Parsi theatre adopted Urdu/Hindustani instead of Gujarati for playwriting and production. The first Urdu adaptation of a Shakespeare play was Edalji Khori's *Sone ke Mul ki Khurshed* in 1871, directed by Dadi Patel for the Victoria Theatrical Company at the Victoria Theatre. The play was initially translated into Gujarati by Khori as *Sunana Mulni Khurshed* and then into Urdu by Behramji Firdunji Merzban. There were two significant reasons for the shift from Gujarati to Urdu/Hindustani. The first was the economic compulsion of the Parsi theatre. Urdu/Hindustani, unlike Gujarati, had broader appeal. Plays in Urdu could be taken to other parts of India which meant more business. In fact, Parsi theatre earned much of its reputation by touring with its productions. The influence of Parsi theatre was so strong that soon various companies mushroomed throughout India. The second reason was related to the reformist discourse that colonial modernity had introduced. It is well-known that songs formed an integral part of Parsi theatre which utilised folk forms like *khayal*, *bhavai*, *garba* and *lavani*.[36] These songs were immensely popular, yet these folk form inclusions posited a problem. Hansen comments that the association of the traditional folk performers seemed a 'threat' to respectable and civic activity of the emerging middle class.[37] This concern is evident on the part of some of the Parsi playwrights who addressed this issue in the prefaces of their plays. Delta wrote in his preface for *Romeyo ane Julyat* (*Romeo and Juliet*), 'rather than the black stamp of immorality that is slapped on the mind of the viewer by the dance of prostitutes, the shows of *Mahlaris*, and the *Bhavai* of the folk-players, the blameless amusement of theatre enlarges the mind, gladdens the heart, cools the eyes, and speeds morality'.[38] Urdu seemed to provide the solution to this problem as it had a rich tradition of poetry and lyric. It was realised that adopting Urdu would, therefore, impart respectability to Parsi theatre. Parsi theatre, thus, adopted Urdu as its language of production from the 1870s onwards. In fact, the most productive and well-known period of Parsi theatre was when Urdu playwrights like 'Raunaq', 'Betaab', 'Kashmiri' and Ahsan Mehdi wrote for it. The use of Indian languages, then, right from the beginning challenged the theatrical modernity brought by the West by appropriating the Western plays in Indian languages.

Shakespeare in Parsi Theatre

Prior to Parsi theatre, the newly established theatre in the Indian metropolis was a private affair of the rich and the educated. Parsi theatre's biggest contribution to modern Indian theatre was to make theatre a public activity by opening it up for the masses. Since Parsi theatre catered to a diverse audience, it drew upon from eclectic sources for its narratives like Persian and Sanskrit mythology, medieval legends, histories and English plays. However, the greatest influence on Parsi theatre was Shakespeare. Shakespeare and Parsi theatre worked well for each other. Shakespeare provided Parsi theatre the necessary material to cater to the needs of this audience and Parsi theatre, in turn, popularised Shakespeare among the masses. The vogue of translating, adapting and appropriating Shakespeare, especially by the Urdu playwrights of Parsi theatre, can be judged by the fact that almost all major playwright of Parsi theatre drew upon Shakespeare for their plays. Because of his successful adaptations of Shakespeare's plays Agha Hashar Kashmiri, one of the most prominent Urdu playwrights of all times, earned for himself the title of *Shakespeare-e-Hind* (Shakespeare of India). Although there is no record of the number of Shakespearean productions by Parsi companies, one can guess by their growing number of plays performed and the translations and adaptations made for the Parsi theatre. Javed Malick lists at least 75 extant play-scripts.[39] Also, Yajnik in *The Indian Theatre* lists over 200 Shakespeare adaptations in various Indian languages by 1934. There may have been many more Shakespearean adaptations since most Parsi play-scripts are lost.

Parsi theatre generally followed a set pattern in adapting Shakespeare's plays. Javed Malick identifies the following as the main strategies in adapting Shakespeare for Parsi theatre.[40]

I. interpolation of songs and later dances into the original text,
II. rewriting and/or rearranging scenes of the original by jettisoning sequences and interweaving motifs derived from other Shakespearean texts into the chosen play with a view to simplify and streamline the bard's highly diversified and complex narrative patterns besides pandering to indigenous tastes and values,
III. changing the Elizabethan blank verse into standard Urdu forms of rhymed 'shers' and *ghazal*s or into rhythmic, ornate and stylized (often stilted) prose known as *nasr-e-muquaffa* and *musajja*,
IV. in the case of tragedies, refashioning the final sequences into a happy ending.

Besides, 'indegenising' the *mise-en-scène* and the use of dazzling sets and costumes to augment the spectacle were common in Parsi theatre. As mentioned earlier, songs were integral to Parsi theatre. Gupt notes that even fighting heroes and dying heroines would sing on the Urdu stage.[41] It is due to its musical character that Parsi theatre has also been referred to as opera. Gupt, crediting Dadi Patel for introducing music on the Parsi stage, notes, 'the addiction to songs grew to such an extent that occasions of joy, deaths, wars, and dialogues were all accompanied by singing'.[42] Lyrics printed on the 'opera book' or programmes were given to the audience and one could find the audience singing their favourite songs from the 'opera book'. While Parsi theatre used classical Indian music like *thumri*, *dadra*, *jhinjhoti* and *kalingara* besides ghazals, one could also find pieces of Western music.[43] Love scenes were often depicted through songs. Ania Loomba observes that a production of *Sher-Dil* (an Urdu adaptation of *Othello* by Najar Dehlvi) staged by the Parsi Alfred Company in 1918, opens with

> Brabantio entertaining Othello with dance and music. The Desdemona-Othello's courtship was often depicted through songs. Roderigo and Iago sing in duet to awaken Brabantio and his kinsmen with the news that the 'peacock is in the house of the thief' or that Desdemona and Othello have eloped.[44]

Khun-e-nahaq, an Urdu adaptation of *Hamlet* by Munshi Mehdi Hasan for Parsi Alfred Company (1898) was transformed into a musical. The play opens in the court of Claudius 'celebrating the nuptials of Claudius and Gertrude with dance and music'.[45] The audience's response to the songs sung on stage is described by Gupt in the following words.

> The audience, when pleased with the actors' songs, would shout 'Once more!' Sometimes, 'once more' was demanded even after the drop scene had fallen. If 'once more' was declared two or three times, the manager would satisfy the audience's desire by having the scene repeated. Sometimes this created the ridiculous effect of slain characters, recently killed in combat, rising from the floor and beginning to fight all over again.[46]

This fad for music increased the demand for trained classical singers. Amir Jan, Moti Jan, Mukhtar Begum, Gohar Jan, Munnibai and Mehrbai (Miss Mary Fenton) for example, who were trained semi-classical singers became popular singer-actors of Parsi theatre.

Most of the Parsi productions of Shakespeare were free adaptations with extreme liberties taken. New scenes were introduced and those which did not fit into the design were dropped. An example of the latter case can be found in Karimuddin Murad's adaptation of *Pericles* as *Khudadad* in which the father-daughter incest motif was dropped for its incompatibility with the 'Indian' sensibility. Instead, the king is poisoned against his son Khudadad by the minister Azlam which makes Khudadad flee from his kingdom.[47] Thrill, intrigue and murder were added to the plots. Yajnik argues that a play like *The Taming of the Shrew* was probably not adapted by the Urdu stage due to the absence of bloodshed and sentimental pathos.[48] On the other hand, a play like *Titus Andronicus*, which no other theatre approached because of blood and gore in the play, was adapted in Urdu by A.B. Latif 'Sad' as *Junune Vafa* (Mad Fidelity, 1910) and staged by the Shakespearean Theatrical Company in 1910. Although a whopping sum of 1,000 pounds was spent by the manager V.K. Nayak on the production for the elaborate Roman costumes and scenery yet the production was a failure, as Yajnik notes, possibly because: '(a) the high-sounding Roman names did not appeal to the people; and (b) scholastic touches given by many Arabic words fell flat on the ears of the illiterate playgoers'.[49] Scenes of pathos were exploited to the fullest. Often new poignant scenes were interpolated showing the characters facing 'even greater misfortunes than are to be met within the originals in order that their virtue might shine the more'.[50] Also, in some cases, scenes from various Shakespeare plays were incorporated within a single production. For example, Agha Hashar Kashmiri's adaptation of *Richard III* as *Saide-havas* for Parsi Theatrical Company incorporated scenes from the last two acts of *King John*. Similarly, scenes from two plays are mixed in *Dil Farosh*, an adaptation of *The Merchant of Venice* by Kashmiri. Mishra notes,

> After a conventional song, Bassanio (Kasim) in the position of Orlando is presented praying to God to protect him from the evil designs of his elder brother Mahmud, who not merely seeks to deprive him of his rightful share in property but also rivals him in his love for Portia.[51]

Some of the Bard's plays were adapted or appropriated by different playwrights for different companies. *King Lear*, for example, was adapted by Munshi Murad Ali for Victoria Theatrical Company (1905) as *Hara-Jita* and by Agha Hashar Kashmiri for Parsi Company as *Safed Khun* (1906). Similarly, *Othello* was adapted by Munshi Mehdi Hasan for The Empress Victoria Company as *Shaheede Vafa*

(1898) and by Najar Dehlvi for Parsi Alfred Company as *Sher-Dil* (1918). Most of the Shakespearean tragedies were transformed into happy endings probably because of the absence of tragedy as a genre in the classical Indian theatre and folk theatres. Thus, although both the versions of *King Lear* as *Hara-Jita* by Munshi Murad Ali for Victoria Theatrical Company (1905) and *Safed Khun* by Agha Hashar Kashmiri for Parsi Company (1906) follow the original text but end happily by uniting Lear and Cordelia and the latter being crowned.[52] Similarly, *Romeo and Juliet's* adaptation by Mehar Hasan as *Bazme Fani* (*The Fatal Banquet*, 1897) is transformed into a tragic-comedy in three acts. Also, *Kali Nagin* (1906), an adaptation of *Antony and Cleopatra* produced by one Joseph David for New Parsi Victoria Company, ends happily with Antony regaining his throne and uniting with his family.

In its early phase, few props or furniture were used on the stage in Parsi theatre similar to the early colonial theatre of Bombay probably due to financial constraints. Also, painted curtains were used in English theatre were employed to make the stage seem 'real'. Later, when Parsi theatre became commercial, professional rivalry among the theatre managers led them to spend huge amounts of money on creating stage spectacle. Company managers would spend thousands of rupees for scenic effects and dazzling costumes in a single production. Painted curtains retained their importance and painters were commissioned from Europe to paint them. Later, Indian artists were employed and names of celebrated painters like Hussain Buksh were advertised in the playbills. To attract the audience, playbills advertised spectacles like 'Transformation Scenes' that the audience could see. Stage effects of storms, seas or rivers in commotion, sieges, steamers, aerial movements and other similar scenes were generally employed and enjoyed by the audience.[53] The following playbill for *Nala and Damyanti* by Pandit Shaida is advertised as 'A Spectacle of Super-Extravagant Splendour in Three Acts'.[54]

NEW PLAY! NEW PLAY!
AT THE
CORINTHIAN THEATRE
ETC.
THE LOVE STORY OF THE AGES
NALA AND DAMAYANTI
A Spectacle of Super-Extravagant Splendour
in Three Acts
etc.
With an All-Star Cast Featuring India's
Popular Stage-Star
MASTER MOHAN
in the principal role of 'Bidushak'
The play is replete with gorgeous dresses, wonderful transformation scenes and weird and enchanting effects…
The entire gorgeous scenery designed and painted by
India's Greatest Living Artist
Mr. K. HUSSAIN BUKSH, of Lahore
See? See? See?
The sleepy Lotuses transform themselves into Fairy visions.
The Vision of Princess Damayanti.
The bursting of a lotus and the appearance of Goddess 'Saraswati' therefrom.
The flight of the Swan.
The 'Swayambara' of Damayanti.
Narad's descent from the clouds.
The miraculous appearance of Kali with the Flaming Sword.
The transformation of five Nalas.
The transformation of 'Karkota' in a forest fire.
The Durbar-Hall of King Nala.
The transformation of seven Fairies, etc.

One cannot miss the focus on 'splendour', 'gorgeous dresses', 'gorgeous scenery', 'flight' and 'transformation scenes' and 'enchanting effects', all of which were so typical of Parsi theatre. Another playbill for Shakespeare's *Cymbeline* by Empress Victoria Theatrical Company in 1899 was advertised as given in Images 2.8 and 2.9.

Image 2.8: Playbill of a Gujarati play *Zoolme Narwa* (*Cymbeline*) directed by Jahangir Pestonji for Empress Victoria Theatrical Company in 1899

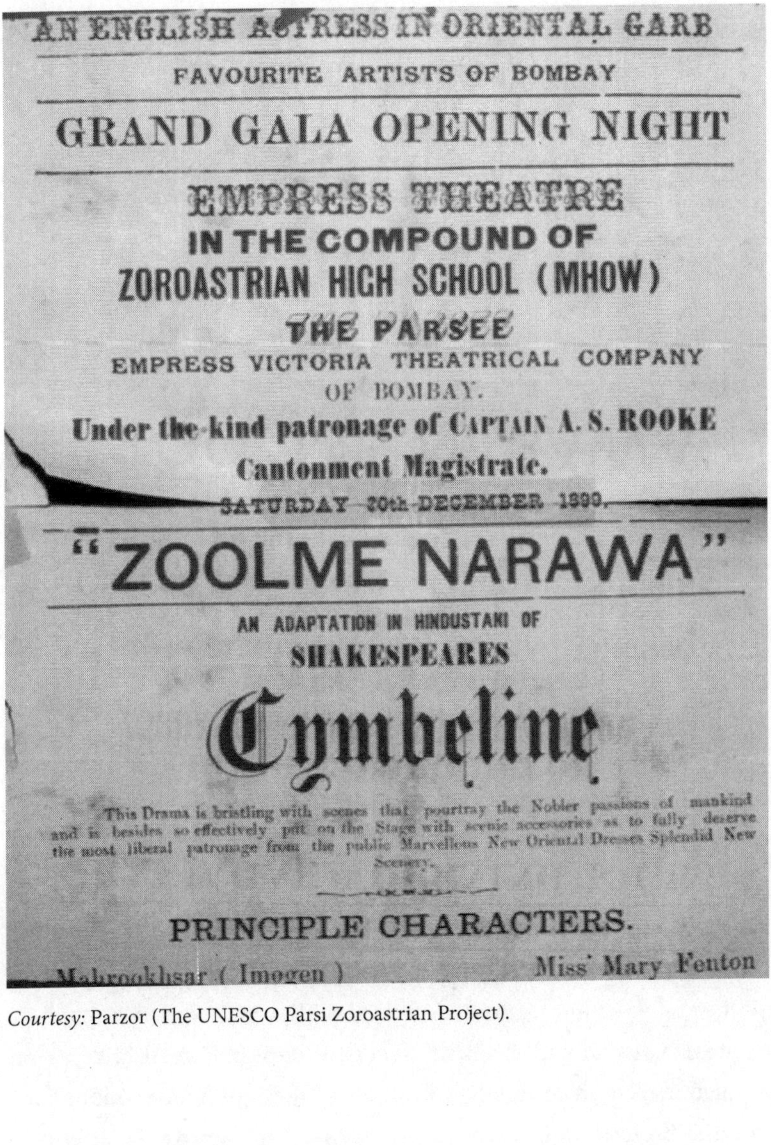

Courtesy: Parzor (The UNESCO Parsi Zoroastrian Project).

Image 2.9: Playbill of a Gujarati play *Zoolme Narwa* (*Cymbeline*) directed by Jahangir Pestonji for Empress Victoria Theatrical Company in 1899 depicting the cast and price of tickets

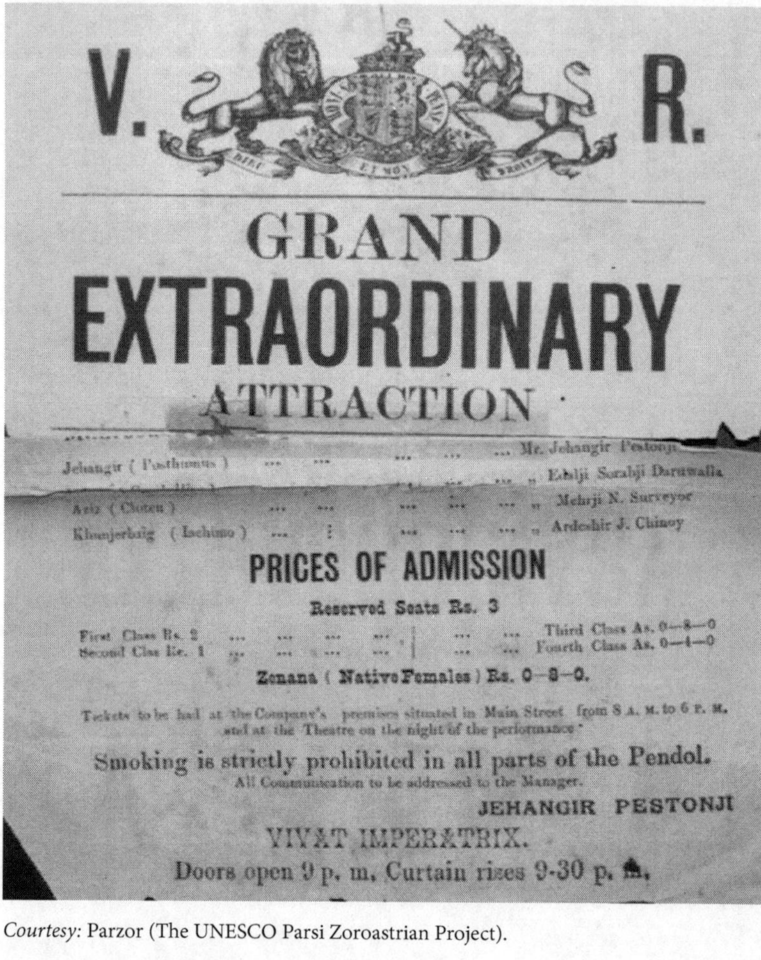

Courtesy: Parzor (The UNESCO Parsi Zoroastrian Project).

While the playbill introduced the actress Miss Mary Fenton, daughter of an Irish soldier and the most successful actor in Parsi theatre, as 'an English actress in oriental garb,' it also highlighted 'marvelous new oriental dresses' and 'splendid new scenery' to capture the attention of the audience (Image 2.7). In fact, the vogue for the spectacle was such that some companies even ordered machinery from England. This fashion for 'spectacle' interestingly gave birth to a new genre called 'mythological' drama. As Anuradha Kapur suggests, stories of gods and miracles that contained supernatural elements could now be presented easily on stage with the help of machinery.[55]

Costumes were another elaborate affair with the Parsi theatre companies that added to the spectacle. The early Parsi theatre used dazzling costumes regardless of their specificity to the periodical or cultural contexts in which the plays were set. Sometimes costumes were indigenised to suit the setting though this was not always the case. For instance, while the playbill for *Ek Bevapha Mitr* (A False Friend), an adaptation of *Othello* staged by The Parsi Stage Players, was advertised in the *Rast Goftar*, 10 October 1865 as a play in Gujarati language and Spanish costume.[56] Another playbill for a production of *As You Like It* by Gentleman Amateurs Club published in the *Rast Goftar*, 2 April 1865 advertised the play to be staged in 'Gujarati language and Italian costume'.[57] Due to such mixture in costumes, Ania Loomba describes the 'result' as 'a strangely hybrid dress, sometimes more Indian than Victorian, sometimes the other way around, and a theatrical look that was common in early Indian cinema as well'.[58] However, more attention was given to the appropriateness of costumes in the later period. For *Khun-e-nahaq* an adaptation of *Hamlet*, Kavasji Khatau followed 'Henry Irving's model for dress and scenery'.[59] Later, to preserve the 'original' flavour of Venice and Cyprus, his son spent vast sums of money on painted curtains and costumes for *Sher-Dil*, an adaptation of *Othello*.[60] The production of *Hara-Jita*, an adaptation of King Lear by Munshi Murad, uses elaborate and spectacular Egyptian costumes and scenery. Sometimes scenes were added into the scripts for the sake of spectacle and costume. One such case was the opening scene in *Bhul Bhullaiyan*, an adaptation of *Twelfth Night*, by The New Alfred Theatrical Company. The scene opens in the Court of Safdarjang, the King of Bokhara, which provides an opportunity to flaunt the grand and spectacular set and also dance and song. Yajnik informs us that the scene was dropped in the later production.[61] Many Shakespeare's plays in Parsi theatre opened with such grand court scenes which provided the theatre-managers an opportunity to display their technological superiority over the other companies. The Alfred Theatrical Company (1871) of Framji Joshi was especially known for its spectacular productions. Within its short life span, the company staged several spectacles. Gupt informs us that in its play *Jahanbakhsh ane Gulrukhsar* (Jahanbaksh and Gulrukhsar) 'mechanical scenes were employed for the first time. The eruption of a volcano, the emergence of a giant from the earth, and the descent onto the stage of flying fairies and other scenes were shown to good effect.'[62] Thus, song and dance, rich costumes, expensive spectacle combined with Shakespearean melodrama provided Parsi theatre with potential and security in the industry. See Images 2.10 to 2.12 for typical Parsi costumes.

Image 2.10: Hamlet's costume in Jal Khambatta's *Hamlet* (n.d. circa. 1940s)

Courtesy: Parzor (The UNESCO Parsi Zoroastrian Project).

Image 2.11: Claudius's costume in Jal Khambatta's *Hamlet* (n.d. circa. 1940s)

Courtesy: Parzor (The UNESCO Parsi Zoroastrian Project).

Image 2.12: Gertrude's costume in Jal Khambatta's *Hamlet* (n.d. circa. 1940s)

Courtesy: Parzor (The UNESCO Parsi Zoroastrian Project).

'Hybridity' in Parsi Theatre

Dennis Kennedy in *Foreign Shakespeare* observes,

> Whereas in Europe the Shakespeare project embraced the translation and outright appropriation of the texts, in Asia the imperial mode tended to bring them in the original language as a demonstration of the linguistic and the cultural superiority of the conqueror. This was most notable in India, of course, where the insertion of the Shakespearean text into native life paralleled the insertion of the power of the master race.[63]

This is but partially true. There is no denying the fact that Shakespeare, as part of English literary studies, was a forced assimilation imposed upon the natives to demonstrate the British cultural and moral superiority. Not only the 'academic' Shakespeare, but the earlier Shakespeare productions also attempted to be 'faithful' to both the text and the conventions of English theatre. But Shakespeare was gradually assimilated into indigenous theatrical activity. The plays were translated and performed in regional languages. Poonam Trivedi observes that the earliest local adaptation of a Shakespeare play in India was *Nathari Firangiz Thekani Avi* (A Bad Foreigner Woman Brought to Sense), a critical adaptation of *The Taming of the Shrew*, 'for it distanced and labeled the shrew as non-Indian, a *firangi*', performed in 1852 in Gujarati.[64] As discussed in the previous section, Parsi playwrights like Agha Hashar Kashmiri, Munshi Mehdi Hasan and Narain Prasad Betab appropriated Shakespeare's plays freely and took liberties with plots, characters and structures. Dances and songs based on Indian classical music and occasionally on Western music were added, scenes were interpolated or discarded, new characters and plots of murders and intrigues were introduced. In fact, Parsi theatre made every effort to fit Shakespeare's plays into the Indian context. Such 'illegitimate' Shakespeare, as some may call it, was the hallmark of Parsi theatre. Such eclectic nature of Parsi theatre may (mis)lead one to theorise it as essentially 'hybrid'.

As Loomba observes regarding the costumes in Parsi theatre which were drawn from different sources and resulted in 'a strangely hybrid dress, sometimes more Indian than Victorian, sometimes the other way around, and a theatrical look that was common in early Indian cinema as well'.[65] Though this might appear as 'hybrid' yet one should be cautious in locating Parsi theatre in general and Parsi adaptations of Shakespeare's plays in particular in the discourse of (post)colonial 'hybridity' for the reasons elaborated further.

'Hybridity' is one of the most contested and widely (mis)used concepts in postcolonial theory. In recent years, the concept has been linked with Homi Bhabha who was inspired by Franz Fanon's view to develop his theory of cultural 'hybridity'. Fanon in *Black Skin, White Masks* argues that the colonised subject is hybrid as s/he attempts to mimic the coloniser but fails in the attempt and in the process becomes hybrid.[66] For Fanon, 'hybrid' means rootless. In his view, this psychic schism leads to the erasure of the identity of the colonized subject as s/he disowns his/her roots and attempts to become white. Fanon writes in *The Wretched of the Earth* that the colonial world is 'a world divided into compartments ... a world cut into two' where the coloniser and the colonised are two clear-cut binaries.[67] Unlike Fanon, Bhabha argues that the relationship between the colonised and the coloniser is 'ambivalent', a constantly fluctuating love/hate relationship and thus interdependent. Bhabha in *Location of Culture* defines colonial mimicry as 'the desire for a reformed, recognisable Other, as a subject of a difference that is almost the same, but not quite'.[68] For Bhabha, mimicry is not a tragic failure as viewed by Fanon. On the other hand, mimicry enables agency in the colonised subject. This is so because according to Bhabha, mimicry is not far from mockery, a kind of parody, thus, making mockery 'at once resemblance and menace'.[69] Bhabha's concept thus provides an alternative understanding of coloniser–colonised relationship as it stresses the dependence of both on each other. If one considers the early amateur English productions by Indian students, many of which were Shakespeare's, one may argue that there was an attempt to 'mimic' the Western theatrical conventions. Also, one can call such productions as a case of colonial 'mimicry' since they were carried out to produce Macaulay's 'mimic men' who could reproduce English culture without losing their brown skins. However, it is important to note that these productions were confined to the exclusive domains of schools and colleges. Even when these performances were staged in more public spaces like the Grant Road Theatre, the audience comprised educated Indians and the European gentry. Moreover, one should remember that such productions were not representative of the Parsi theatre as it came to be identified later—a flamboyant, dynamic and popular style of performance. This kind of Parsi theatre was, on the contrary, best represented by plays staged in various Indian languages like Hindi, Urdu, Gujarati and Marathi and characterised by the features mentioned in the previous section of this chapter. The need for localising foreign plays became strong during the later years of Parsi theatre that student theatre clubs like Elphinstone Dramatic Club which had performed Shakespeare in English earlier started performing his plays in Gujarati and Urdu by the 1870s. The desire for 'mimicry' in the case of Parsi theatre reflects on the *indigenisation* of the English traditions rather than the 'Englishisation' of Indian traditions. In a sense then, Parsi theatre's mimicry is not targeted towards becoming like the coloniser. Consequently, what Parsi theatre creates is a syncretic form of theatre by yoking together elements of Indian and English theatrical traditions without any obvious foreignness about it. The materiality of Parsi theatre, as against the textuality of academic Shakespeare, allows it to invert the logic of colonial mimicry.

Bhabha, as mentioned earlier, acknowledges the coloniser–colonised relationship as 'ambivalent' and 'unfixed'. He generalises this state as common to the colonial subject anywhere in the world. According to Bhabha every colonial subject is 'hybrid' and every cultural identity is negotiated and formed in the 'third space of enunciation'.[70] He does not take into account various factors like gender, nation or class/caste that could nuance the coloniser–colonised relationship that could make it different. Loomba raises this important question and argues that.

> The colonialist presence was felt differently by various subjects of the empire some never even saw Europeans in all their lives, and for them authority still wore a native face. For others, but even for some of the elites … the foreign presence was daily visible, but physical as well as cultural space was still divided into 'their' sphere and 'ours'. In other parts of the world colonialism had penetrated much deeper into the everyday existence of natives of all classes. These patterns also shifted over time. Thus the resonances of both 'hybridity' and mimicry are enormously variable and we need to peg the psychic splits engendered by colonial rule to specific histories and locations.[71]

Both Bhabha and Fanon argue that the colonial subject undergoes the split in identity in the colonial world. An intimate and interdependent relationship between the coloniser and the colonised makes the base for such an argument. It may be true for the educated elite subject who might have shared an 'element of intimacy' which is central to the postcolonial view of hybridity. However, this argument may not be applied to every colonial subject anywhere. Not every colonial subject shared an 'intimate' relationship with the coloniser The post1870s Parsi theatre explains this refusal of 'hybridity' on behalf of the colonised subject. Bhabha assumes that mimicry and hybridity can be potentially subversive. He states,

> Mimicry is, thus the sign of a double articulation; a complex strategy of reform, regulation and discipline, which 'appropriates' the Other as it visualizes power. Mimicry is also the sign of the inappropriate, however, a difference or recalcitrance which coheres the dominant strategic function of colonial power, intensifies surveillance, and poses an immanent threat to both 'normalized' knowledges and disciplinary powers.[72]

Also, according to Bhabha, 'Hybridity is the sign of the productivity of colonial power, its shifting forces and fixities; it is the name for the strategic reversal of the process of domination through disavowal.'[73] However, Parsi theatre's 'hybrid' Shakespeare does not subvert the Shakespearean authority by 'appropriating' it since it does not recognise that authority in the first place. It 'appropriates' Shakespeare not because Shakespeare is great but because Shakespeare seems to cater to the melodramatic nature of Parsi theatre which, in turn, was determined by the audience's craving for a spectacle that had a song, dance, declamation, action and thrill. There is no doubt that Parsi theatre took a great deal from the Western theatre including Shakespeare. However, Parsi theatre thoroughly appropriated the European theatre for the native mass consumption. As Rustom Bharucha observes, 'these derivations [i.e. Western theatrical conventions] had been thoroughly "Indianized" through music, song, colour, pathos, melodrama and the histrionic delivery of lines that are intrinsically a part of the popular theatrical tradition in India'.[74] Although Parsi productions were staged in proscenium with box sets, painted curtains and transformation scenes, they incorporated folk forms like *bhavai*, *yakshagan*, or *lavani* and Urdu, Gujarati or Persian ghazals, and thumris. As Willmer has argued,

> the whole style of performance suggests an established idiom that owes little or nothing to colonial influences. The customary appearance of Ganapati and Saraswati (the latter riding a peacock), usually accompanied by the angelic child gods Bal and Gopal, that opened each performance immediately located the performance within a different tradition, and the incorporation of the songs, acrobatics and jests of the clowns point to another (secular or popular) aspect of this different tradition.[75]

It does not seem that there was a desire to 'mimic' European theatre in order to 'become like that'. Thus, there was no reverence towards either European theatre or Shakespeare on behalf of Parsi theatre. Even the early Bollywood films based on Parsi theatre productions, states Rajiva Verma, were not reverential adaptations of a master text but a case of 'one professional playwright borrowing plots and situations and other tricks of the trade from another'.[76] Thus, the material conditions of Parsi theatre allowed it to borrow freely from European theatrical traditions and mixing them with indigenous theatre. Such eclecticism, coupled with its commercial compulsions prevented Parsi theatre from 'mimicking' its colonial masters with an intention to become like them. In this context, the hybridity of Parsi theatre can then be understood, as Willmer puts it, as:

> a kind of publicly-mediated 'hybridity of form' that characterizes Parsi theatre, rather than the internal distortions and mutations that mark postcolonial hybridity. This hybridity of form is the means by which Parsi theatre 'acts out' the narrative transformations brought about by the encounter with empire, its cultural components ('the civilizing mission'), and imperial capital, rather than an essential transformation of self produced by the experience of colonization.[77]

A more fundamental problem with the concept of 'hybridity' is that although it aims to deconstruct the notion of 'authenticity' but it assumes the presence of the latter in the first place against which 'hybridity' is set as a binary. However, the existence of 'authentic' itself is problematic. Loomba, for instance, argues, 'every culture can be said to be hybrid—in fact even 'authentic' identities are the result of ongoing processes of selection, cutting and mixing of cultural vocabularies. In practice, hybridity and authenticity are rarely either/or positions'.[78] Also, Bart Moore-Gilbert argues,

> the term 'hybridity', only has a conceptual force by the virtue of the assumption that there are such things as 'non-hybrid' cultures, which by no one has yet been able to demonstrate. Inevitably, some such accounts tend to homogenize the centre (and the Third World, to a lesser extent) more or less implicitly and make it monolithic in a way which simply does not do justice to the realities.[79]

If one works by the reverse logic it can be argued since there is no 'purity' there can never be 'hybridity'. The question of 'purity'/'authenticity' and 'hybridity'/'inauthenticity' gains particular significance in the context of Parsi productions of Shakespeare since the 'hybrid' (read: eclectic) nature of such productions may tempt a bardolator to consider them as 'inauthentic' Shakespeare. For instance, Sisson in his 1926 lecture to the Shakespeare Association at King's College, London observed.

> The orthodox Shakespearian would experience many a shock if he ventured into this [the theatres of Bombay] strange temple of his idol. He might accustom himself to the Oriental costume and mise-en-scene, to the disturbing medley of the audience, even, with some study, to the foreign language. But he would be amazed to find that he was being provided with an opera, and a ballet as well as a play, …, and horrified when he realized the extreme liberties that were being taken with the text and plot.[80]

Sisson's view is decidedly Eurocentric since the 'authenticity' of a Shakespeare production, to him, is determined by the way Shakespeare's plays were staged in England. The 'authenticity' of Shakespeare is debatable at textual as well as performance level. How is one to believe that the Shakespeare text that has come down to the modern readers is 'authentic'? Shakespeare himself was a reviser of scripts. Moreover, Shakespeare texts have been mediated by numerous editors, compositors and scribes. Such multiplicity of Shakespeare texts makes it impossible to claim a version as the 'authentic' text of Shakespeare. Lurie E. Osborne notes,

> All Shakespearean editions are copies; there is no recoverable original, even for those plays like *All's Well that Ends Well* for which bibliographers suggest that the edited text was taken from Shakespeare's foul papers. In fact, the more vigorously textual bibliographers search for some singular, original authorizing text, the more obvious it becomes that there is no original to be found.[81]

In addition to the Shakespeare text, present-day performance conditions even in England are very different from the Elizabethan times. As Loomba argues,

> For even the New Globe is, as Dennis Kennedy has put it, 'a form of staged authenticity', combining aspects of the shrine with those of the amusement park. In this situation, the inauthenticity of the 'foreign' or indeed any other devotee should matter less than it once did, just as the authenticity of Shakespeare himself is less important to both audiences and vendors.[82]

Another useful insight into the 'authenticity' and 'hybridity' debate can be W.B. Worthen's idea of the 'citational environment' defined as 'generic and cultural fields that incorporate specific stances towards source materials and rules for handling them'.[83] According to Cartelli and Rowe, '[A]ll adaptations make their habitations not only in specific geographic milieu and media but also in citational environments.'[84] Worthen has developed the idea of citational environment from Joseph Grigely's notion of 'iteration' and states that the concept of iteration refers to 'not only the transmission of texts but also the ongoing negotiation of the meaning of artworks in culture'.[85] For Grigely, any act of 'transmission of art … necessarily involves surrogation, a continual "process of being unmade (as an object) and remade (as a text and as memory)," a kind of performance he calls "textualterity."'[86] Understood in this sense, every attempt to produce a Shakespeare play, or for that matter any other play, is a palimpsest rather than 'authentic'. Thus, any attempt at producing an 'authentic' Shakespeare play would invariably be 'inauthentic'. Grigely's 'textualterity', thus, relieves Shakespeare of the burden of 'authenticity' and justifies the difference posited by each performance from another.

Thus, one finds that Parsi theatre is 'hybrid' in the sense of being eclectic not necessarily characterised by the mutations of the postcolonial hybridity. Driven by its own material and economic compulsions Parsi theatre borrowed only those elements from English theatre that it considered would add to its commercial value. In the process, Parsi theatre created a syncretic theatrical form devoid of any foreign pretensions about it. It is this syncretism of Western and Indian aesthetics, dramatic and theatrical conventions, techniques and devices that characterise the later period of Indian theatre and which would be carried into Indian cinema. Parsi theatre enjoyed its hey-day till the 1920s after which it started declining with the advent of cinema in Bombay.[87] Many of the actors and playwrights of Parsi theatre joined the cinema. Though cinema was influenced by Parsi theatre and it continued to exert its influence for decades to come especially with its legacy of melodrama, dance and song. Parsi theatre, without any doubt, succeeded in popularising Shakespeare in India to the extent that no other theatre has been able to do since then.

Notes

1. C.J. Sisson, *Shakespeare in India: Popular Adaptations on the Bombay Stage* (London: The Shakespearean Association, 1926), 7.
2. There are several challenges involved in researching on Parsi theatre. To trace the beginnings of Parsi theatre one needs to rely on newspaper advertisements and reviews, play scripts, memoirs, song books, biographies and letters. Sometimes, the reliability of some such documents may be doubtful. For example, the colonial agenda of the Anglo-Indian newspaper *Bombay Telegraph and Courier* or the reformist agenda of Parsi-Gujarati weekly *Rast Goftar* determined the nature of the review of a particular production in the mid-19th century Bombay theatre. Second, many of the extant play-scripts may not be the 'original' plays written by the Parsi playwrights but afterthoughts. Another problem arises due to the fact that plagiarism was a common practice. A popular play was quite often published by another playwright with some alterations. One such example is the extant play-script of *Khudadad* in Urdu which is a translation of Shakespeare's *Pericles, the Prince of Tyre*. Javed Malick in 'Foreign Origins/Native Destinations' notes that although the play was originally written by a playwright called Karimuddin Murad, the extant version bears the name of Mahmood Mian Zarif [Lata Singh, ed., *Theatre in Colonial India: Play House of Power* (New Delhi: Oxford University Press, 2009), 170.] In all probability, the extant play is a pirated version of Murad's *Khudad*. Also, *Dil Farosh* (*The Merchant of Hearts*, 1900) is an adaptation of *The Merchant of Venice* by Agha Hashar Kashmiri. But there is another play by this name which is attributed to Munshi Mehdi Hasan 'Ahsan' by Ganga Prasad Arora who represented the play in Devnagari script. Yet another challenge is that a good amount of source material on Parsi theatre is spread across a number of Indian languages such as Gujarati, Urdu and Marathi in addition to English and Hindi limiting the access

to the non-speaker of the regional languages. Lastly, the archival material in many cases is in such a dilapidated condition that it is almost impossible to use the original. There are efforts now being undertaken especially by Parzor, a UNESCO Parsi Zoroastrian project to digitally archive the material.

3. Colaba, Old Woman's Island, Bombay, Mazagaon, Worli, Parel and Mahim.
4. I use the two terms 'imperialisation' and 'capitalisation' as used by David Willmer. According to Willmer,

> The narrative of imperialisation is one that, rather than the more limited and prescriptive subject-object relationship of colonization by itself, suggests the possibility of a greater degree of participation on the part of the subject/s in question. The latter may be able to participate in the greater project of empire building in an active way, 'collaborative' way, even if they might, arguably, take part objectively in their own repression, whereas the experience of being merely colonized must always be seen as an essentially passive one. Likewise, with the narrative of capitalization, which often comes hand-in-hand with that if imperialisation, but is not necessarily marked by all the same defining characteristics (such as the civilizing mission), the colonized subjects can also be willing and instrumental participants in its unfolding. The narrative of capital in general has an added dimension in that the colonized subject's participation in it can both precede and continue independently of the intervention of empire. [David Willmer, 'Theatricality, Mediation and Public Space: The Legacy of Parsi Theatre in South Asian Cultural History,' PhD diss. (University of Melbourne, 1999), 12–13]

5. Quoted in D. Menant, *The Parsis In India, Vol. 1*, tr. M.M. Marzban, (Madras: Modern Printing Works, 1917), 74.
6. Quoted in Shroff, *The Contribution of Parsis*, 12.
7. Jesse S. Palsetia, 'Partner in Empire: Jamsetjee Jeejeebhoy and the Public Culture of Nineteenth-century Bombay,' *Parsis in India and the Diaspora*, eds. John R. Hinnells and Alan Williams (London: Routledge, 2008), 82.
8. Ibid.

9. See Eckehard Kulke, *The Parsees in India: A Minority as Agent of Social Change* (Munich: Weltforum-Verlag, 1974); Jesse S. Palsetia, *Jamsetjee Jeejeebhoy of Bombay: Partnership and Public Culture in Empire* (New Delhi: Oxford University Press, 2015); John R. Hinnells and Alan Williams, eds. *Parsis in India and the Diaspora* (London: Routledge, 2008); Zenobia Shroff, *The Contribution of the Parsis to the Development of Education and Social Change in Bombay City (1820–1920)* (Mumbai: Himalaya Publishing House, 2001); David L. White, 'From Crisis to Community Definition: The Dynamics of Eighteenth Century Parsi Philanthropy', *Modern Asian Studies* 25(2) (1991): 303–320.
10. Willmer, 'Theatricality, Mediation and Public Space,' 48.
11. Palsetia, 'Partner in Empire,' 83.
12. Willmer, 'Theatricality, Mediation and Public Space,' 104.
13. Kathryn Hansen, 'Language, Community, and the Theatrical Public: Linguistic Pluralism and Change in the Nineteenth-century Parsi Theatre,' in *India's Literary History: Essays on the Nineteenth Century*, eds. Stuart Blackburn and Vasudha Dalmia (Delhi: Permanent Black, 2008), 63.
14. Ibid., 65.
15. Eckehard Kulke, *The Parsees in India: A Minority as Agent of Social Change* (Munich: Weltforum-Verlag, 1974).
16. Kathryn Hansen, 'Parsi Theatre and The City: Location, patrons, audiences,' *Sarai Reader* 2002: The Cities of Everyday Life (2002): 43.
17. The wealthy Bombay merchants, many of whom were Parsis, had been watching English theatre at the Bombay Green even before the 1850s. When this theatre faced financial crisis in 1835, Jamsetji Jeejibhoy bought the theatre for ₹ 50,000. The proceeds after paying the debts were used ten years later to establish Grant Road Theatre. Also by the 1850s, some Parsi students of Elphinstone College were holding theatre performances on Saturday nights. Since these performances proved profitable, many others were encouraged to follow suit. The recognition of theatre as a viable commercial enterprise led to the development of several Parsi theatrical companies.
18. S.K. Das, *A History of Indian Literature: 1800–1910: Western Impact, Indian Response* (New Delhi: Sahitya Akademi, 1991), 183–184.
19. Gupt, *Parsi Theatre*, 129.

20. Somnath Gupt, *Parsi Theatre: Its Origins and Development*, ed. and tr. Kathryn Hansen (Calcutta: Seagull Books, 2005), 7.
21. Willmer, 'Theatricality, Mediation and Public Space,' 1.
22. Ibid., 1–2.
23. Gupt, *Parsi Theatre*, 23.
24. R.K. Yajnik, *The Indian Theatre: Its Origins and its Later Developments under European Influence* (London: George Allen & Unwin Ltd., 1933), 116.
25. Gupt, *Parsi Theatre*, 19.
26. See Hannah Scolnicov and Peter Holland, eds., *The Play Out of Context: Transferring Plays from Culture to Culture* (Cambridge: Cambridge University Press, 1989); Linda Hutcheon, *A Theory of Adaptation* (London and NY: Routledge, 2006) and Margaret Jane Kidnie, Shakespeare and the Problem of Adaptation (Oxon: Routledge, 2009).
27. Sisson, *Shakespeare in India*, 8.
28. Kumudini Mehta, 'English Drama on the Bombay Stage in the Late Eighteenth Century and in the Nineteenth Century,' PhD diss. (University of Bombay, 1960), 178–185.
29. Willmer, 'Theatricality, Mediation and Public Space,' 204.
30. Hansen, 2008, 64.
31. Willmer, 'Theatricality, Mediation and Public Space,' 178–179.
32. Quoted in Gupt, *Parsi Theatre*, 48.
33. Hansen, 'Language, Community, and the Theatrical Public,' 69.
34. Quoted in Willmer, 'Theatricality, Mediation and Public Space,' 206.
35. Hansen, 'Language, Community, and the Theatrical Public,' 66.
36. *Khayal* is a form of north Indian classical music which literally means imagination. This style of singing originated in opposition to *Dhrupada* which had rigorous and fixed rules. *Bhavai* is a folk drama while *garba* is a folk dance of Gujarat. *Lavani* is a folk dance of Maharashtra.
37. Hansen, 'Language, Community, and the Theatrical Public,' 72.
38. Quoted in ibid.
39. Javed Malick, 'Appropriating Shakespeare Freely: Parsi Theater's First Urdu Play Khurshid,' in *India's Shakespeare: Tradition, Interpretation, and Performance*, eds. Poonam Trivedi and Dennis Barthlomeusz (Delhi: Pearson Longman, 2005), 82.
40. Malick, 'Foreign Origins/Native Destinations,' 160.
41. Gupt, *Parsi Theatre*, 115.
42. Ibid., 182.

43. Ibid., 181.
44. Ania Loomba, 'Shakespearean Transformations,' in *Shakespeare and National Culture*, ed. John J. Joughin (Manchester: Manchester University Press, 1997), 119.
45. Yajnik, *The Indian Theatre*, 161.
46. Gupt, *Parsi Theatre*, 174.
47. Malick, 'Foreign Origins/Native Destinations,' 165.
48. Yajnik, *The Indian Theatre*, 135.
49. Ibid., 156.
50. Gupt, *Parsi Theatre*, 233.
51. Mishra, *Shakespeare's Impact*, 41.
52. Yajnik, *The Indian Theatre*, 171.
53. Ibid., 113.
54. Ibid., 114.
55. Anuradha Kapur, 'The Representation of Gods and Heroes: Parsi Mythological Drama of the Early Twentieth Century,' *Journal of Arts and Ideas*, 23–24 (1993): 86.
56. Quoted in Willmer, 'Theatricality, Mediation and Public Space,' 200.
57. Quoted in ibid., vii.
58. Loomba, 'Shakespearean Transformations,' 121.
59. Yajnik, *The Indian Theatre*, 161.
60. Ibid., 167.
61. Ibid., 140.
62. Gupt, *Parsi Theatre*, 128.
63. Dennis Kennedy, 'Afterword: Shakespearean Orientalism,' in *Foreign Shakespeare: Contemporary Performance*, ed. Dennis Kennedy (Cambridge: Cambridge University Press, 1993), 291.
64. Poonam Trivedi, '"Folk Shakespeare": The Performance of Shakespeare in Traditional Indian Theater Forms,' in *India's Shakespeare*, eds. Trivedi and Bartholomeusz, 153.
65. Loomba, 'Shakespearean Transformations,' 121.
66. Frantz Fanon, *Black Skin, White Masks*, tr. Charles Lam Markmann (London: Pluto Press, 1986).
67. Fanon, The *Wretched of the Earth*, tr. Constance Farrington (NY: Grove Press, 1963), 37–38.
68. H.K. Bhabha, *The Location of Culture* (London: Routledge, 1994), 86.
69. Ibid.

70. Bhabha, *The Location of Culture*, 37.
71. Ania Loomba, '"Local-manufacture made-in-India Othello fellows": Issues of Race, Hybridity and Location in Post-colonial Shakespeares,' in *Post-Colonial Shakespeares*, eds. Ania Loomba & Martin Orkin (London: Routledge, 1998), 147–148.
72. Bhabha, *The Location of Culture*, 86.
73. Ibid., 112.
74. Rustom Bharucha, *Theatre and the World: Performance and the Politics of Culture* (London: Routledge, 1993), 194.
75. Willmer, 'Theatricality, Mediation and Public Space,' 127.
76. Rajiva Verma, 'Shakespeare in Hindi Cinema,' in *India's Shakespeare*, eds. Trivedi and Bartholomeusz, 243.
77. Willmer, 'Theatricality, Mediation and Public Space,' 16.
78. Loomba, 'Local-manufacture made-in-India,' 146–147.
79. Bart Moore-Gilbert, *Postcolonial Theory: Contexts, Practices, Politics*, 3rd ed. (London, NY: Verso, 2000), 193–194.
80. Sisson, *Shakespeare in India*, 8.
81. Laurie E. Osborne, 'Rethinking the Performance Editions: Theatrical and Textual Productions of Shakespeare,' *Shakespeare, Theory and Performance*, ed. James C. Bulman (London and NY: Routledge, 1996), 169.
82. Ania Loomba, 'Shakespeare and the Possibilities of Postcolonial Performance,' *A Companion to Shakespeare and Performance*, eds. Barbara Hodgdon and W.B. Worthen (Malden, MA: Blackwell Publishing, 2005), 123.
83. Thomas Cartelli and Katherine Rowe, *New Wave Shakespeare on Screen* (Cambridge: Polity Press, 2007), 29.
84. Ibid.
85. W.B. Worthen, 'Drama, Performativity, and Performance,' *PMLA* 113.5 (October 1998): 1101.
86. Ibid.
87. This does not mean that there were no plays staged by Parsi companies. Jal Khambatt, for instance, staged Zoolme Narwa, an adaptation of Cymbeline in the 1940s and *Merchant of Venice* in 1948.

III

Shakespeare in Marathi, Kannada, Malayalam and Hindi Theatres

Although Shakespeare's presence was felt the most in Calcutta and Bombay, it does not imply that his plays were limited to these regions. Shakespeare's plays travelled across the length and breadth of India. The 1964 survey of Shakespeare's translations and adaptations by the Indian National Library, Calcutta, provides the following data: Out of the total of 670 productions, 128 were produced in Bengali, 97 in Marathi, 70 in Hindi and 66 in Kannada. In this chapter, I have limited the study to a few regions with relatively higher theatre activity. Shakespeare's influence on Bengali and Parsi theatre has already been discussed at length in the earlier chapters. Other theatre traditions like Marathi, Kannada, Malayalam and Hindi, which are equally rich and have registered a considerable influence of Shakespeare, cannot be ignored. The chapter is structured into four sections—each section representing Shakespeare in one language respectively- Marathi, Kannada, Malayalam and Hindi.

Shakespeare in Marathi Theatre

Like Bengali and Parsi theatres, modern Marathi theatre also began in the 19th century. Scholars like P.G. Sahasrabuddhe believe that the modern Marathi drama began in 1880 when Balwant Pandurang Kirloskar's *Sakuntala* was staged.[1] Vijaya Mehta also traces the history of Marathi to the latter half of the 19th century.[2] However, G.P. Deshpande, a Marathi playwright, theatre scholar and activist, believes that modern Marathi theatre began in the 1840s with Vishnudas Bhave's attempts at producing mythological plays using traditional art forms of Maharashtra like *tamasha* and *dasavatara*.[3] His plays are usually referred to as '*akhyans*' and not plays. It should be mentioned here that Bhave tried to minimise the crude elements of the folk forms, such as symbolic meanings and the battle scenes, to suit the sensibility of the royal court. Bhave was employed in the court of Sangli in south Maharashtra and wrote plays for the entertainment of the royal court. His musical *Sita Svayamvar* (1843) was an instant hit and Bhave was asked by the king to write more plays. However, after the king's death, Bhave had to move out of the court. He formed his company called Sanglikar Natak Mandali and toured Maharashtra with his plays. Bhave reached Bombay in 1853 and performed his *khel-akhyans* successfully. However, the real success came when Bhave once visited the Grant Road Theatre in 1853. Bapurao Naik informs:

> He was so impressed by the production technique and the stage aids, including changeable scenery etc., that he set his heart on it and decided to have the theatre for at least one show. He composed a new play, *Raja Gopichand*, in Hindi, to cater for a mixed audience composed of Parsis, Gujaratis, Muslims and even Europeans. The theatre was reserved for a night and ticket sales reached Rs. 1,800 on the day of the show.[4]

Inspired by Bhave's success, other companies such as Shahunagarwasi Natak Mandali, Amarchand Wadikar Natak Mandali and Mumbaikar Natak Mandali were established. Thus, modern Marathi theatre began its journey after 1853. It should be noted here that Bhave's company was an important influence on Parsi theatre as well. After watching Bhave's plays, the first Parsi company performed a play in the same year. Bhave's plays were predominantly musical and this was to exert a major influence on the Marathi theatre in the coming years. Although Kirloskar, fondly called Annasaheb Kirloskar, is credited to have developed *sangeet natak* (musical drama) in Maharashtra, the seeds had been sown some 40 years earlier by Bhave.

Marathi theatre got a boost with the establishment of the University of Bombay in 1857. The introduction of the English curriculum exposed native students to English literature. Shakespeare, too, was a part of the new curriculum. This exposure to English literature, mainly Shakespeare, coupled with English theatre in Bombay led to the staging of the Bard's plays by school and college students. Similar to the students in Calcutta, the students in Bombay and Pune too involved themselves in annual Shakespeare productions. Ramu Ramanathan informs that the students of Vishrambaug High School staged *Julius Caesar* in their school courtyard in 1872 and that the students of Baba Gokhale School presented *The Merchant of Venice*.[5] In all probability, these productions attempted to present Shakespeare 'faithfully' (even if they could enact only select scenes) as the students were guided by their English teachers in such endeavours. Besides such efforts, British Shakespeare actors such as Miss Elisa May and Miss Chloe Player, were invited by Deccan College (Pune) to read Shakespeare's plays to the students for 500 rupees.[6] Along with English education, came a deep nostalgia for Sanskrit literature. The educated natives also looked towards their own classical tradition for inspiration. However, scholars like Sunita Deshpande argue that:

> [T]he tradition of classical Sanskrit drama lost its hold when Marathi writers became familiar with English and European drama. Between 1870 and 1920 the Marathi stage was dominated by translations and adaptations, most of Shakespeare's plays being translated during this period, along with some of Moliere, Schiller, Goldsmith, Sheridan and others.[7]

This is but partially true. While there was an increase in translations from Shakespeare and other English writers, Sanskrit plays too were translated, though few were successfully staged. Table 3.1 shows a list of Marathi translations of Sanskrit plays provided by H.N. Dasgupta.

Table 3.1: Marathi translations of Sanskrit plays in the 19th century

S. No.	Play	Year	Translator
1.	*Uttar Ramcharit*	1859	Parshhurampant Godbole
2.	*Parvati Parinaya*	1872	Parshhurampant Godbole
3.	*Mrichhkatik*	1881	Parshhurampant Godbole
4.	*Sakuntala*	1881	Parshhurampant Godbole
5.	*Venisamhar*	1881	Parshhurampant Godbole
6.	*Viratparva*	1884	Parshhurampant Godbole
7.	*Mudra Rakshas*	1867	Krishna Shastri Rajawade
8.	*Malati Madhava*	1861	Krishna Shastri Rajawade
9.	*Vikramorshivaya*	1874	Krishna Shastri Rajawade
10.	*Malavikagnimitra*	1867	Ganesh Shastri Lele
11.	*Vidhhashalbhanjika*	1869	Ganesh Shastri Lele
12.	*Prasanna Raghava*	1859	Shivaramshastri Palande

Source: H.N. Dasgupta.[8]

To this educated new breed of intellectuals, Bhave's plays seemed crude and not worthy of being staged. The attitude of the growing educated class towards mythological plays using traditional and folk forms is reflected in the 'Epilogue' for the translation of Bhatta Narayan's *Venisamhar* (The Binding of the Braid) written by Krishnaji Parashuram Gadgil, a student from Deccan College, Pune.

Though some might laugh us out and set at naught,
Because they see no feats no duels fought
No freakish monkey, no delirious yell,
No Lanka's tyrant fierce with fury fell,
No absurd songs, no din, no wild attire,
No meaningless uproar, no senseless ire;
Let them, what can they, indiscrete tools,
In turn we laugh them down and deem them fools,
Illiterate players have usurped the stage,
With scenes obscene depraved this rising age.[9]

Critical of Bhave-type plays, students made an important intervention in the development of Marathi theatre by introducing a new kind of drama hitherto unfamiliar to Maharashtra. The new playwrights who were influenced by the Western drama, especially Shakespeare, wrote prose plays or 'bookish' plays which had elaborate written scripts to be rehearsed and performed, unlike Bhave's impromptu productions.[10] As seen in the epilogue quoted previously, the new generation of Marathi playwrights were critical of the musical element of the Marathi theatre and developed prose drama unheard of in Marathi theatre. In 1861, Vinayak Janardan Kirtane (1840–1891) became the first playwright to write a Marathi play *Thorle Madhavrao Peshwe* (Peshwa Madhavrao the Elder). Interestingly, this was also the first Marathi play to use history instead of mythology as its subject. It was a prose drama and did not have any songs. About a performance by Sanglikar Players, *Belgaum Samachar* of 11 December 1865 reports that although the play was hailed by the educated Marathi as a landmark in Marathi theatre, the masses, used to watching musical plays of Bhave and folk performances like *tamaṣha*, did not respond well.[11]

The influence of Sanskrit tradition on Marathi theatre can also be seen in the development of *sangeet natak*. In fact, Kirloskar made his debut with a performance of Kalidasa's *Sakuntala* in *sangeet natak* in 1880. *Sangeet natak* as a form was developed by Balwant Pandurang Kirloskar. Although songs and music were important constituents in Bhave's plays, they were not made integral to the structure. Moreover, the *sutradhar* would sing all the songs. Dialogues were sparse and had to be improvised by the actors. Kirloskar introduced important changes. Maya Pandit observes that Kirloskar 'perceived the importance of classical and folk music, the organized structure of Sanskrit and English drama, and the romantic and comic aspects of Sanskrit theatre'.[12] Kirloskar combined these elements and developed Marathi *sangeet natak*. He differed from Bhave in that he wrote the scripts for his plays. Also, the songs were sung by actors and not by the *sutradhar* as in Bhave's plays. The first *sangeet natak* to be presented by Kirloskar was *Sakuntala* which had 209 songs. With the success of *Sakuntala*, *sangeet natak* was established as an important genre in Marathi theatre. Soon, there were companies such as Natyakala Company, Mahalakshmiprasada Company and Balvant Company that followed Kirloskar's footsteps and began staging *sangeet nataks*.

Marathi theatre, thus, seems to grow in two directions in the later part of the 19th century: prose or 'bookish' plays and *sangeet natak*. Though the two had their own characteristics, Shakespeare was common to both. Performances of Shakespeare's plays on the Marathi stage entertained both the educated elite and the masses. However, there was a difference in the way Shakespeare was adapted. The English-educated adaptations were close to Shakespeare's text but transformed his poetry into prose. *Sangeet natak* moulded Shakespeare into musicals and took liberties with plot and structure following Parsi theatre. In fact, there were seriously debated issues of translation versus adaptation during this time. G.G. Agarkar, a college principal, wrote in the 'Preface' to his version of *Hamlet*: 'Does not the mere mention of "a free adaptation" serve as a cloak for all possible license and abuse of the original?'[13] However, he also agreed that the Bard's plays needed to be 'modified' for the Marathi stage. So, his versions along with those of V.M. Mahajani, V.B. Kelkar and others were transcreations rather than literal translations. An important influence that the English education and the English theatre had on the educated Marathi population was that the latter took to theatre in order to 'improve' the Marathi stage.

One of the earliest attempts in this direction was made by three students of Pune Engineering College—G.B. Deval, A.V. Patkar and Vamanrao Bhave. They formed a company by the name of Aryodharak in 1879. It was not a commercial enterprise but, as H.N. Dasgupta suggests, aimed at introducing novel ideas and contribute the earnings towards public welfare.[14] The company is known to have performed *Othello*, *King Lear* and *Tara* (an adaptation of *Cymbeline* by V.M. Mahajani). Deval himself played the title role in *Othello* and Patkar played Iago. The company closed down as all three founders left it one by one. Deval joined Kirloskar Natak Mandali while Bhave, with support from Mahajani and others, established Ichalkaranjikar Natak Mandali.

Ichalkaranjikar Natak Mandali was known for producing prose plays. Among various plays that the company staged were *Taruni Shiksha*, *Manorma* and *Gunotkarsh*, two were Shakespeare's adaptations—*Tara* and *Tratika*, an adaptation of *The Taming of the Shrew* by V.B. Kelkar (*Tratika* will be discussed later with reference to another production). *Tara* was a successful comedy on the Marathi stage. The play was performed by at least three companies, Aryodharak (1879/1880), Chittakarshak Company (1879) and Ichalkaranjikar Natak Mandali (1880). Ichalkaranjikar Natak Mandali performed the play in 1880 at the joint wedding function of the King of Baroda to a Princess of Tanjore and his sister Tara Bai to the Prince of Savantwari. A review of the production that lasted close to six hours by an Englishman, Harold Littledale, throws light on various aspects of the performance.

> The theatre was a temporary structure of bamboo-poles and canvas. The stage, a whitewashed sandbank forming an oval about three feet height, twenty feet in breadth, and forty feet in depth, was partly concealed behind a drop-curtain, on which an elephant and tiger fight was depicted, and by a proscenium of canvas, adorned with full-length portraits of three-headed gods and mythic heroes in strange attire. Three uprights—one of them a growing tree—on either side [of] the stage, sustained the 'foot-lights'—some twenty kerosene lamps.[15]

The play, in accordance with the Sanskrit theatre tradition, begins with the *purvaranga*, the *sutradhar* singing an invocation to Lord Narayana to bless the production, followed by a *nandi* after which Saraswati, the goddess of knowledge and arts, appears, dances and exits. Littledale then observes the changes that the Indian adapter had incorporated in order to make the play acceptable to the audiences. For example, the soothsayer of Act V was substituted by a Brahmin astrologer, 'who promised victory to Iachimo's side if they took care to give the Brahmin a feed'.[16] Further, in the love-scenes between

Imogen and Posthumus, instead of running to embrace her husband, the traditional Indian wife usually veils her face at his approach and 'ventures perhaps to peep timidly towards him from beneath the folds of her *sari*, but takes refuge in a corner if her lord become at all demonstrative in his affection'.[17] Littledale's comments on the costumes and make-up reveal that although the costumes were Indianised in order to match the setting, not much attention was paid towards their propriety. Imogen, for instance, wore

> a dark green *sari* with gold edges, golden armlets, and earrings. Her face was fair as any English maiden's and her cheeks bloomed with very conspicuous rouge. Unfortunately, she had not taken the precaution of whitening her arms to match her face, and the contrast was rather marked when she lifted her nut-brown hand, as she frequently had occasion to do, to adjust the cumbersome pearl ornaments which adorned her lily-white nose.[18]

The play was a prose translation of the original but the playwright made some modifications in the original text. The play was completely Indianised as names of characters and locales were substituted with Indian proper names. Imogen became Tara, Cymbeline became Sambhaji, Guiderius was Shivaji, Arviragus was Rajaram, Belarius was Malharrao, Cloten was Murarrao, Posthumus was Hambirrao, Iachimo was Khanduji and Pisanio was Sadoba. Similarly, Britain became Suvaranpuri and Italy became Vijaipura.[19] Also, to suit the audience sensibility, the queen is not a widow who has remarried and Tara (Imogen) too is unmarried. According to Littledale, other Shakespeare productions by this company were *The Tempest*, *Comedy of Errors*, *Othello* and *The Taming of the Shrew*.[20]

One of the most well-known companies that frequently performed Shakespeare's plays in prose was Shahunagarwasi Natak Mandali. The company was steered by one of the best actors of the Marathi theatre—Ganpatrao Joshi. Generally called the 'Garrick of Maharashtra', he was famous for playing Shakespearean characters like Hamlet, Othello and Macbeth. The company had a band of brilliant actors that ensured its immense success. Apart from Ganpatrao Joshi, there were Govindrao Supekar and Balvantrao Jog, famous for playing female characters like Lady Macbeth, Katharina, Ophelia. Among various plays that the company produced over a period of 25 years, the more successful were G.B. Deval's *Zunzarrao* (*Othello*), G.G. Agarkar's *Vikarvilasita* (*Hamlet*, 1883), V.B. Kelkar's *Tratika* (*The Taming of the Shrew*, 1891) and *Viramani ani Sringarasundari* (*Antony and Cleopatra*, 1893), S.M. Paranjpe's *Manajirava* (*Macbeth*, 1896), L.N. Joshi's *Kapidhvaja* (*King John*, 1904) and *Visvamitra* (*Timon of Athens*, 1905). *Zunzarrao* was a stage version of M.G. Kolhatkar's adaptation of *Othello* (1867). Kolhatkar's adaptation was a failure on the stage in which G.B. Deval played the title role. Later, Deval adapted Kolhatkar's version for the stage and called it *Zunzarrao*. Deval's version was staged by Shahunagarwasi Natak Mandali as a prose adaptation which remained close to the original although dialogues had a colloquial language. Like other scholarly adapters, Deval too felt the need to make changes in the original text to suit the audience's taste while retaining the spirit of the original. Yajnik notes,

> The medieval tragic story of a lovelorn Hindu princess (for Barbara) finds a most melodious expression of its poignant sentiments pertaining to the condition of the banished Sita. These words have been set to an intensely melancholy strain of music. This perfect lyric has become a household song in Maharashtra.[21]

The play was quite successful and was staged many times. Two such revivals were in the 1950s, one featuring Baburao Pendharkar, a Marathi film actor, as Othello and Jeevankala as Desdemona, and the other had Nanasaheb Phatak as Othello and Vijaya Mehta as Desdemona. The first production was directed by Chintamanrao Kolhatkar. Others in the cast were Durga Khote, Balgandharva, Nanasaheb Phatak, Jayamala Shiledar, Keshavrao Datey and Chintoba Gurav, a veteran actor from Kirloskar Natak Mandali (Mankar).

Shahunagarwasi Natak Mandali staged G.G. Agarkar's *Vikarvilasita* (*Hamlet*) in 1883. The production went on to become the most sought after due to Ganpatrao Joshi's rendition of Hamlet. Joshi and Balbahu Jog, who had rendered the part of Ophelia, got appreciation not only from Indian audiences but also from some of the English gentlemen who witnessed the performance. L.N. Joshi provides an account of the praises showered upon the actors.

> Mr. E. H. Atkin was 'taken by surprise' in 1894, as he could follow Shakespeare scene by scene and as the acting was 'good and powerful throughout'. To Mt. J. R. Roberts, in 1902, it was a 'revelation that the dramatic art had attained to so high a pitch in India as that displayed by the Shahu Company. Ganapatrao's rendering of the great characters of Shakespeare is beyond all praise. He is a finished actor of the highest quality and of marvelous talent. I would say the same of Balbhau, who does the female parts'. Mr. F.B. Younghusband was 'astonished at the ability and talent' of Ganapatrao and Balwantrao in 1902.[22]

Some scholars attribute the success of this production to Agarkar's strategies employed for translation. The text more or less follows the original faithfully but Agarkar replaces the foreign references with episodes well known to the Indian audiences. For instance, Priam's death in the play is replaced by Ashwathama-Drona episode from the *Mahabharata*.[23] Whether it was because of Joshi's acting or Agarkar's adaptation, the play was certainly a hit with the audiences who would come again and again to watch it.

Tratika is a prose adaptation of *The Taming of the Shrew* by V.B. Kelkar. Actually, *The Taming of the Shrew* had been produced by various companies with different titles like *Sangita Chaudave Ratna* by Balvant Company and *Karakasdaman* by Patnakar Company. Both these productions were musicals in the tradition of *sangeet natak*. *Tratika* is generally believed to be the most successful version. Kumud Mehta observes that in the 'Introduction' to the play,

> Kelkar frankly admits that he has put in a great deal that is his own and he asks the reader not to judge his work as a translation....

> It reproduces the situation of *Taming of the Shrew* but the words in it can under no circumstances be described as Marathi equivalents of the original.[24]

Whether a translation of *The Taming of the Shrew* or not, the play was a success on the stage. L.N. Joshi notes that *Tratika* did so well on the stage that the company easily cleared its debts.[25]

Macbeth has been an all-time favourite with Marathi audiences. The play has been adapted by several playwrights for several companies. However, the two important ones are *Manajirava*, a prose adaptation of *Macbeth* by S.M. Paranjpe in 1896 and *Rajmukut* by V.V. Shirwadkar in 1954. *Manajirava* was staged by the Shahunagarwasi Natak Mandali in 1896 in which Ganpatrao played the title role. The play was a success especially due to the actors involved. L.N. Joshi gives an account of a production of this play in Bombay.

> When the troupe went to Bombay, on the night of its first production the tumultuous enthusiasm of the audience reached such a high pitch that they continued shouting 'Once more!' (meaning repeat the walking scene), declaring that they would not allow the play to continue until they were satisfied. Then the great Ganapatrao, who played Macbeth with distinction, came forward and lectured the audience: 'This is not a music-hall, where you can encore a song as many times as you like. If you still persist in your demand, realize that such a consummate piece of acting cannot be repeated devoid of its context. Yes, I shall start the whole play again, and will need three more hours to reach this point. It is already one in the morning, but I have no objection if you get the necessary police sanction'. The effect was instantaneous; the play proceeded.[26]

The other adaptation *Rajmukut* was done by V.V. Shirwadkar for Mumbai Marathi Sahitya Sangh in 1954. The play was directed by Herbert Marshall, a British director and featured actors such as Nanasaheb Phatak as Macbeth and Durga Khote as Lady Macbeth. The production does not seem to have done well despite leading film actors of the day performing. Dhyaneshwar Nadkarni attributes the production's failure to the 'Indianising' of *Macbeth*:

> What does one make of the powerful banquet scene? Does one ask the guests to sit on wooden planks on the floor and serve them *laddoos*? The entire frustrations of this trans-cultural effort came tumbling down on the heads of directors and actors. The debate has since then still been going on whether Shakespeare should be adapted or translated. In the latter case Macbeth's guests will at least eat at the dining table—more stageworthy, more dignified![27]

Nadkarni's observation raises important questions about Shakespearean production in the Bombay of the 1950s. With a rich tradition of Parsi Shakespeare and Marathi *sangeet natak* in Bombay, it is ironical that Nadkarni would find a 'straight' version of Shakespeare more acceptable than an adaptation. He seems to have forgotten that in India almost all 'straight' versions of Shakespeare had failed. There are ample examples of such failures—Girish Ghosh's *Macbeth* in 1893, as mentioned in Chapter I, failed because he had translated the original text 'faithfully' and did not bother to Indianise it. Nadkarni seemed to suggest that Shakespeare could be produced in Indian languages with all the 'Englishness' of the original text. Perhaps, it was for this reason that although there were innumerable literal translations of Shakespeare's plays, not all could be successfully staged.

Shakespeare in Kannada Theatre

> *Kannada scholars have pointed out that a newly developing modern Kannada intellectual community accepted Shakespeare to such an extent that he was popularly referred to as Sekh Pir.*[28]

Kannada theatre, unlike various other theatre traditions in India, was late to respond to Shakespeare. There is a general consensus that the first translation/adaptation of Shakespeare was Channabasappa Basavalingappa Dharwad's *Nagadavarannu Nagisuva Kathe* an adaptation of *The Comedy of Errors* published in 1871, much later than its Gujarati or Bengali versions. It was during this time that Kannada writers were also busy translating Sanskrit dramas though it was only in 1870 that the first Kannada translation of a Sanskrit play was done. This was Shesha Ramachandra Churamuri's translation of *Sakuntala* as *Sakuntala Natakavu.* Inspired by these two traditions, the Kannada playwrights tried to develop indigenous drama. This period is generally understood to be the beginnings of 'modern' Kannada theatre. However, according to K.V. Akshara it is a general misconception to think that the 'modern' Kannada theatre began in the 1880s with the emergence of theatre companies and new forms of dramatic writing.[29] According to him, the 'modern' Kannada theatre began much before when the *yakshagana* troupes started touring outside Karnataka during the early 19th century.[30] One needs to remember here that it was a *yakshagana* troupe from Karnataka that had performed in the royal court of Sangli (in southern Maharashtra) in 1842 that sowed the seed of modern Marathi drama. Thus, for a region like Karnataka where the performance tradition was so strong it is no surprise that Shakespeare made inroads into performance. In fact, a Shakespeare play had already got into a *yakshagana* script much before his plays began to be translated or adapted in the rest of India.[31] This was *As You Like It* adapted as *Sankalpa Siddhiyu* incorporated into a *yakshagana* script in the 1860s. This gradually gave rise to more Shakespeare translations and adaptations in Kannada which, along with Sanskrit drama, played an important role in the development of modern Kannada theatre. T.S. Satyanath suggests that, 'the early precursors of modern Kannada drama, which include several Shakespearean translations, should be seen as an interface that continued the sensibilities of an earlier performing tradition into the newly emerging literary (text-centered) sensibilities'.[32]

Modern Kannada theatre absorbed the influence of the various travelling theatre companies that staged their plays in this region. *The Handbook of Karnataka* states,

> [T]he British colonialists also contributed in a great way for the development of the theatres. They brought with them theatre troupes, which performed plays of Shakespeare and other popular English plays. Encouraged by this, translations of these plays appeared and were staged successfully.[33]

However, the most important influence on Kannada theatre were the touring Parsi and Marathi theatre companies. During the 19th century, itinerant drama companies travelled from one region to another. It is useful to consider this influence because professional Kannada theatre companies, which later established a style of their own, known as *company nataka*, modelled themselves on the Parsi and Marathi companies. The plays of these companies were well received in Karnataka. For instance, the plays of Kirloskar Natak Mandali like *Sangeet Sakuntala* and *Sangeet Saubhadra* were quite popular in Karnataka. Satyanath informs that a Parsi company, the Balliwala Company, so impressed the Maharaja of Mysore that the King encouraged the establishment of Chamarajendra Karnataka Nataka Sabha which was later renamed as the Palace Company.[34] From another source, it is learned that it was Sangli Nataka Company's performance of *Padmavati Parinaya* (Padmavati's Marriage) in Mysore that impressed the Maharaja to the extent that he formed a company called Sakuntala Nataka Company in 1881 to perform *Sakuntala* and that the company was later named Chamarajendra Karnataka Nataka Sabha.[35] Whichever company might have influenced the Maharaja, the fact is that the interaction of various companies from different regions created an environment congenial for the growth of new theatre in Karnataka. It is important to know that Chamarajendra Karnataka Nataka Sabha with the Maharaja as its patron held the earliest performances of Shakespeare in Karnataka. The Maharaja also invited companies to perform Shakespeare's plays and interested himself in the Shakespearean performances staged by the Palace Company. Vijaya Guttal notes that this company was the first to give public performances of *Shursena Charitre* (an adaptation of *Othello* by Basappa Shastri) and *Panchali Parinaya* (an adaptation of *The Merchant of Venice* by A. Anandrao) in 1882.[36] The Maharaja invited a British officer Frazer for the show who was 'all praises for artiste Subanaa, who played Devdatta (Iago in *Othello*), and Veeraraghavacharya who played Mohane (Desdemona). He exclaimed that famous English artiste Henry Irwin's portrayal of Iago's role looks dull before Subanna and no English women can match Mohane in acting'.[37] Also, as in schools and colleges of Calcutta, Bombay and Pune, the Maharaja College of Mysore often performed either scenes or whole plays of Shakespeare under the tutelage of their English teachers. In fact, the dramatic society of the college, 'invested a good bit of money on stage-equipment and period costume—or what would pass for period costume'.[38] The dramatic society was invited by the Maharaja to perform in the court as well. In 1901 after Krishnaraja Wadiyar IV ascended the throne, the theatrical activity of the Palace Company expanded. Like his predecessor, he encouraged theatre and other arts. During his reign, various companies visited Karanataka to stage plays. *Tratika*, the Marathi adaptation of *The Taming of the Shrew* by Kelkar, was performed in Dharwar in 1908. The king himself was an accomplished actor and made sure that his company did well. A guess can be made about how professional the company must have been by the fact that,

> A committee of royal court scholars, musicians like Bidaram Krishnappa, Dodda Ramarya, Chikka Ramarya and others screened the artistes for selection. It was mandatory for the artistes to sing well. The men played the female characters. The rehearsal was also carried out under the supervision of these scholars regularly. Nalwadi himself supervised the rehearsals sometimes when a particular play was to be staged for a royal guest or a British delegate or officers.[39]

Thus, Kannada theatre did not grow in isolation but was influenced by the travelling companies. It took, from such companies, elements such as, '[T]heir distinct theatrical idiom with painted curtains, appealing songs, melodramatic acting, and mesmerizing special effects [which] reigned supreme over the popular imagination of Karnataka till the advent of films.'[40]

Shakespeare has been translated and adapted in Kannada for more than a hundred years. According to the Indian National Library, Kolkata, the number of Kannada translations and adaptations of Shakespeare were 66 till 1964. According to Satyanath, by 1964 there were around 93 translations and adaptations covering about 20 plays of Shakespeare, which reached 111 by 1992. There have been a good number of Shakespearean translations and adaptations in Kannada since 1871 and it might be possible that many more translations and adaptations might have gone unnoticed. Similar to the Marathi tradition discussed previously, the approach of Kannada translators/adapters has not been uniform. As Satyanath notes, 'Kannada's response to Shakespeare represents two ambivalent and parallel streams of sensibilities, one corresponding to the literary tradition and the other to the stage tradition.'[41] One is led by the love for Shakespeare and the other, by love for the stage. G.S. Amur identifies three generations of Kannada writers who have appropriated Shakespeare: the first generation (1870–1920) writers engaged themselves in free adaptations of Shakespeare; the second generation (1920–1960) attempted 'faithful' translations of Shakespeare's plays; and the third generation (1960 onwards) translated Shakespeare to address contemporary problems and for creative expression.[42] One may find exceptions too where the trend of one generation is found in another.

The first generation adaptations of Shakespeare are more of transcreations as they, like Parsi adaptations, took extreme liberties with the originals. The scarce availability of archival material, at least in English, on the performative aspect of the Kannada *nataka* companies poses a great challenge to a researcher. It is, therefore, difficult to imagine the kind of performances that must have been held. Even scholars like Satyanath, who are deeply rooted in the

Kannada tradition, have referred to this fact. He states, '[L]ong ago, Kurtakoti (1969) made an appeal for a historiography of Kannada theatre performances, an appeal that has remained unfulfilled to this day.'[43] However, one can guess, knowing full well, that Kannada theatre companies were influenced by Parsi and Marathi theatres. Melodrama, dance and music, spectacle and complete indigenisation of plays which were the hallmark of Parsi and Marathi theatres would have been followed by the Kannada companies. Some common characteristics of early Kannada adaptations were indigenisation of names, places, characters and plot, transformation of tragedies into comedies and the use of songs and music. Music has always been an integral part of the theatre in India. Like Parsi, Marathi and Bengali theatres, Kannada theatre incorporated music and songs. The same formula was applied to Shakespeare adaptations as well. As it happened quite often on the Parsi stage, even in the popular Kannada theatre, Guttal notes, people often 'came to listen to particular songs by particular singer-actors,' who would shout for encores and the actors had to oblige.[44]

While dealing with the early adaptations of Shakespeare in Kannada, one must remember that these were done with an eye on the performance. From 1870 to 1920, there were around 57 translations and adaptations available of the Bard's plays. This suggests that the majority of the translations and adaptations of Shakespeare emerged from this period—a fact that reflects Shakespeare's contribution to the development of modern Kannada theatre. As mentioned earlier, since these adaptations were done keeping the stage in mind, it became important for the adapters, to render the text in an idiom familiar to the common audience. Ramchandra Dev argues that

> it was also a strategy to circumvent the onslaught of an alien culture and preserve self-identity by substituting a construct from their own language and cultural milieu. This belief is reinforced by the fact that Sanskrit plays that came into Kannada almost at the same time did so through literal translations and through adaptations, as the question of alien domination did not arise there.[45]

It is my contention that the early Kannada adapters preferred to adapt rather than translate for theatrical compulsions. Translating and presenting Shakespeare to the audience unfamiliar with the English culture would not have made much sense. Srikantesha Gowda and M.S. Puttanna justified the appropriation on the basis of cultural difference in their prefaces. Since they were writing for the stage it was important to make Shakespeare's plays intelligible to the audience. K.G. Kundangar observes in this connection:

> Social customs being the same these afforded no difficulty in their translations. *Hamlet's* mother marrying her brother-in-law a few days after her husband's death, the parting of the hero and the heroine soon after their marriage in *The Taming of the Shrew*, and similar other incidents could not be retained consistently with Indian customs. It was very hard, therefore, to translate the English dramas to suit the Indian stage and to win the estimation of the lovers of literature, and the theatergoing public. Some say that these should be rendered closely, and not adapted to suit Indian customs. In that case the mind trained to view eastern society will not feel at home.[46]

Thus, the Parsi and Marathi adaptations of Shakespeare provided the models for Kannada adapters. Another point that Dev seems to forget is that many of the early Kannada adapters of Shakespeare were not all English educated university scholars well versed with the language. Writers like Somnathayya S. Bellave, Venkatacharya and G.H. Honnapuramath used Telugu, Bengali and Marathi translations of Shakespeare's plays which were in turn based on Charles Lamb's prose renderings of Shakespeare.[47] Similarly, Basappa Shastri used C. Subbarao's translation of *Othello* for *Surasena Charithre* (1895).

Srikantesha Gowda's *Pramilarjuniya* (1890), an adaptation of *A Midsummer Night's Dream*, provides an example of thorough 'Indianisation' of the English text. G.S. Amur observes:

> Srikantesha Gowda borrows his structural plan from *A Midsummernight's Dream* but brings about a total cultural transformation in the content. The story of Theseus and Hyppolita is substituted by the story of Arjuna and Pramila and Greece changes

> into Kerala. The fairy king and queen are replaced by Manmatha and Rati and the Elizabethan artisans make room for Mayachari and his friends who obviously belong to Karnataka. Interestingly enough the *Pyramus and Thisbe* interlude finds a parallel in *Ramavarma and Lilavati*, the name under which *Romeo and Juliet* had been translated into Kannada. The opening of the play, in the form of a dialogue between *Sutradhara* and *Nati*, follows the conventions of Sanskrit drama.[48]

Even close to being considered translations, most notably those of Basappa Shastri and Puttanna, made some changes to the original. Amur informs us that Puttanna who translated *King Lear* as *Hemachandrarajavilasa* (1889) gave the characters,

> Indian names in order to make the play appear natural to Kannada readers. There are two important changes in the translation. The first relates to English customs and habits for which substitutes have been found deliberately to suit the genius of the Kannada language and facilitate understanding by the Kannada people. The other is a result of misreading or imperfect knowledge of the text.[49]

Satyanath makes an interesting observation that not only the content was appropriated, but also the genre was 'conceived in terms of indigenous genres', as is clear from the titles of these adaptations, named as *nataka* (drama), *charite/charitre* (life-story), or *kathe* (story).[50] The comedies usually ended with *vijaya* (victory) or *vilasa* (romance) or *parinaya* (marriage).[51]

Romeo and Juliet seems to have drawn the attention of many adapters of the time. There were at least six adaptations of the play prior to 1930. The play under the name *Ramavarma Lilavati* was adapted and staged by at least three different companies. While Ratnavali Nataka Sabha led by the actor, director and owner, A.D. Varadachar, who was known for playing Shakespeare's heroes, used his own adaptation, Chamarajendra Karnataka Nataka Sabha used Jayarajacharya's 1889 adaptation *Ramavarma Lilavati Charitre*, and Rajdhani Nataka Mandali used Anandrao's 1889 adaptation. However, all those who adapted the plays made it a point to transform the tragedy into a happy ending. This transformation has often been criticised by Kannada scholars on account of doing 'injustice' to Shakespeare. Shamaraya, for instance, has made the following observation regarding the happy ending in Anandrao's (1889) adaptation:

> The absurdity par excellence is the self-conceived last act of the play, in which Pujyapada Yogishwara (Friar Lawrence) prays to Lord Vishnu, who appears on the stage, appreciates Ramavarma's (Romeo) love for Lilavati (Juliet) and Lilavati's chaste virtues and brings them back to life. The translator, in an attempt to bring Ramavarma and Lilavati back into life, has murdered the great dramatist (*sekspiyar mahakavi*). The saying that 'translators are traitors/murderers' has actually become true here.[52]

Criticism like this has often been raised by those who take a literary approach towards Shakespeare and forget the fact that these early adaptations were done for the stage. Shamaraya's argument renders the whole idea of adaptation as a useless activity. However, he fails to acknowledge that any playwright, however great, would make sense to the masses if he speaks to them in their language and context. Instead of taking fidelity to Shakespeare as an index of their contribution towards Shakespeare scholarship, these adaptations should be 'understood and appreciated as cultural maneuvers of an interface in transforming culture in which the nature of the text and its performance was in a state of flux and change'.[53]

If adaptation was the mode preferred by the first generation writers, the next generation (1920–1960) was more 'faithful' to Shakespeare in their translations. Many of the translators of this period were university-educated who had read Shakespeare as part of the curriculum. In order to understand this transition from adaptation to translation of Shakespeare, one needs to look at various forces in operation during the 1920s. The change was brought about by two main developments in Karnataka: the theatrical and the literary. As mentioned earlier, the first half of the 20th century was dominated by the *company natak* in Karnataka. However, one can also notice the rise of amateur theatre during the second decade of the century. By the 1920s, a good number of amateur theatre groups and playwrights had come up. Akshara notes that the important role in the growth of amateur theatre in Karnataka was played by T.P. Kailasam in Bangalore, K. Shivarama Karanth in South Karnataka and Sriranga (Adya Rangacharya) in north Karnataka.[54] On the one hand, all of them criticised *company natak* especially for its 'artificiality and anachronism' and, on the other, advocated social drama and realism in theatre.[55] K. Marulasiddappa writes, 'As a negative reaction to the pomp, din and festive atmosphere of this [company] theatre, naturalist theatre appeared in the thirties. It was a theatre of the sophisticated, urban middle class. They were too shy to act or write on broad emotions.'[56]

Another impulse that was instrumental in guiding the Kannada drama of this period came from literature. The period between 1920 and 1960 is generally referred to as *navodaya* (Renaissance) in Kannada literature. The period saw the growth of modern Kannada poetry and novel. However, some of the writers also wrote drama mainly as closet plays. These writers also translated Shakespeare following the original faithfully. To mention some of the important ones who translated Shakespeare were D.V. Gundappa, B.M. Srikantia, K.V. Puttappa (Kuvempu) and Masti Venkatesh Iyengar. Most of them were English educated which made it possible for these writers to render 'faithful' translations of Shakespeare. The representative of this approach to Shakespeare can be seen in Gundappa's 'Preface' to his translation of *Macbeth* (1936):

> It is my intention to represent the world of Shakespeare as far as possible as it really is and not merely to tell the story. It is my effort to retain the names used by him, the atmosphere he created, his descriptions ... on the whole his representation of the world as it is. I believe that this is necessary for the enhancement of Kannada literature and the sensibility of the Kannada people and for the broadening of their vision of the world. If human civilization and peace are to last, it is of foremost importance that the different races of the earth attain a world vision. In order to achieve this the people of the West should read our epics, the *Ramayana* and the *Mahabharata* sympathetically as we must acquaint ourselves with their poetic tradition.[57]

As *navodaya* was predominantly a poetic renaissance and most of the Shakespeare translators of this period were poets, it was obvious for them to bring out the poetry in Shakespeare in Kannada which the earlier generation had neglected. For instance, Masti Venkatesa Iyengar, the renowned poet, fictionist and playwright, observed that a translator ought to 'reproduce not just the meaning or the emotion but to the cast of mind behind the poetry'.[58] Guttal observes that in order to bring out the poetry in Kannada translations, translators like Kuvempu, Iyengar and Gundappa, employed *Sarala Ragale*, a Kannada poetic meter, which could substitute the English blank verse and as a result of which most translations became more poetic than dramatic.[59] This is probably the reason that except for Kuvempu's *Raktakshi* (*Hamlet*) no other translation of this period has been staged.[60] There were other reasons as well which prevented the staging of Shakespeare's translations during this period. On the one hand, the company theatre was losing its vitality mainly due to the influence of cinema. On the other, new playwrights like Kailasam, Sriranga and G.B. Joshi were focusing their attention on social plays with realistic themes and so did the amateur theatre. It was in the 1960s, that playwrights and translators adapted and translated Shakespeare for creative expression.

The post-Independence Kannada theatre, like other theatres in India, has seen various forces at work. While the early post-Independence Kannada theatre addressed existential issues in the plays of P. Lankesh, Girish Karnad and Chandrashekhar Kambar, the 1970s witnessed a revival of folk and traditional art forms to address contemporary issues. Karnad, for example, has incorporated elements from Kannada folk and traditional theatre in writing his plays *Hayavadana* (The One with a Horse's Head, 1971) and *Nagamandala* (Play with a Cobra, 1987–1988). By the 1960s, B.V. Karanth had started experimenting with folk and traditional forms of Karnataka in his productions to address contemporary issues. Amidst such theatre developments, the approach towards Shakespeare too witnessed a change. It is neither a mere rendering of the Shakespearean story like the first generation nor a close translation of the second generation. It is rather a reworking of Shakespeare to suit creative and contemporary needs. On his approach to Shakespeare, Ramchandra Deva observes, 'I was trying to bring Shakespeare to Kannada through myself, to understand myself and my times through Shakespeare!'[61] This seems to be the guiding principle of other playwrights and translators as well who have either reworked or translated Shakespeare in the post-Independence Indian theatre in general and Kannada theatre in particular. The representatives of this approach in Kannada theatre are Ramchandra Deva, H.S. Shivaprakash and Nissar Ahmed. Some of the important translations of Shakespeare that have often been staged during this period are Ramchandra Deva's *Macbeth* (1976) and *Hamlet* (1978) and Shivaprakash's *Lear Maharaja* (*King Lear*, 1988) and *Maranayakana Drishtanta* (*Macbeth*, 1990). However, one production of *Macbeth* that has been influenced by Kannada traditional forms and has proved quite successful on the stage is *Barnam Van* (*The Birnam Wood*, 1979), an adaptation of *Macbeth*. Directed by Karanth in Hindi for Bharat Bhavan, *Bhopal*, the play experiments with the Kannada folk form *yakshagana*. I would discuss this production at length in Chapter IV.

Shakespeare in Malayalam Theatre

Theatre in Kerala has a long history dating back to the 9th century. Kerala can boast of a great number of traditional and folk forms of performance many of which are still in practice. In fact, the oldest performance form of India which is extant belongs to Kerala. *Kutiyattam*, as it is called, is based on the classical Sanskrit plays. Other traditional forms of performance of Kerala are *teyyam*, *tullal* and kathakali. However, it is paradoxical that despite such theatrical activity in Kerala, dramatic literature in Malayalam is a recent phenomenon dating back to the latter half of the 19th century.

There were, of course, written texts that *kutiyattam* and kathakali used but these were ancient Sanskrit texts. However, an important intervention in the traditional theatre of Kerala was made by the Portuguese who were the first foreigners to establish contact with Kerala. As a result of the contact there developed a form of theatre in the late 17th century Kerala called *Chavittunatakam*. The dramas presented Western stories and Christian themes of saints and war heroes translated into Malayalam and interpolated with local music and dance. Some of the popular dramas were *Genoa Natakam*, *Caralman Natakam*, *Napolean Charitram* and *Yakoba Natakam*.[62] This was the first Western influence on the theatres of Kerala. Although this form did not receive much favour from the high-caste Hindus, yet it was quite popular with the masses for some time.

Despite a good number of performances in Kerala it is noteworthy that actual Malayalam drama began with the Malayalam translation of Kalidasa's *Sakuntalam* by Kerala Varma in 1882. This was also the time when efforts were being made to develop the idea of the 'stage' in Kerala. During this time, *Sakuntalam* was staged in various parts of Kerala by a theatre troupe called Manmohanam Nataka Company under the direction of Thiruvattar Narayana Pillai. K.S. Narayana Pillai observes that this company seems to grow after Tamil commercial troupes visited Kerala and staged musicals in the form of *sangeet natak*.[63] The staging of *Sakuntalam* was successful and 'the Tamil model influenced Kerala artists to such an extent that they organized troupes to perform similar plays in Malayalam, signifying the commencement of Malayalam theatre as we know it today'.[64] The success of this translation encouraged other writers to translate more Sanskrit plays. Within two decades there were Malayalam translations of all the major Sanskrit classics like *Uttar Ramcharit* (Ram's Last Act), *Malatimadhav* (Malati and Madhav) and *Malavikagnimitram* (Malavika and Agnimitra). Malayalam playwrights did not confine themselves to the translations of Sanskrit plays only but also attempted original plays in Malayalam. The first such attempt was Kochuni Tampuran's *Kalyani Natakam* (1891) set against the background of contemporary society. Thus, one finds that Malayalam dramatic literature was growing in three directions: Sanskrit translations, English translations and original plays in Malayalam.

Although the Portuguese, Dutch and French had come to Kerala before the British, they were not able to influence Malayalam literature to the extent the English did. English education in Kerala encouraged the educated Malayalam writers to translate English works and then write Malayalam plays by borrowing the Western dramatic techniques. Ayyappa Paniker informs,

> The first English school was established by the London Mission Society as early as 1806, by the Church Missionary Society in 1815, and by the Government of Travencore in 1834. This led to the greater use of English for official purposes and closer intellectual contact with England. The work of the Christian missionaries speeded up this process of westernization. With the establishment of printing presses and the publication of newspapers there was a tremendous change in the lifestyles of the native population.[65]

Once the educated class of Kerala was exposed to the English literary traditions, it took up the translation of English works and also shaped Malayalam literature along the Western lines. New genres from the West like the short story, novel, essay and biography were welcomed. As in other regions, Shakespeare exerted a significant influence on the early playwrights in Kerala. The first translation of a Shakespeare play came in 1866 as *Almarattam*, an adaptation of *The Comedy of Errors* by Oomman Philipose. Jayasree Ramakrishnan Nair notes that this translation inaugurates the trend of writing Malayalam drama based on the Western models.[66] However, this adaptation does not follow a dramatic form but is rather a story much like Lamb's *Tales from Shakespeare*. A notable point is that most of the Malayalam translations of Sanskrit or English plays were not performance-oriented. The reason could be that the already available performing forms like kathakali and *kutiyattam* satisfied people's desire for the visual.

Translations, adaptations and performances of Shakespeare's plays had a relatively lesser presence in Kerala as compared to Maharashtra, Karnataka or Bengal in pre-Independence India. There could be many possible reasons for this conspicuous absence of Shakespeare in the literary and theatrical tradition of Kerala. First, unlike in Calcutta or Bombay, the British did not have a very visible presence in Kerala. There were hardly any play-houses set up by the British in Kerala. Probably due to the absence of the Western theatrical model Shakespeare did not receive much attention in Kerala. Second, the neglect of Shakespeare in Kerala could possibly be due to the general indifference towards the stage. As mentioned earlier, unlike other regions of India, Kerala has strong traditional and folk performance traditions such as *teyyam*, *tullal* and kathakali which might have discouraged the staging of new plays in general and Shakespeare in particular. P.K. Parameswaran Nair argues that the reason,

> for the sad neglect of the stage would be that the poets were too fond of the *Kathakali* to go in for any other dramatic forms. The repertoire of Sanskrit was always before them, and they were not averse to translating, adapting and imitating a great part of its literature.[67]

Thirdly, the development of prose farce in Kerala in the first decade of the 20th century, that was to have a considerable influence on dramatic literature as well as on theatrical staging, could have proven detrimental to Shakespeare. Instead of focusing their attention on Sanskrit classics or on Shakespeare, writers like C.V. Raman Pillai and later E.V. Krishna Pillai and N.P. Chellappan found inspiration in the English comedy of manners of Sheridan and Goldsmith. The new plays that emerged were C.V. Raman Pillai's *Kuruppillakkalari* (A School without a Master, 1909), *Pantatte Pacchan* (Good Old Pacchan, 1918) and E.V. Krishna Pillai's *Koallapramanam* (Spurious Document, 1931) as social critiques. Lastly, by the 1930s, Malayalam drama, like the Marathi drama, had come under the influence of the Norwegian dramatist Henrik Ibsen. Ibsen was in fact the most influential Western playwright to have affected Malayalam drama. His dramas like *Ghosts*, *Rosmersholm*, *Wild Duck* and *Enemy of the People* were translated and adapted by Malayali translators. The 1930s and the 1940s witnessed the rise of political theatre in Kerala. The 1950s were influenced by the influential Indian People's Theatre Association (IPTA) and several agitprop theatre groups committed to staging progressive plays came up. In a politically charged atmosphere, it was no surprise that instead of paying attention to Shakespeare or Kalidasa the playwrights and theatre practitioners chose to write, adapt and stage radical plays like C.J. Thomas's *Avan Veendum Varunnu* (He Comes Again! 1949) and Toppil Bhasi's *Ningalenne Communistakki* (You Made me a Communist, 1951).

This is not to say that there were no translations or adaptations of Shakespeare's plays in Malayalam. Although there were translations and adaptations of Shakespeare, these were not done with an eye on the stage but as literary exercises by the poets of Kerala. Jayasree Nair argues,

> The early translators of Shakespeare's plays were drawn to the wealth of poetry in the originals and proceeded to render the plays in a medium intermingling verse and prose, exploiting the facilities of metre, rhyme and rhythm for the verse passages. This was during the latter half of the 19th century, when the writers were influenced by the style and structure of Sanskrit Dramas such as those of Kalidas, Bhasa and Bhavabhuti which were being translated into Malayalam at that time. The translators of the Sanskrit classics and those of Shakespeare's plays were identical in that both groups concentrated on the poetic beauty of the originals, giving little importance to the theatrical features. Consequently, these versions are more suitable for literary appreciation rather than actual performance.[68]

An example can be Kodungallur Kunjikuttan Thampuran's translation of *Hamlet* as *Hamlet Natakam* (1897). Nair informs us that Thampuran used poetic metres from Sanskrit like '*sardulavikriditam*, *Kusumanjari* and a host of others' to correspond with Shakespearean blank verse.[69] There were some minor attempts at translating Shakespeare for the stage. As mentioned earlier, Tamil commercial companies would frequently visit various parts of Kerala. The musicals staged by these companies had an influence on the theatre in Kerala. As a result, some writers composed Malayalam musicals on the lines of Tamil *sangeet natak*. The two *sangeet nataks* in Malayalam that set the tone for further musicals were T.C. Achyuta Menon's *Sangita Naishadham* (Musical on Nishadha, 1892) and K.C. Kesava Pillai's *Sadarama* (1903). It is worth mentioning that Malayalam *sangeet natak* marks the first attempt at evolving professional theatre in Kerala. Like Marathi and Kannada *sangeet natak*, Malayalam *sangeet natak* too was predominantly musical in nature and the main purpose of this kind of drama was entertainment. K.M. George writes about the Tamil *sangeet natak*,

> The [C]hief actors were always first-class musicians. No one bothered about the quality of acting or dialogue. People enjoyed the songs and the colourful costumes and stage settings. Soon their technique was adapted into Malayalam, and a few musical plays came to be written.[70]

One can notice similarity among the Marathi and Kannada musical theatres which followed the same pattern. The dramatic style of *sangeet natak* seems to have influenced at least one Shakespearean adaptation. This was Chunakkara Krishna Warrier's *Vasantikasvapnam* published in 1905, a *sangeet natak* version of *A Midsummer Night's Dream* as adapted by R.V. Krishnamacharya in Sanskrit. Following the norms of *sangeet natak*, Warrier incorporates into the play many songs based on various *ragas* like *kalyani*, *hamsvadhani*, *toti*, *hindustani*, *kinnari* and so on.[71] Nair gives the following information regarding the transformations incurred by the playwright in the original:

> The location is Avantidesam (Athens) ruled by Indravarma Maharaja (Theseus) married to Kanakalekha (Hippolyta). The central characters are Vasantan (Lysander), Makarandan (Demtrius), Kaumudi (Hermia) and Saudamini (Helena). The story follows the original without change. The supernatural world of the fairies is adapted

> to the world of the kinnaris and kinnaras who are demi-gods and celestial musicians in the Indian culture. The figures introduced here are Pramohan (Puck), Bhadramukhi and so on. Oberon is Pradosan, the *kinnara* ruler who is at loggerheads with Nimbavati (Titania), his queen. The sub-plot involving the artisans Quince, Snug, Bottom, Flute, Snout and Starveling is also introduced through the characters Dhanyakan, Adharakan, Dhanakan, Vasuvalitan, Rajasan and Sadhakan. The original play within the play, 'Pyramus and Thisbe' is localized as 'Bhanumatyasmakendra.' The conclusion of the play is slightly different. When the original closes Oberon, Titania and their train entering on stage to bless the couples, the adaptation picturises Pradosan, Nimbavathy and the *vidyadharas* looking down from heaven and singing joyous songs. Flowers are showered and the play closes with a Bharatavakya by Vasantan, which is a *mangalasloka* for Indravarma Maharaja.[72]

There is, however, no documentary evidence about the staging of the play.

It is in the post-Independence Malayalam theatre, that Shakespeare's plays have received attention by various theatre groups of Kerala. There have been attempts at producing at least three plays, namely *King Lear*, *Othello* and *Julius Caesar* in kathakali besides staging Shakespeare's plays in schools and colleges. One such theatre club is that of S.B. College, Changanassery called The Shakespeare Theatre. The Shakespeare Theatre had staged 19 productions of Shakespeare's plays between 1937 and 2011 as given in Table 3.2.

Table 3.2: Shakespeare productions between 1937 and 2011 by S.B. College, Changanassery, Kerala

S. No.	Year	Play
1.	1937	*Macbeth*
2.	1947	*Macbeth*
3.	1951	*The Merchant of Venice*
4.	1952	*The Merchant of Venice*
5.	1952	*King Lear*
6.	1953	*Hamlet*

S. No.	Year	Play
7.	1961	*King Lear*
8.	1964	*Othello*
9.	1965	*Othello*
10.	1969	*Macbeth*
11.	1971	*Macbeth*
12.	1983	*The Merchant of Venice*
13.	1986	*Macbeth*
14.	1989	*Julius Caesar*
15.	1991	*Othello*
16.	1994	*Romeo and Juliet*
17.	1997	*Antony and Cleopatra*
18.	1999	*Hamlet*
19.	2007	*Macbeth*

Source: The Shakespeare Theatre.[73]

An unconventional rendering of Shakespeare's *Othello* as *kathaprasangam*, a story-telling form in Malayalam was attempted by V. Sambasivan (1929–1996). Sambasivan not only rendered his own stories but also adapted Malayali writers like Vallatol and Asan, Russian writers Tolstoy, Dostoevsky, Pushkin and the English playwright Shakespeare. What is interesting about this form is that it is highly popular among the masses and has helped popularise Shakespeare in Kerala among the masses. Sanju Thomas in her work on *Othello* in *kathaprasangam* brings forth an important distinction between a popular performance form like *kathaprasangam* and a more elaborate and classical form of performance such as kathakali. She writes,

> What marks *kathaprasangam* from other narrative classical art forms of Kerala such as *ottamthullal* and *kathakali* is the simplicity of language and form which would appeal to the common man and the illiterate. *Kathaprasangam* offers a rich contrast to *kathakali* which is a more elite classical performing art that demands detailed arrangements at all levels and an understanding of the nuanced aesthetics of the art.

> But *kathaprasangam* is a more broad-based popular art. The story is narrated plainly and simply with minimal accompaniments so that it reaches the common man with clarity. *Kathakali* involves more than one performer and the *kathakali padams* are sung by trained experts while a *kathaprasangam* artist most often is not a trained singer or an orator, but only has a talent for singing and story-telling. In short, the success of a *kathaprasangam* performance depends entirely on the dramatic skills of the narrator, and his ability to engage with the audience.[74]

Though *Othello* has been performed in both the forms, in their distinct styles, one may assume that Sambasivan's *Othello* is simpler yet more popular among the masses as compared to Sadnam Balakrishnan's *Othello* (1996) or Annette Leday/Keli Company's *King Lear* (1999) in kathakali which is highly codified form, has a complex structure and expects from the audience familiarity with the nuances of the form in order to appreciate it. Other than these two, there have also been individual efforts like K.N. Panikkar's production of *Kodumkattu*, a translation of *The Tempest* (2000), Chandradasan's *Chatthankattu* (*The Tempest*, 1995) and *Macbeth* (2002) and M.G. Jyothish's *Macbeth* (2009). *Chatthankattu* is an allegory of colonisation. Chandradasan writes in the 'Programme Note' of his production of *Chatthankattu*:

> The first colonizer Prospero reaches this island with his daughter Miranda by fate, barely escaping the conspiracy of his brother Antonio. He relieves Azhakan Chathan the primitive 'element' of the island from a magic bondage and converts 'it' to be his trustworthy slave. The other creature Karumadan Chathan, the prospective ruler of the island too has been tamed by Prospero with love, education and punishment.... Each of the westerner reaching the island after the shipwreck has colonial instinct, which is highlighted in this production. Antonio, Sebastian, Gonzalo, Stephano and even Trinculo are dreaming of converting the island into a colony and are discussing the means to sell the 'tribal sub-humans' of the island in a western market.[75]

For the production, the director draws on eclectic sources like folk music, beliefs and myths and shamanistic and ritualistic traditions to give the production a local colour. Chandradasan presents a highly stylised production before the audiences. Another Malayalam production that deserves mention is *Macbeth* directed by M.G. Jyothish (2009) which went on to win four META (Mahindra Excellence for Theatre Awards) awards in 2014. The production dwells on the theme of overpowering ambition and immorality which leads to the tragedy. The familiarity with the original text makes Jyothish focus not on the entire story but only on the psychological deterioration of Macbeth and Lady Macbeth. Hence, the text is edited to a large extent. Guilt, which is a recurring motif in the play, comes alive on the stage as the director makes use of large mirrors that continuously reflect Macbeth and Lady Macbeth who feel traumatised by what they see. While in Chandradasan's *Macbeth*, Lady Macbeth appears as a 'suppressed and weeping presence that is tortured and neglected by Macbeth in his relentless pursuit of power,' Jyothish's Lady Macbeth sticks to the more conventional devilish woman who coaxes her husband to murder the king.[76] Jyothish successfully brings out on stage the internal fears, appresios and turmoils of Macbeth through powerful visuals and haunting music.

Shakespeare in Hindi Theatre

> *Shakespeare has been translated a number of times, the same play at a different period of time in the same language. There is a significance of repeating the translation every twenty years. The target language grows—the meaning of the original text grows.... This need for a Shakespeare translation after every generation, emphasizes both the eternal Shakespeare and the evergrowing Shakespeare. And that is Shakespeare's challenge.*[77]
>
> Raghuvir Sahay

Unlike Marathi, Bengali and Kannada theatres, Hindi did not have professional theatres during the colonial period. Hindustani was employed by Parsi theatre for its performances but Hindi theatre per se distanced itself from Parsi theatre for its 'vulgarity', 'crudity' and 'commercialism' from the very beginning. It was largely in reaction to Parsi theatre that Hindi drama was established by Bhartendu Harishchandra (1850–1885) who is generally referred to as the 'father of modern Hindi theatre' in the mid-19th century. Critical of Parsi theatre, Bhartendu propagated a theatre which would have an edifying effect on the society. He not only wrote plays but also staged them and often travelled to various towns. Among his important plays are *Vaidiki Himsa Himsa na Bhavati* (Vedic Violence is not Violence, 1876), *Bharat Durdasha* (India's Plight, 1875), *Satya Harishchandra* (Truthful Harishchandra, 1876), *Andher Nagari* (City of Darkness, 1881) and *Nildevi* (1881). He was also a prolific translator and translated a number of plays from Sanskrit, Bengali and English. His translation of *The Merchant of Venice* as *Durlabh Bandhu* (*A Rare Friend*, 1880) was the second translation of a Shakespeare play in Hindi, the first being Munshi Imdad Ali's *Bhram Jhalak* (*Comedy of Errors*, 1879).

Bhartendu translated *Durlabh Bandhu* from the Bengali translation titled *Surlata Natak* (1877) by Pyarilal Mukhopadhyay. In his version, Bhartendu replaces the names of characters and places with Indian names but maintains their phonetic similarity. Thus, Antonio is Anant, Bassanio is Vasant, Salerio is Saral, Portia is Purashree, Shylock is Sherlaksh and Venice is Vanshnagar. No changes are made to the original plot. However, foreign references are substituted with familiar ones. For instance, Portio's lines (72–81) in Act I, sc. ii,

> Portio: You know I say nothing to him, for he understands not me, nor I him: he hath neither Latin, French, nor Italian; and you will come into the court and swear that I have a poor pennyworth in the English. ... I think he bought his doublet in Italy, his round hose in France, his bonnet in Germany, and his behaviour; everywhere.

These are translated as follows.

> *Purashri: Woh na Hindi janta hai na Braj bhasha na Marwari aur tum shapathpurvak keh sakogi ki Maithil mein mujhe kitna nyoon abhyaas hai. Usne apna ang Marwaar mein mol liya hai, pajama Mathura mein*

> *banvaya hai, topi Gujrat se mangani laya hai, aur chaal-dhaal thodi thodi sab jagah se bheekh maang laya hai.*[78]

Here, Latin, French and Italian have been replaced by Hindi, Braj and Marwari. Also, doublet is substituted by kurta (shirt), round hose by pajamas and bonnet by cap. One of the major challenges for Indian translators translating *The Merchant of Venice* is the Christian-Jew conflict. While some have made it a conflict between castes, Bhartendu transforms this conflict into a Hindu–Jain tussle to provide a familiar context to the readers. However, it does not bring out the complexity of the Christian anti-semitism. The famous speech of Shylock, 'He hath disgrac'd me and hind'red me half a million…I will better the instruction' in Act 3, sc. i has been rendered as follows.

> *Usne mujhe apratishthit kiya hai aur kam se kam mera paanch lakh ka laabh rok diya hai; woh sada meri hani par hansa hai, mere labh ki ninda ki hai, meri jati ki apratishtha ki hai, mere vyavharon mein taanch mari hai, mere mitron ko thanda aur mere shatruyon ko garam kiya hai; aur yah sab kis liye? Keval isliye ki mai Jaini hu. Kya jaini ki aankh, naak, haath, paanv aur dusre ang aryon ki tarah nahi hote? Kya uski sundhi, sukh aur dukh, preeti aur krodh aryon ki bhanti nahi hota? Kya woh wahi ann nahi khata, unhi shastron se ghayal nahi hota, wahi rog nahi jhelta, unhi aushadhiyon se achha nahi hota, usi garmi aur jade se sukh aur kasht nahi uthata jaise ki koi arya? Kya yadi tum chutki kato toh hum logon ke rudhir nahin nikalta?…Jo paajipan tum log mujhe apne udahran se sikhlaate ho use main kar dikhlaunga aur kitni hi kathinata kyun na pade main badla lene mein avashya tumse badhkar rahunga.*[79]

Nandi Bhatia interprets the play as a 'struggle between Indians and British, a struggle in which Anant resembles the colonized, and Shailaksha, a foreigner in Vanshnagar, symbolizes the foreign foe'.[80] She perceives Anant's victory over Shailaksha as an important model of resistance and that 'the appropriation of the play conveys that knowledge of colonial models can be turned into a tool for striking back at the colonizer'.[81] Whether the play was ever staged is debatable as there is no documentary evidence available. With the early death of Bhartendu at an age of 35, Hindi theatre suffered a setback though there were sporadic attempts by amateur groups to sustain its activities. In the absence of regular theatrical activity, Shakespeare's translations were largely confined to literary circles.

It is clear then that most of the Shakespearean translations in Hindi, prior to Independence, were done as a literary exercise rather than for the stage. These are 'faithful' literary translations. As the translators did not have to cater to an audience as in Parsi theatre, they did not indigenise or transcreate the English plays to the extent Parsi or Marathi theatres did. However, it is important to look at the pre-Independence translations because Shakespeare exerted an important influence on the emerging Hindi drama between the mid-19th and early 20th centuries. The Hindi translations of Shakespeare's plays can be broadly classified into two categories: prose narratives introducing Shakespeare to Hindi readers; and 'faithful' translations as plays. Lala Sitaram, a prolific translator, translated 15 plays of Shakespeare between 1900 and 1926. His translations follow the original plays closely intending to counteract the 'demoralising effects upon the minds of the readers' made by the works of the 'vernacular romancers'.[82] His *Bhul Bhullaiyan* (*The Comedy of Errors*, 1915) is a faithful rendition in prose. The names of the characters and the places are changed to Indian ones while maintaining the phonetic affinity with the original, as for example, Silanidhi for Solinus, Ajina for Aegeon, Antapal for Antipholus, Damaru for Dromio, Amalika for Aemilia, Adra for Adriana. The lines (Act II, sc. ii; 43–52) spoken by Dromio are translated so literally that it loses all its charm.

> Dromio: Return'd so soon; rather approached too late:
> The capon burns, the pig falls from the spit,
> The clock hath stricken twelve upon the bell:
> My mistress made it one upon my cheek:
> She is so hot because the meat is so cold;
> The meat is cold because you come not home;
> You come not home because you have no stomach;
> You have no stomach, having broke your fast;

> But we, that know what it is to fast and play.
> Are penitent for your default today.

The Hindi translation is:

> *Damaru: Itni jaldi aya. Mujhko toh badi der ho gai, mrig jal jata hai, masa sika se aag mein gir raha hai aur jab ghante mein barah baja to bahuji ne mere sir par ek bajaya. Khana thanda ho raha hai isse vah bahut garam ho rahi hai aur kahati hai ki khana thanda hota hai aur aap ghar par nahi aate aur aapke ghar par na aane ka kaaran yahi hai ki aapko bhuk nahi hai kyonki aap kahi aur bhojan kar chuke hai. Parantu ham log jaante hai ki upvas karna aur devata ka manana kya hai. Ascharya yah hai ki aap aparadh karen aur ham vrat kare.*[83]

His other translations like *Man Mohan ka Jaal* (*Much Ado About Nothing*, 1912), *Apni Apni Ruchi* (*As You Like It*, 1915), *Bagula Bhagat* (*Measure for Measure*, 1915), *Sati-Pariksha* (*Cymbeline*, 1915), *Jangal men Mangal* (*The Tempest*, 1915) and *Prem Kasauti* (*Romeo Juliet*, 1931) indigenise the names and places but otherwise follow the original texts closely. Among the histories, Sitaram translated *Richard II* as *Raja Richard Dwitiya* (1915) and *Henry V* as *Raja Henry Pancham* (1915). Harish Trivedi writes that no other translator has tried to translate these two histories in Hindi probably because of 'wide unfamiliarity in India with these historical backgrounds'.[84] Since Shakespeare's history plays are steeped in the English history, it is difficult for the Indian translator to 'Indiannise' them. As Mishra observes, '[A]s the translation is too literal, it becomes a mere catalogue of historical facts, and has little appeal to a reader.'[85] Among the Shakespearean tragedies, Sitaram keeps the original names and places and follows the text closely. His *Hamlet* (1915) is in prose with occasional verse. Mishra notes that this translation 'decidedly marks an advance upon all its predecessors. The prose is chaste, noble and dignified; the sense becomes crystal-clear and the verses … do not degenerate into mere doggerel.'[86] Similarly, Sitaram translated *Othello* as *Jhutha Sandesh* (1915), *King Lear* as *Raja Lear* (1915) and *Macbeth* (1926) following the original closely. Rajiva Verma states that although Sitaram's translations have not been rated highly, 'he did succeed in popularizing Shakespeare in the Hindi-speaking regions. Some of his translations were so popular that they went through several editions during the course of a few years.'[87] Other Hindi translators of Shakespeare during this period were Ganga Prasad, Kashinath Khattri, Jai Vijay Narain Singh Sharma, Seth Govind Das, Mathura Prasad Chaudhari and Govind Prasad Ghidiyal. Some of the plays translated or adapted for Parsi theatre were also put into Devnagri script like Narain Prasad Betab's *Gorakh Dhanda* (*Comedy of Errors*, 1912) into Hindi by B. Sinha (1917), Munshi Mehdi Hasan Ahsan's *Bhool Bhullaiyan* (*Twelfth Night*, 1905) and Munshi Arzu Sahib's *Khun-e-nahaq* (*Hamlet*) by Shivaram Das Gupta.

Only in the post-Independence India, Hindi translations of Shakespeare were done for the stage although literary translations continued. Rangeya Raghav's translations, for instance, are largely done in prose and have not been staged often. His 15 translations during the 1957–1958 are instead a hasty exercise. Raghav observes, 'A language which does not have translations of Shakespeare can never be counted among developed languages [sic.].'[88] All his translations follow the original texts closely. He retains all the original names, places, allusions and references. Shakespearean puns too are sometimes retained and at other times explained in the footnotes. In *Barhevin Raat* (*Twelfth Night*, 1957), for instance, the translator retains the pun on 'dear' (Act III, sc. ii: 60–63):

> Fabian: This is a dear manikin to you, Sir Toby
> Sir Toby: I have been dear to him, lad, some two thousand
> strong, or so.

In the Hindi translation, Raghav replaces 'dear' by '*amulya*' and the pun is retained.

> *Fabian: Sir Tobi yah bhi aapke amulya aadmi hain.*
> *Sir Tobi: Are main isko amulya hu. Jab se yeh yahan hai,*
> *tab se iske karib do hazaar pound kharch ho gaye hain.*[89]

On the other hand, in the opening scene of *Twelfth Night*, Curio asks the Duke (Act I, sc. i: 15–22).

Curio: Will you go hunt, my lord?
Duke: What, Curio?
Curio: The hart.
Duke: Why, so I do, the noblest that I have.
O! When mine eyes did see Olivia first,
Methought she purg'd the air of pestilence.
That instant was I turn'd into a hart,
And my desires, like fell and cruel hounds,
E'er since pursue me.

In the footnotes, Raghav explains the pun Shakespeare plays upon 'hart' as 'hunt' and 'heart' and also states that since there is no pun for 'hart' in Hindi that has both the meanings, it could not be used in translation (I. i). One exception to his prose translations is *Ek Sapna* (*A Midsummer Night's Dream*) in which he has retained poetry for poetry. In the 'Introduction' to his translation, he writes:

> While translating I realized that if I translate it in prose, like my other translations, it will not represent Shakespeare suitably. For this reason, I have translated Shakespeare's prose into prose and his poetry into poetry.... The prose translation has been kept keeping in mind the dialogues. Despite being poetry, it can be spoken in prose like the Shakespearean poetry. At places, there are contexts of some old stories that have proven incomprehensible in Hindi. I have changed them a little taking recourse to affective translation and have mentioned the original in the footnotes.[90]

For instance, the song 'Over hill, over dale ... here anon' sung by Fairy in Act 2, Scene i has been rendered poetically by Raghav as:

Pari (Fairy): *Parvat, ghati, van, hariyali,*
Agni, lahar sab par matwali,
main sarvatra ghoomti rahti
Chandrakala se bhi tvar chalti.
Pariyon ki rani ki dasi
Main hun chapla nahin udasi,
Haritima par sajjit karti
Niharo ko jhilmil rachti.
Peele kusumon ki chhaviyon mein

Rahte laal bindu mukhrit se,
Pariyon ko ve hain ati bhaate
Maansal dal lagte pulkit se.
Chalun kahin nihar dhundh lun,
Kusum-kusum ke kaanonon mein ab
Latka dun moti se ujjwal,
Vida, vida lo, jaati hun ab.
O hey aatma! Samay paas hai
Pariyon ki rani aayegi
Pariyon ki rani aayegi,
bela unki bohot paas hai.[91]

In the same scene, references to Apollo and Daphne in Helena's lines 'The wildest hath not … valour flies,' have been explained, due to the Hindi reader's unfamiliarity with Greek mythology, in the footnotes as: 'Apollo: *Surya* (Sun), Daphne; *Usha* (dawn) [In Vedic Sanskrit: *Dahna*]. It's a Greek story, the sun pursues the dawn. Griffin is an imaginary creature whose body and paws resemble a lion's and beak and head is believed to be an eagle's.'[92] Raghav's translations have not found much favour with theatre directors for being too literal. Other Hindi translations of Shakespeare in the post-Independence India include *Mano na Mano* (*As You Like It*, 1960) and *Athens ka Raja Timon* (*Timon of Athens*, 1960) by Dharam Pal Shastri; *Barehvin Raat* (*Twelfth Night*, 1961) by Kuldeep Kapoor; *Barehvin Raat* (*Twelfth Night*, 1962) by Shyam Sunder Suman; *Othello* (1962) by Vidyarthi Diwakar Prasad; and *Hamlet* (1988) by Amrit Rai. Most of these translations as short prose narratives or prose translations follow the original closely. Kuldeep Kapoor's *Barehvin Raat*, for instance, is in the form of a novel. There is no record of these translations being staged.

In Hindi, two translators have stood out during this period—Harivansh Rai Bachchan and Raghuvir Sahay. As powerful poets, they were able to translate Shakespeare's plays into verse, a rare feat achieved in Hindi translations of Shakespeare. The success of their translations is evident in the fact that they have been successfully staged. Sahay's *Barnam Van* (*Macbeth*, 1979) has become one of the path-breaking productions in Indian theatre. Bachchan translated *Macbeth* (1957), Othello (1959), *Hamlet* (1969) and *King Lear* (1972). *Macbeth* was the first telecast as a radio play by All India Radio (AIR) in February 1958 and was subsequently published in 1959. The play was staged by the Hindi Shakespeare Stage on 18, 19 and 20 December 1958 at the Fine Arts Theatre in Delhi after six months of rehearsals. Bachchan's *Macbeth* is significant because it was the first Hindi version of a Shakespeare play in verse to be staged. It appears that the biggest problem that Hindi translators have faced in translating Shakespeare is that of metre. Hindi does not have a metre that corresponds to the Shakespearean blank verse. Bachchan's success in translating *Macbeth* and *Othello* (1959), lies in devising an unrhymed verse using the traditional *rola* metre that comes quite close to blank verse. In the 'Introduction' to *Othello*, Bachchan justifies his use of *rola* as follows:

> Like blank verse, *rola* too has that rhythm which, being suitable for poetry, does not leave the naturalness found in the spoken prose. The biggest strength of blank verse is that it is the closest to the rhythm of spoken English. During the staging of Macbeth most of the audiences did not even realize that verse is being spoken. While criticizing the acting, many well-known newspapers wrote that the translation is in prose-verse. But this mistake made the fact of the translation clear. The translation gave the feeling of verse and the sound of prose.[93]

His choice of *rola* metre has been questioned by some as it is more suited for descriptive poetry rather than the dramatic. Though Rajiva Verma finds the metre a suitable substitute for iambic pentameter, she finds Bachchan's use of it 'mechanical and monotonous'.[94] She argues that

> [T]he metre is too emphatic and draws attention to itself all the time. Further, in trying to stick to his metre closely, Bachchan has often distorted the syntax of the spoken language. His verse thus sounds too much like verse and too little like speech and thus fails to capture the

> characteristic rhythm of Shakespearean blank verse, which never loses touch with the spoken language.[95]

Look for example Banquo's lines 'I' the name of truth … nor your hate,' spoken to the weird sister in Act I, Scene 3 translated as:

> Banquo: … *Sach sach bolo,*
> *tum chhalana ho, ya ki theek jaisi bahar se*
> *deekh rahi ho? Mere bhagyavaan saathi ka*
> *tum abhivaadan kartin uske vartman pad,*
> *aagaami sampad, bhavishya mein rajbhog ki*
> *asha se bhi, jiske karan wah apne mein*
> *khoya-sa hai: mujhse tum kyun naghin boltin?*
> *agar kaal ke antaraal mein paith tumhari,*
> *aur jaan sakti ho daanaa kaun ugega,*
> *kaun sookh jaayega, toh kuch mujhe batao;*
> *go tum karke kripa bana dogi kya mera,*
> *aur ghrina karke bigaad hi kya paaogi!*[96]

However, Bachchan has rendered Shakespeare's poetry brilliantly as is evident in Lady Macbeth's oft-quoted soliloquy, 'The raven himself is hoarse … To cry "Hold, hold!"' in Act 1, Scene v:

> Lady Macbeth: *Kauua bhi apne bharraye svar se kahta,*
> *mere parkote mein pag dharna Duncan ko*
> *ghaatak hoga. Aao, hey maarak mansubon*
> *par mandranewali ruhon, meri saari*
> *naari-janit komalta har lo, bhar do mujhmein*
> *aidi se choti tak, khoob labaalab,*
> *kathin kroorta! Mera khoon bana do gadha,*
> *roko saare maarg aur sab dwaar daya ke;*
> *jis se jeevan ki koi bhi karun bhavana*
> *paith hriday mein mere nirmam, dridh nishchay ko*
> *diga na paaye, au' na iraade aur nateeje*
> *mein khaai ban kar aa jaaye! O hatya ke*
> *prerak preton, jahan kahin bhi ho tum apne*
> *alakh roop mein, duniya ke paapon ke upar*
> *aankh lagaaye, aa jaao meri naari ki*
> *chhati mein jo doodh use tum zahar bana do.*
> *Ghani raat, aa, kajjal-kaale, narak dhuein se*

apne sab angon ko dhak le, jis se meri
tez chhuri jo ghaav kare who dekh na paaye,
aur svarg tam ki chaaar ko utha na jhhanke
aur pukaare, 'thahro' 'thahro!'

While Bachchan has translated the English speech retaining the Shakespearean spirit intact, it reads like an original piece in Hindi. This is the most important reason that many theatre directors have used Bachchan's translation for staging Shakespeare in Hindi. In his 'Preface' to *Macbeth*, Bachchan reproduces a review published in *The Indian Express* which suggested that

> along with the Hindi translation of *Macbeth* the characters too should have been Indiannised—i.e. Macbeth should have been made a Hindu king and so too other characters, because English characters speaking in Hindi seem fake and unnatural. Such mentality reveals sheer ignorance towards the tradition of translation and that of drama.[97]

Even though Bachhan does not Indiannise his *Macbeth* yet his translation surpasses many others, only to be matched by Raghuvir Sahay's *Barnam Van* which would be discussed in Chapter IV.

Thus, one finds that Shakespeare's presence was felt in dramatic and theatrical traditions of Maharashtra, Karnataka, Kerala and North India other than Bengali and Parsi theatres strongly. While Shakespeare's plays helped some languages in developing traditions of literature and translation, they also aided other languages in giving their theatrical traditions a particular direction.

Notes

1. Quoted in G.P. Deshpande, *Dialectics of Defeat: The Problems of Culture in Postcolonial India* (Calcutta: Seagull Books, 2006), 26.
2. Vijaya Mehta, 'Inter-culturalism and Intra-culturalism in Theatre: A Personal Response,' in *Culture and the Making of Identity in Contemporary India*, eds. Kamala Ganesh and Usha Thakkar (New Delhi: Sage Publications, 2005), 144.
3. Deshpande, *Dialectics of Defeat*, 26. *Tamasha* is a Marathi folk form of performance comprising dance and music; *dasavatara* is a traditional

theatrical form of Konkan and Goa based on the ten avatars of Lord Vishnu—Matsya (fish), Kurma (tortoise), Varaha (boar), Narasimha (lion-man), Vamana (dwarf), Parashurama, Rama, Krishna (or Balarama), Buddha and Kalki.

4. Bapurao Naik, 'The Beginning (1843–1880),' in *The Marathi Theatre: 1843–1960*, ed. V.A. Naik (Bombay: Popular Book Depot, 1961).
5. Ramu Ramanathan, 'Shakespeare in India,' accessed 30 March 2018, http://stellamaristheatre.blogspot.in/2010/01/shakespeare-in-india-by-ramu-ramanathan.html.
6. Ibid.
7. Sunita Deshpande, *Encyclopaedic Dictionary of Marathi literature, Vol. I* (New Delhi: Global Vision Publishing House, 2007), 250.
8. Hemendranath Dasgupta, *The Indian Stage, Vol. III: Girish Centenary Edition* (Calcutta: Metropolitan Printing & Publishing House, 1944), 201.
9. Quoted in Shanta Gokhale, *Playwright at the Centre: Marathi Drama from 1843 to the Present* (Calcutta: Seagull, 2000), 11.
10. Ibid.
11. Quoted in ibid., 13.
12. Maya Pandit, 'Sangitnatak,' in *The Oxford Companion to Indian Theatre*, ed. Ananda Lal (New Delhi: Oxford University Press, 2004), 410.
13. Quoted in R.K. Yajnik, *The Indian Theatre: Its Origins and its Later Developments Under European Influence* (London: George Allen & Unwin Ltd., 1933), 125.
14. Dasgupta, *The Indian Stage, Vol. III*, 205.
15. Harold Littledale, 'Cymbeline in a Hindoo House,' *Macmillan's Magazine* XLII (May–October 1880): 65.
16. Ibid., 67.
17. Ibid.
18. Ibid., 68.
19. Ibid., 66.
20. Ibid.
21. Yajnik, *The Indian Theatre*, 166.
22. Quoted in ibid., 160.
23. Ibid.
24. Kumud A. Mehta, 'Shakespeare's Marathi Translators,' *Journal of the Asiatic Society of Bombay* 41–42 (1966–1967), 246.
25. Quoted in Yajnik, *The Indian Theatre*, 136.

26. Quoted in ibid., 173.
27. Dhyaneshwar Nadkarni, 'Shakespeare in Maharashtra,' in *A Tribute to Shakespeare*, ed. Sunita Paul (New Delhi: Theatre and Television Associates, 1989), 18.
28. T.S. Satyanath, 'How Does Shakespeare Become Sekh Pir in Kannada?' *Translation Today* 1, no. 2 (October 2004), 46.
29. K.V. Akshara, 'Kannada Theatre,' in *The Oxford Companion to Indian Theatre*, ed. Ananda Lal (New Delhi: Oxford University Press, 2004), 189.
30. Ibid.
31. Ibid.
32. Satyanath, 'How Does Shakespeare Become Sekh Pir,' 65–66.
33. S.A. Jeelani, ed. 'Culture,' *A Handbook of Karnataka* (Government of Karnataka, 2010), 505, accessed 4 July 2019, http://www.gazetteer.kar.nic.in/gazetteer/hand%20book/Chapter-13_477-458.pdf.
34. Satyanath, 'How Does Shakespeare Become Sekh Pir,' 67.
35. K.R. Singh, Eswar, 'A Royal Heritage Restored,' *The Deccan Herald*, 1 October 2010.
36. Vijaya Guttal, 'Translation and Performance of Shakespeare in Kannada,' in *India's Shakespeare: Translation, Interpretation, and Performance*, eds. Poonam Trivedi and Dennis Bartholomeusz (New Delhi: Pearson Longman, 2005), 97.
37. Eswar, 'A Royal Heritage Restored.'
38. A.N. Moorthy Rao, 'Shakespeare in Kannada Literature,' *Indian Literature* 7, no. 1 (1964): 63.
39. Eswar, 'A Royal Heritage Restored.'
40. Akshara, 'Kannada Theatre,' 189.
41. Satyanath, 'How Does Shakespeare Become Sekh Pir,' 48.
42. G.S. Amur, 'Shakespeare in Kannada,' in *Shakespeare in Indian Languages*, ed. D.A. Shankar (Shimla: Indian Institute of Advanced Studies, 1999), 116.
43. Satyanath, 'How Does Shakespeare Become Sekh Pir,' 65.
44. Guttal, 'Translation and Performance of Shakespeare,' 97.
45. Quoted in ibid., 96.
46. K.G. Kundangar, 'Development of the Kannada Drama,' *Journal of the Bombay Branch of the Royal Asiatic Society* VI (December 1930), 321.
47. Satyanath, 'How Does Shakespeare Become Sekh Pir,' 54.
48. Amur, 'Shakespeare in Kannada,' 118.

49. Ibid., 119.
50. Satyanath, 'How Does Shakespeare Become Sekh Pir,' 54.
51. Ibid.
52. Quoted in ibid., 58–59.
53. Ibid., 66.
54. Akshara, 'Kannada Theatre,' 191–192.
55. Ibid., 192.
56. K. Marulasiddappa, 'Drama (Kannada),' in *The Encyclopaedia of Indian Literature, Volume II (Devraj To Jyoti)*, ed. Amaresh Datta (New Delhi: Sahitya Akademi, 1988), 1077.
57. Quoted in Guttal, 'Translation and Performance of Shakespeare,' 98–99.
58. Quoted in Amur, 'Shakespeare in Kannada,' 121.
59. Guttal, 'Translation and Performance of Shakespeare,' 99.
60. Ibid.
61. Quoted in Amur, 'Shakespeare in Kannada,' 122.
62. P.K. Parameswaran Nair, *History of Malayalam Literature*, tr. E.M.J. Venniyoor (New Delhi: Sahitya Akademi, 1977), 145.
63. K.S. Narayana Pillai, 'Malayalam Theatre,' in *The Oxford Companion to Indian Theatre*, ed. Ananda Lal (New Delhi: Oxford University Press, 2004), 245.
64. Ibid.
65. Ayyappa Paniker, 'Modern Malayalam Literature,' in *Modern Indian literature: An Anthology*, Vol. 2, ed. K.M. George (New Delhi: Sahitya Akademi, 1992), 232–233.
66. Jayasree Ramakrishnan Nair, 'Towards a Malayalee Shakespeare: The Search for an Ideal Form of Expression,' in *Shakespeare in Indian Languages*, ed. D.A. Shankar (Shimla: Indian Institute of Advanced Study, 1999), 125.
67. P.K. Parameswaran Nair, *History of Malayalam Literature*, 145.
68. Jayasree Ramakrishnan Nair, 'Towards a Malayalee Shakespeare,' 128.
69. Ibid.
70. K.M. George, *Western Influence on Malayalam Language and Literature* (New Delhi: Sahitya Kala Akademi, 1998), 147.
71. Jayasree Ramakrishnan Nair, 'Towards a Malayalee Shakespeare,' 130.
72. Ibid., 132.
73. 'College History,' accessed 25 March 2018, http://sbcollege.ac.in/college-history/.

74. Sanju Thomas, 'The Moor for the Malayali Masses: A Study of *Othello* in *Kathaprasangam*,' *Multicultural Shakespeare: Translation, Appropriation and Performance* 13 (2016): 109.
75. Chandradasan, 'Programme Note,' *Chatthankattu* (1995).
76. Ibid.
77. Raghuvir Sahay, 'Interview by Reeta Sondhi and Dhyaneshwar Nadkarni,' The relevance of Shakespeare in India, in *A Tribute to Shakespeare*, ed. Sunita Paul (New Delhi: Theatre and Television Associates, 1989).
78. Bhartendu Harishchandra, 'Durlabh Bandhu,' in *Bhartendu Samagra*, ed. Hemant Sharma (Varanasi: Hindi Pracharak Sansthan, 1987), 492.
79. Ibid., 507–508.
80. Nandi Bhatia, *Acts of Authority/Acts of Resistance* (New Delhi: Oxford University Press, 2004), 63–64.
81. Ibid.
82. Quoted in Rajiva Verma, '*Macbeth* in India with Special Reference to Some versions in Hindi,' *Shakespeare Worldwide* 14/15 (1995): 33.
83. Quoted in Jagdish Prasad Mishra, *Shakespeare's Impact on Hindi Literature* (New Delhi: Munshiram Manoharlal, 1970), 35.
84. H.K. Trivedi, 'Hindi Translations of Shakespeare,' *Shakespeare Translation* 5 (1978): 83.
85. Mishra, *Shakespeare's Impact*, 53.
86. Ibid., 60.
87. Verma, '*Macbeth* in India', 33.
88. Rangey Raghav, *Ek Sapna* [*A Midsummer Night's Dream*] (Delhi: Rajpal and Sons, 1957), 4.
89. Rangey Raghav, *Barahvin Raat* [*Twelfth Night*] (Delhi: Rajpal & Sons, 2006), 69.
90. Rangey Raghav, *Ek Sapna,* 6–7.
91. Ibid., 29–30.
92. Ibid., 41; translation mine.
93. H.R. Bachchan, 'Macbeth,' in *Bachchan Rachnavali*, Vol. 5, ed. Ajit Kumar (New Delhi: Rajkamal Publications, 1983), 118; translation mine.
94. Verma, '*Macbeth* in India', 35.
95. Ibid.
96. Bachchan, 'Macbeth,' 36.
97. Quoted in ibid., 'Preface,' 24; trans. mine.

IV

Performing Shakespeare in Post-Independence India

This chapter looks at productions of Shakespeare's plays in post-Independence India. As discussed in the previous chapters, the number of Shakespearean productions, translations and adaptations had decreased considerably in the post-1920s India. An important reason for this decline between the 1920s and 1940s was the emergence and growth of the Indian People's Theatre Association (IPTA) which had shifted the focus of theatre from entertainment to voicing social and political issues of the time. During this time, Shakespeare seems to have lost his appeal. It is not my contention that IPTA did not perform Western plays in India. In fact, a perusal of IPTA performances reveals that it did adapt plays like Clifford Odet's *Waiting for Lefty* (1935) and Sergei Mikhailovich Tretiakov's *Roar China* (1924) for the Indian masses in 1942. Such plays were picked for their anti-fascist sentiment which went well with the IPTA's professed aim. Shakespeare, however, was unable to provide any anti-imperialist theme to the politically and culturally committed IPTA. It was only in the post-Independence India that Shakespeare's plays found favour again on the stage.

This chapter is divided into three sections. Section I traces the growth of Indian theatre in independent India. It is important to situate the select Shakespearean performances in postcolonial Indian theatre discourse since 'historicity of text and textuality of history' (performance as text in this case) are interlinked and cannot be separated.[1] Hence, this discourse on Indian theatre presents a context to these productions and also functions as a co-text to be read to understand the complexity of the appropriation of Shakespeare's works in India. Section II discusses some Shakespearean productions that employ folk and traditional idioms from varied sociocultural and linguistic sectors in post-Independence India. Christy Desmet in *Shakespeare and Appropriation* describes the process of postcolonial appropriations of Shakespeare as the one 'in which post-colonial societies take over those aspects of imperial culture … that may be of use to them in articulating their own social and cultural identities.'[2] In this context, Utpal Dutt's *Macbeth* (1954) and *Bhuli Nai Priya* (*Romeo Juliet*, 1970), B.V. Karanth's *Barnam Van* (*Birnam Wood* 1989), Habib Tanvir's *Kamdev ka Apna Vasantritu ka Sapna* (*A Mid-Summer Night's Dream*, 1993), Lokendra Arambam's *Macbeth: Stage of Blood* (1997) and M.K. Raina's *Badshah Pather* (*King Lear*, 2009) illustrate practical application of this process. Section III provides the conclusion to the chapter. These productions cannot claim to be truly 'folk' theatre. In fact, what they represent is a true blend of folk and modern theatres which is representative of any postcolonial society. My focus, here, is to understand the cultural alterity that these productions bring forth in the context of Shakespeare performance and distinguish them from other Shakespeare productions across the world.

Decolonising Indian Theatre

> *the most important area of domination was the mental universe of the colonized, the control, through culture, of how people perceived themselves and their relationship to the world. […] To control a people's culture is to control their tools of self-definition in relationship to others. For colonialism this involved two aspects of the same process: the destruction or the deliberate undervaluing of a people's culture, their art, dances, religions, history, geography, education, orature and literature, and the conscious elevation of the language of the colonizer. The domination of a people's language by the languages of the colonizing nations was crucial to the domination of the mental universe of the colonized.*[3]

After the political Independence was achieved by India in 1947, one of the major concerns for the nation was to decolonise the minds of its people. The colonists had gone but colonialism remained a perpetuating influence. Aimé Césaire, Frantz Fanon and Ngugi wa Thiong'O, the most vociferous proponents of decolonisation, have stressed the need to decolonise every aspect of life to make independence worth. In this context, during the early decades of the post-Independence era, Indians were faced with the task of reshaping a culture that would be 'authentically' Indian free from the colonial influences. This would mean the creation of a cultural community distinct from other such communities/nations. Theatre was a part of cultural deliberations in post-Independence India. Emphasising the need to reimagine Indian theatre, P.V. Rajamannar, the first chairperson of Sangeet Natak Akademi, in his welcome address to the First Drama Seminar, 1956 observed:

> The important place that theatre occupies in the cultural life of a nation cannot be denied. Rabindranath Tagore once said that a nation's culture is judged by the standard of its theatre.... If the theatre is to be of any moment and significance, it must necessarily be an embodiment of the contemporary life of the nation. Otherwise, the theatre would cease to be a living force. It might then provide a certain amount of entertainment, but otherwise it would be worthless and insignificant.... I use the expression 'contemporary life' in a very wide and comprehensive sense.... Contemporary life would include not merely the present but everything in the past which has still a meaning and influence ... history and biography, myths and folklore, would also serve to supply themes for a living theatre.[4]

The *Akademi* sought to search for indigenous idioms for Indian theatre to decolonise Indian theatre and provide it a new direction. The contact with the West had brought about a transformation in almost every sphere of Indian life—social, economic, political and cultural—during the colonial rule. Theatre too had experienced change. The theatrical modernity brought by the West had introduced a new kind of theatre quite different from the traditional performances. Some of the important features that differentiated the two theatrical traditions were the use of fixed proscenium stage replacing open air performances of folk theatre; western realism and naturalism in the place of inherent symbolism in Indian traditional forms; Western commercial theatre instead of Indian theatre tradition based on patronage. The 'new' theatre introduced by the English was taken up by the educated Indian elite as a civic activity. Gradually this kind of theatre was assimilated into the indigenous performance traditions and a distinct theatre emerged during the colonial period that subtly blended the two traditions. In the years immediately after Independence, there was opposition to this kind of theatre which seemed 'derivative, 'imitative' and 'colonial' to many (as discussed later in the chapter). It was argued that theatre needed to be decolonised for it to flourish in India. The collective support was for a theatre inspired equally by the classical Sanskrit tradition as well as folk theatre—merging elements from both the 'great' and the 'little' traditions.

It was with this idea that Sangeet Natak Akademi was established in Delhi in 1953 as the national institution for performing arts to monitor and guide, provide patronage and conserve Indian traditions of performance. Maulana Abul Kalam Azad, then the Union Minister for Education, said in his opening address at the inauguration of the Akademi

> India's precious heritage of music, drama and dance is one which we must cherish and develop. We must do so not only for our own sake but also as our contribution to the cultural heritage of mankind. Nowhere is it truer than in the field of art that to sustain means to create. Traditions cannot be preserved but can only be created afresh. It will be the aim of this Akademi to preserve our traditions by offering them an institutional form.... In a democratic regime, the arts can derive their sustenance only from the people, and the state, as the organized manifestation of the people's will, must, therefore, undertake ... maintenance and development [of arts] as one of [its] first responsibilities.[5]

The Akademi intended to organise a seminar every four years for each of the arts—dance, drama, music and film. The first drama seminar was organised in 1956 and inaugurated by S. Radhakrishnan, the then Vice-President of India. Aparna Dharwadker refers to this seminar as 'the first sustained exercise in historical self-positioning—an early postcolonial reflection on the singular problematic of a multilingual theatre tradition that had classical and pre-modern as well as colonial antecedents, the emergent modernity of which was synchronous with colonialism.'[6] The objective of the seminar was to conceive the future of Indian theatre as it should develop in independent India. It was formally recommended in the seminar that,

> the regeneration of the Indian theatre can only be possible by revitalizing the traditional folk forms so as to narrow the gulf between the dramatic forms that have developed during the last hundred years and the survivals from the past. The Seminar recommends that adequate steps be taken not only for the careful and scientific study of the folk drama in different parts of India but also for preventing their decay and disappearance and for giving them recognition and new life.[7]

Thus, the major concern for theatre practitioners was to 'decolonise' Indian theatre in terms of—form, content, conventions and so on.

The most important and visible colonial metaphor in modern Indian theatre was 'Western naturalism' manifest in the form of the proscenium stage. The discussion regarding the proscenium was based on the assumption that this Western convention along with naturalism had disturbed the traditional styles of performance. The subject generated interesting discussions. Almost all the participants in the seminar agreed that the urban proscenium was a Western imposition on Indian theatre that destroyed the elasticity of spatial use in traditional performances by creating fixed and enclosed theatre space. The proscenium created an unwanted divide between the performer and the audience. For instance, Mulk Raj Anand argued that Indians '... cannot follow the Western system of founding a chain of grandiose closed theatres in India, in blind imitation of the West and merely mount plays in those theatres according to the commercial techniques already discarded by the most advanced experts of Europe.'[8] One cannot miss irony in Anand's argument that India should discard the proscenium as even the West has done the same. My contention is that the probability of the proscenium stage harming the traditional theatres seems little since the former was largely urban-centric while traditional performances were based majorly in rural India. Even if the latter were performed in the urban areas they co-existed with the former. In fact, as I have discussed in Chapter II, Parsi theatre did bring elements from folk forms into the proscenium theatre. Moreover, certain traditional forms had already started to decay even before the advent of the British theatres in India. Anand, for example, commented on the already decaying status of Indian traditional forms before the arrival of the British.

> The decay of ritual through rigid ill-understood forms, and the whole tradition, which was becoming increasingly more conventional through formalism, was degraded by the low position to which actors and dancers were reduced in the cast hierarchy that bound Hindu society into a compact but corrupt social organism. The puritanism of the Muslim invaders made the situation in the arts more difficult still, because Hindu religious practices were often an exposition of their sense of value.[9]

Thus, some traditional performance forms were already in decay by the 18th century before Indians were introduced to the Western proscenium theatre. Moreover, in the 19th century, indigenous forms of performance had come under severe criticism by the emerging middle class and social reformer movements as discussed in Chapter I. The important consequence of the seminar was that it recommended construction of theatres across the country, establishment of a Central Institute to provide training to theatre professionals, providing financial help to artists, doing away with Dramatic Performances Control Act of 1876 and preservation and promotion of folk drama among other things. Consequently, there were attempts to revive folk theatre on the one hand and Sanskrit drama on the other as an 'ingredient of national theatre for restoring an "authentic" Indian tradition, which, in the nationalistic post-colonial imagination, had been interrupted by colonialism.'[10] The revival of Sanskrit theatre led to contemporary productions of Sanskrit drama by almost every notable theatre director for the next 30 years or so, aided by centrally-funded festivals like the *Kalidasa Festival* and *Nehru Shatabadi Natya Samaroh*.

The National School of Drama (NSD) was established in 1959 in Delhi to realise the aim of developing a 'national theatre' based on the rich cultural heritage of India. The issue gained further impetus with Suresh Awasthi becoming the secretary of Sangeet Natak Akademi in 1965. Awasthi's role in decolonising Indian theatre is clear in his comments,

> As part of the great cultural renaissance generated during the post-independence period, there has occurred a most meaningful encounter with tradition in various fields of creative activity. The return to and discovery of tradition was inspired by a *search for roots and a quest for identity*. This was part of a whole process of decolonization of our life style, values, social institutions, creative forms and cultural modes. The modern Indian theatre, product of a colonial theatrical culture, felt the need to *search for roots most intensely to match its violent dislocation from the traditional course.*[11]

Efforts to establish theatre based on the Indian past had already begun through events like 'First Drama Seminar' (1956) and seminar on 'Contemporary Playwriting and Play Production (1961). Such efforts gained momentum then and tried to establish Awasthi's 'theatre of roots' a pan-India movement through Sangeet Natak Akademi's policies and the state-sponsored conferences, seminars and festivals such as 'Roundtable on the Contemporary Relevance of Traditional Theatre' (1971), Conference on 'Emergence of the National Theatre' (1972) and the 'Scheme of Assistance to Young Theatre Workers' especially promoted the creation of indigenous theatre. Theatre festivals like *Kalidasa Festival* and *Nehru Shatabadi Natya Samaroh* helped in strengthening the status of 'theatre of roots'. Erin B. Mee argues that the 'theatre of roots really went national' during the 1970s by carefully projecting a constructed image of Indian theatre.[12] Such a policy left theatre workers in search for grants, with no other option but to take up traditional forms sometimes without adequate knowledge of these forms. Soon, theatre of roots came under severe criticism from theatre persons for promoting a particular kind of theatre. Satish Alekar, a well-known Marathi playwright, objected against the 'Scheme of Assistance to Young Theatre Workers' which laid down the mandatory condition that,

> for the play to be performed in the scheme [it] should have [some] bearing on the folk theatre traditions of India. Due [to] this condition all the directors who had no knowledge of folk theatre traditions were made to use these forms in order to be in the scheme and as a result a lot of substandard plays were produced.[13]

International theatre festivals furthered the projection of the 'Immortal India' image. Initiated in the 1980s, the Festival of India was to play a major role in the 'marketing drive to introduce India to the highly industrialized G7 countries as a viable locale for investment.'[14] Thus, the Festivals projected a carefully constructed image of 'India' for an economic end. The economic gain for the government through these festivals becomes the clearly-stated official intention:

> S.K. Mishra, director-general of the Festival of India, and an ex-tourism top official from the state of Haryana, explained the Festivals in terms of the following: '… it's a perfect moment for India to cash in, to change existing prejudices about India in the western world and to signal a new era of Indo-American cooperation.' And Niranjan Desai, the Washington-based minister counsellor for culture, talking about economic potentials in the field of tourism, books, movies, investment and trade: 'These are things we want but cannot get until we alter our image. We are still trapped in the Heat and Dust and Indiana Jones syndrome. We have to show that India is not only exotic but contemporaneously exotic as well as modern and competent.'[15]

To meet the aim of the festivals, it was required to feature only those productions that were cast in typically traditional and folk idioms. Productions like Habib Tanvir's *Charandas Chor* (Charandas the Thief), K.N. Panikkar's *Karnabharam* (The Anguish of Karna) and *Madhyam Vyayog* (The Middle One), M.K. Raina's *Andha Yug*

(The Blind Age) and Ratan Thiyam's *Chakravyuha* (The Wheel of War) which incorporated elements from traditional Indian forms were clear choices for the festivals. Projecting such a constructed image of Indian culture at international fora has led Rustom Bharucha to argue that,

> At the international level, we have projected a most cosmetic and superficial image of 'Indian culture'.... At home, these festivals have merely mechanised and commodified our rural and tribal cultural resources, apart from making showpieces of our 'classical art'. They have disrupted social relationships by creating false hierarchies within the communities of performers. They have increased the role of impresarios and cultural dalals, intensifying deference's to power structures rather than facilitating a critique of their role.[16]

Another source that helped to crystallise the indigenising trends in post-Independence Indian theatre was Bertolt Brecht. Theatre practitioners found in Brecht's theatre characterised by its rejection of Western theatrical traditions, anti-realism, epic theatre mode, a performative style that would accommodate traditional forms of India, China and Japan. Nissar Allana, one of the leading designers of Indian theatre, observes that the elements used by Brecht were already present in folk theatre and, therefore,

> brought about a wider awareness of the possibility that such elements could become a part of the modern idiom in the Indian context [...] In India there was already an awareness of the importance of discovering a link with the tradition, and Brecht's theatre soon became exceedingly relevant.[17]

In the 1960s, Brecht was taken as the model for developing 'modern' theatre based on indigenous traditions of performance. Also, the sponsorship provided by the German Democratic Republic in the 1960s provided the opportunity to Indian directors like M.S. Sathyu and Shama Zaidi to visit the Berliner Ensemble. Later Ebrahim Alakzi's participation in the 'Brecht Dialog 1968' in East Berlin and Fritz Bennewitz's collaboration with National School of Drama in the early 1970s affirmed Brecht's place in Indian theatre.[18] The period that followed witnessed Brecht being produced by eminent directors around India. Some of the major productions include Fritz Bennewitz's *The Threepenny Opera* in the *swang* style of Uttar Pradesh (1970); Vijaya Mehta's adaptations of *The Good Woman of Setzuan* and *The Caucasian Chalk Circle* in the *tamasha* and *dashavtar* styles (1972 and 1974); M.K. Raina's Punjabi folk version of *The Caucasian Chalk Circle* (1976); Habib Tanvir's Chhattisgarhi folk version of *The Good Woman of Setzuan* (1978); and B.V. Karanth's Bundelkhandi folk version of *The Caucasian Chalk Circle* (1983). All of these productions attempted to indigenise Brecht within the performative styles of different traditional forms.

Thus, the period from the 1960s onwards was engaged with the search for 'roots'. There is no denying the fact that the theatre of roots gave direction to Indian theatre, especially at a time when directors and playwrights were struggling to find suitable idioms that could be described as 'Indian'. However, excesses started bothering them when 'folk' became the only 'genuine' expression of Indian theatre, thwarting the development of any other form of expression. Such theatre received criticism not only by those who did not practice it but also from those who had once engaged with it. Shanta Gandhi, for instance, who had played a major role in revitalising traditional theatre observed,

> It has become the fashion to incorporate in one's productions some of the features of traditional theatre which the actors can learn without much strain. [...] With rare exceptions, these forms are used without an adequate understanding of their basic nature and without sensitive apprehension of the inherent relationship that exists between the forms and their content.[19]

Thespians like G.P. Deshpande critiqued such an approach and equated this with the West's enthusiasm for 'ethnic' and 'exotic' India. According to Deshpande, such an approach was nothing but 'Orientalism in reverse' which,

> dismisses nearly two hundred years of modern proscenium theatre in India. It rules out contemporary experience and therefore

contemporary sensibility. All this has political meanings. Quite often they are unintended but their impact cannot be avoided. Modern Indian Theatre is a victim of a particular kind of politics—the politics of cultural nationalism which is monolithic, blind and anti-creative.[20]

Despite these debates on theatre of roots, it cannot be denied that it was an influential movement that marked the dominant style of post-Independence Indian theatre. It is amidst such theatre discourse that we look at a few Shakespeare performances in the following section.

Shakespeare Performances in 'Urban-folk' Theatre

Utpal Dutt's Productions of Shakespeare

Shakespeare must be done, but he must be done for the common people.[21]

Utpal Dutt

Utpal Dutt (1929–1993), a theatre director, playwright and actor, was one of the major figures in independent India to engage with Shakespeare. His initiation into theatre dates back to his school and college days where he acted in various Shakespeare plays directed by the Jesuit Fathers. His induction into professional theatre was by Geoffrey Kendall who toured India with his English theatre troupe Shakespearana during the 1950s performing Shakespeare plays in schools and colleges. Kendall invited Dutt to act in his plays and Duttt did act as 'Antonio in *The Merchant of Venice*, Horatio in *Hamlet*, Brutus in *Julius Caesar*, Mercutio in *Romeo and Juliet*, Ross in *Macbeth*, and Roderigo in *Othello*.'[22] It was from Kendall that Dutt learned the nuances of theatre and discipline in acting. Dutt recalls an anecdote when he was beaten up by Kendal in Allahabad after a performance of *Romeo and Juliet*:

I had Mercutio's part, I died in the middle of the play. Having finished my part, I went back to the hotel. Around midnight, Kendall entered my room with a pair of heavy boots in his hand and, before uttering

> a single word, he beat me mercilessly. Then I remembered that I was supposed to conduct the music in the last scene. As there were only fourteen of us in the group, we had to do practically everything ourselves. As I had neglected my duty for various personal reasons, Kendall became furious and constantly repeated the words: 'Shame on you, you don't belong'. You don't belong—you are not one of theater. You are not a man of this profession. The Guru's reprimands hurt me more than the boots. That night I learned a lot. Kendall was an old type of British professional, who had learned by being beaten up and who used to teach by beating.[23]

The tour with the Kendalls and his brief involvement with IPTA brought about a major change in the Dutt's philosophy of theatre. Dutt and his group Little Theatre Group (LTG) had hitherto produced Shakespeare exclusively in English for select audiences which comprised either a few Englishmen in Calcutta or a few Calcuttans who were more British than the British. Dutt remembers the diminishing audience for English theatre in Calcutta who 'sat there with clenched fists—pretending to enjoy it.'[24] Later, Dutt regretted doing Shakespeare in English and observed, '[T]hose were years wasted performing Shakespeare before an intellectual audience.'[25] After the tour with the Kendalls, Dutt decided that LTG would stage plays in Bengali for a wider and more inclusive audience. Himani Bannerji notes,

> No matter how political a play may be—the very fact that it is in English, he [Dutt] felt, kills the politics of the play, since it must be played to an audience which is upper class and generally right-wing. Utpal therefore looked to Bengali and European classics and sought out primarily a Bengali speaking audience.[26]

The first play to be produced was Jatindranath Sengupta's translation of *Macbeth* (1954). Dutt toured with the play, surely influenced by Kendalls's touring company, and performed a hundred shows in the villages of West Bengal. Dutt noted in an interview:

> Shakespeare must be done, but he must be done for the common people. We did *Macbeth* in Bengali, and in one season we did ninety-seven performances in the villages. The people took to Shakespeare

> enthusiastically. To them Shakespeare was in the proper *Jatra* style—the action, the violence, the robustness charmed them.[27]

Dutt observed in another interview that while he found the emotional emphasis in plays like *Macbeth* and *Othello* popular with the *jatra* audience, the violence and melodrama of *jatra* were also compatible with Shakespeare's plays.[28] Dutt, however, did not believe in taking liberties with Shakespeare's plays. In Bengali *Macbeth*, Dutt retained the original names of places and characters and Western costumes. He remained as close as possible to the original text despite some minor alterations. Though the rural audience could not understand some references about Scotland and England but the production was a huge success since human elements such as 'ambition and kingship, loyalties and morality, emotions, poetry, passion and human weakness' were well understood.[29]

Various arguments have been put forward by theatre scholars regarding Dutt's production of *Macbeth*. Some of them equate the production to *jatra*. Rustom Bharucha describes Dutt's production of *Macbeth* as *jatra*. According to him, '[I]t was only by immersing *Macbeth* in the ritual world of *jatra* and by transforming Shakespeare's language into a bold, declamatory form of incantation that the Little Theatre Group could reach a Bengali working-class audience with an Elizabethan classic.'[30] Similarly, Jyotsna Singh observes that Dutt drew on the conventions of *jatra* 'to create the spectacle that he believes is an essential aspect of a non-elitist revolutionary theatre.'[31] While the production was certainly non-elitist, it did not belong to Dutt's famed revolutionary phase. Dutt himself admits about the production was not revolutionary theatre.[32] Helen Gilbert and Joanne Tompkins too laud Dutt's efforts in taking Shakespeare to the rural masses:

> In an attempt to undermine both the elitism and the Anglocentrism associated with the Shakespearian theatre of the time, Dutt took translations of such plays as *Macbeth* to the rural masses, dispensing with the conventions of the proscenium stage and infusing his

> productions with the ritual traditions of *jatra*, the folk theatre of Bengal. By using Shakespearian texts in this manner, Dutt's work presented a way not only of indigenizing the imperial canon but also of disrupting its cultural clout.[33]

Although Dutt took *Macbeth* to villages away from the fixed proscenium, he did not use a *jatra* stage. Tapati Gupta argues that the stage for Macbeth was 'a temporary proscenium—a boxlike, three-walled platform, winged and curtained—with the audience sitting in front.'[34] The arguments put forward by Bharucha, Singh and Gilbert considering Dutt's *Macbeth* as *jatra* seem to be based on the assumption that Dutt had used a bold and declamatory style. Gupta disagrees and maintains that '[S]ince Dutt did not believe in hyper-emotional postures, he explored the natural potentialities of Shakespeare to captivate the imagination of the masses.'[35] Whether it was *Macbeth* in *jatra* or *jatra* in *Macbeth*, it can be safely said that the production was the first Shakespearean performance in the post-Independence India to be taken away from elite circuits to the masses staging 97 shows in one season. Dutt had observed elsewhere that 'the classics were not a prerogative of an elite. They would cease to exist unless they were brought to the people.'[36] The play was later mounted in a Calcutta proscenium but could not achieve the earlier impact. According to Bharucha, the faults lay in the production being 'blatantly operatic,' and 'the production exemplified some of the worst excesses of the nineteenth-century theatre—melodramatic acting and posturing, a pretentious delivery of lines, and a fundamental lack of belief in the social and political resonance of the play. It was one of Dutt's most pointless productions.'[37]

It was much later in 1970 that Dutt produced his first Shakespeare play as *jatra*. This was *Bhuli Nai Priya* (I Have Not Forgotten, My Love), a radical transformation of *Romeo and Juliet*. For the first time, Dutt reworked a Shakespeare text in the *jatra* form for the *jatra* audience. The play was staged by professional *jatra* actors with the spatial arrangement of a traditional *jatra*. Minimum props were used and the audience sat all around, unlike in the case of the earlier *Macbeth*. However, Dutt had to introduce some changes to the traditional *jatra* format. For instance, he reduced the time to two to three hours whereas traditional *jatra* is usually ten to twelve hours long. Also, the traditional *jatra* had innumerable songs. He also cut down the number of songs to four or five. In his own words,

> Originally I think (there's a controversy as to whether the songs or the dialogue came first), it was all sung. But we can understand why during the late nineteenth and twentieth centuries the Jatra had to rely mostly on songs. It is much easier to project song than speech. And continuous acting would be very strenuous in a play lasting from early afternoon until midnight. So the actors would act a little, and then various kinds of singers would come on. There was a character called Vivek ("Conscience") who would enter at particularly dramatic moments and sing a song about what was to be learned from the incident. There was another conventional device—the *juri*—a group of singers sitting on the edge of the arena throughout the performance. In the middle of a scene they would suddenly stand up and start singing in chorus. The action would resume after they finished their song and sat down. That's how the form used to be.... Today the main audience comes from the working class and not the peasants—tea garden workers, railway workers in Assam, coal and steel workers in Bengal. They pay well and the *Jatra* is now oriented towards them. They won't sit and listen to a *Jatra* for twelve hours—they have a work shift the next day—so the plays must be shortened. Naturally the songs are the first to go out, and now instead of thirty, there are never more than five or six, usually only three. Also, *Vivek* is no longer used. We are trying to reintroduce these elements but the paying audience is already conditioned.[38]

Traditional *jatra*, like other folk forms, is declamatory, melodramatic and has exaggerated expressions. According to Gupta, in *Bhuli Nai Priya*

> Dutt naturalized the action and expression, introducing subtlety, racy conversation, natural intonation, and restrained body language. He carefully trained veteran *jatra* actors, whom he admired greatly, and ultimately they discarded their mannerisms and adopted such a finesse that the *jatra* acquired a modernity that was not at odds with the indigenous flavour that Dutt was careful to retain.... The didactic element of *jatra* was retained.[39]

> As far as the narrative is concerned, Dutt's play follows the original story but localises it. Verona is transformed to Murshidabad and Mantau to Calcutta. Escalus becomes Nawab Sirajuddaula. The Montague-Capulet families are changed into Hindu-Muslim families. As Gupta observes, '[B]y making the two families Hindu and Muslim, the historical and post-Partition significance was enhanced.'[40] As the play was thoroughly indigenised for the *jatra* audience, it was natural that the costumes too would be Indian unlike Dutt's previous Shakespeare productions. Thus, the bright and colourful costumes of *jatra* were used. The music composed by Pancham Mitra used a mixture of Indian classical and western instruments like harmonium, *nakkara*, *dholki*, saxophone, clarinet and violin and also incorporated *baul*, *kirtan*, folk tunes and north Indian classical music.[41]

The play *Bhuli Nai Priya* was probably the only play of Shakespeare to be performed in *jatra* by Dutt. By then his theatre had become more revolutionary and Dutt produced *Rifle* (1968), *Jallianwala Bag* (1969), *Delhi Chalo* (March to Delhi, 1970), *Jai Bangla* (Victory for Bengal, 1971), *Sannyasir Tarabari* (The Sword of the Monk,1972), *Jhad* (The Storm, 1973), *Mao Tse Tung* (1974), *Seemanta* (The Border, 1975), *Turuper Tash* (The Ace of Card, 1976), *Mukti Deeksha* (The Indoctrination of Freedom, 1977), *Shada Poshak* (The White Uniform, 1979), *Kuthar* (The Axe, 1980), *Swadhinatar Phanki* (The Lapse of Liberty, 1981), *Bibighar* (The Wife's Room, 1982) and *Damama Oi Baje* (The Beating of the Drum, 1988)—all for professional *jatra* companies. Though *Bhuli Nai Priya* might not be one of Dutt's popular plays it certainly was among the earliest attempts in postcolonial India to bring Shakespeare closer to masses by casting it into an indigenous performance form.

B.V. Karanth's *Barnam Van* (Birnam Wood)

> *Coming face to face with Shakespeare is an awe inspiring and challenging experience for any director, and I am no exception. But Shakespeare, approached with tender submission, yields new dimensions and fresh possibilities begin to reveal themselves.*[42]
>
> B.V. Karanth

B.V. Karanth (1928–2002) was one of the most innovative theatre directors of post-Independence Indian theatre. Born in Manchi village in Karnataka, he was trained as a child actor in theatre by Gubbi Veeranna Company, a well-known company in Karnataka. Gubbi Veeranna later sent Karanth to Banaras Hindu University, Varanasi, to do M.A. Hindi where he was also trained in Hindustani classical music by well-known classical singer and teacher Pandit Omkarnath Thakur. Karanth then graduated from NSD (New Delhi) and later became its director (1977–1981). He also served as Director, Rangmandal Bharat Bhavan, Bhopal (1981–1986) and later Rangayana, Mysore (1989–1995).

The two major influences on Karanth that get reflected in his work are his deep involvement with folk and traditional performances since his childhood and his training in classical music. In fact, theatre personalities like Vijay Tendulkar and G.P. Deshpande considered Karanth more of a music person than theatre. He made use of folk music not only of Karnataka but also from other parts of the country in his productions. Although trained in classical music he did not mind adjusting the rules of classical music to suit the musical needs of theatre. He could create music from stones, wood pieces, chairs or scrap. This was a characteristic feature of many of his productions. Karanth used music not only as an ornament for embellishment but for interpreting a play. Along with folk music, Karanth also used the performance traditions of Karnataka and various other regions for his productions. Deeply rooted in traditional and folk forms of performance, Karanth created individualistic forms for his theatre deriving from these conventions. In his own words,

> Our folk theatre is extremely pliant, but we have completely lost sight of its immense potential. So whenever we look for our own identity or legacy, our quest automatically ends at the same emotional destination ... there ... at folk theatre. However modern and urbanized we think we may have become, our roots still lie somewhere in the villages. It is in the rural countryside that our 'instincts' are essentially grounded. So, it is right to associate ourselves with the folk theatre, while exploring the spirit of the Indian theatre. Whenever we discuss the Indian theatre in the same way as we discuss Indian music and drama, which other forms can we speak about except *Tamasha*, *Yakshagan*, *Bhavai* and so on?[43]

The significance of folk theatres for Karanth is evident from the fact that when he became the director of NSD (1977–1981) he made it mandatory for students to undergo a month-long workshop in folk forms. Karanth's intentions might have been noble but he also received criticism from theatre practitioners and scholars for fostering a unidirectional trend in theatre. Reeta Sondhi, for instance, critiqued Karanth for shifting 'the emphasis in the training programme ... it appears as though it has become a messy splash of colour, comedy and caricature. Credit is to the consummate artistes who have managed to sustain interest in their new productions!'[44] This might be true to some extent but Karanth had the ability to blend the traditional with modern to create the contemporary which was the hallmark of his theatre. While Karanth directed Girish Karnad's *Hayavadana* (The One with a Horse's Head), Vijay Tendulkar's *Ghasiram Kotwal* and Chandrashekhar Kambar's *Jokumaraswamy* all of which had folk elements already embedded in the play-texts, he also adapted Shakespeare's *Macbeth* in indigenous performance idioms.

Karanth produced *Macbeth* as *Barnam Van* in Hindi for the National School of Drama Repertory in 1979. Influenced by the Indian theatre traditions he cast the play in a non-realistic and stylised form. Karanth justifies his choice of *yakshagan* for his production in the 'Director's Note' as follows:

> I do not find myself capable of producing Shakespeare the way he is produced in his own country. Were I to do so, it would be false of me. Therefore, my use of the *Yakshagana* form is not for my own sake, but because it is a part of my awareness and expression. The tragedies of Shakespeare, specially *Macbeth*, overflow with rasas, such as valour, wrath, terror and wonder, and the characters and situations have a universality and larger-than life quality which can be well expressed in the *Yakshagana* style.[45]

Macbeth had already been translated into Hindi by Rangeya Raghav and Harivansh Rai Bachchan, among others. Also, the NSD had produced two plays of Shakespeare—*King Lear* (1964) and *Othello* (1969) under the direction of Ebrahim Alkazi, then Director of the institute. While these productions had used the existing translations, Karanth, commissioned Raghuvir Sahay, a well-known Hindi poet, for his production. But even before the translation of the play had begun, the format was decided. Thus, it was for the translator to fit the play in the form. Unlike Bachchan who had used the *rola* metre for his translation, Sahay chose to translate the play using the '*kavitta* metre whose subtle rhythm gives infinite freedom for creative vocal expression and lends itself to the entire spectrum of moods.'[46] Although, much of the translation follows the original verse pattern a scene or two have been rendered into prose. For example, Lady Macbeth's speech in Act I, sc. vii, which is in prose has been rendered into verse by Sahay.

> Lady Macbeth: I have given suck, and know
> How tender 'tis to love the baby that milks me:
> I would, while it was smiling in my face,
> Have pluck'd my nipple from his boneless gums,
> And dashed the brains out, had I so sworn as you
> Have done to this.
> Macbeth: If we should fail,
> Lady Macbeth: We fail!
> But screw your courage to the sticking-place,
> And we'll not fail.

In Sahay's translation the prose becomes verse as follows:

> Lady Macbeth: *Main pila chuki hun doodh*
> *Aur jaanti hun pyaar aanchal mein kaise umadta hai*
> *par godi mein pade iktak niharte*
> *dudhmunhe ke munh se main chhuda leti stan*
> *patak kar kapaar phod daalti*
> *agar koi pran aisa kiye hue hoti teri tarah*
> Macbeth: *Yadi asaphal hum rahe?*
> *Lady Macbeth: Asaphal hum?*
> *Apne saahas ko tu chaanpe reh usi thor*
> *to hum honge na viphal.*[47]

Instead of translating the original in a literal manner, as in Rangey Raghav's case, Sahay concentrated 'on capturing the sound patterns of sentences as they occur in the original so as to recreate the resonance of the language that was heard on the Elizabethan stage.'[48] Although the names of the characters and places have been retained, topical references to Scotland and England were dispensed with. For instance, in Act 1, scene ii when a soldier talks with Duncan he addresses him as Mark, King of Scotland. However, in the translation Sahay omits the reference of Scotland and the soldier addresses Duncan as *raja* (king). As Sahay explains, '[D]espite being burdened by the ostentatious verbosity of its times, Shakespeare's language at places glows with quiet simplicity, wherein rests his genius and which I have found essential to my translation.'[49] An example of this simplicity of language may be found at the outset of the play where Sahay translates the dialogues of the witches in a very simple and rustic language (Act I, sc. i):

> First Witch: When shall we three meet again
> In thunder, lightning, or in rain?
> Second Witch: When the hurlyburly's done,
> When the battle's lost and won.

as,

> *Daayan 1: Aaj mile hain hamm*
> *pher milenge kabb?*
> *Daiv garjai bijuri chamkai meha barse tabb*
> *Daayan 2: Hum milenge jabb*
> *kattajhujh hui le.*[50]

Or,

> All: Fair is foul, and foul is fair
> Hover through the fog and filthy air.

As,

> All: *Dhoop dhund au dhund dhoop hui jaaye*
> *Daayan toil dhuan mein mandraaye.*[51]

Finally, Sahay left the play to the director to edit it to suit the form.

Barnam Van was first staged at the open-air stage of NSD in 1979. Karanth's mise-en-scène for *Barnam Van* gave him an opportunity to interpret the play in an interesting manner. The open-air stage had a huge banyan tree with its branches coming on to the stage which cast a maze of shadows on the stage, with the help of lights, creating a scene of a jungle. The setting is made more eerie and haunting as the witches appear on the stage. For Karanth, the powerful and haunting visual symbolises the theme of *Macbeth*: 'the labyrinthine jungle of ambition, which ensnares and destroys man.'[52] Karanth's approach to witches is also unusual. Unlike *Macbeth*, in which Shakespeare introduces the witches probably because of the English obsession with witches as destroyers of human lives in the 16th century, Karanth interprets his witches as 'creation of his [Macbeth's] own mind.'[53] This is doubly supported by the fact that Karanth's witches had branches painted on their costumes as if emerging from the jungle which itself is Macbeth's own creation. Such an interpretation then holds *Macbeth* directly responsible for his fate.

As mentioned earlier, Karanth made use of elements from *yakshagan* 'especially for characters' entry and exit, battle scenes, and the expression of emotional tensions through the rhythm of body movements.'[54] In *Barnam Van*, characters enter and exit with stylised dance steps taken from *yakshagan*. Unlike kathakali, *yakshagan* relies on the movements of the whole body and not just face and hands. In traditional *yakshagan*, characters usually enter from behind a half-curtain called *tere* held by two stagehands. In *Barnam Van*, Karanth uses the half-curtain for the entry of characters and for more dramatic purposes to conceal the witches' entry by shaking the curtains and making circular dance movements, draping the curtains around their bodies and suddenly removing them.[55] Such creative use of the conventional half-curtain makes the scene dramatically effective and also enhances the suspense. The last scene showing the moving Birnam Wood has always been challenging for directors. Karanth makes ingenious use of half-curtains to meet the challenge. Malcolm's army enters the stage draped in half-curtains having branches painted on them around their bodies. This gives the impression of the Birnam Wood proceeding towards Macbeth. Other than stylised movements, music is central to *yakshagan*. A traditional *yakshagan* troupe has one or two singers and at least three instrumentalists—a *maddale* drummer, one for *chende*, and one to provide the drone on a harmonium.[56] Karanth, himself a trained classical singer, makes music integral in all his productions. *Barnam Van* is no exception, especially when he borrows so much from *yakshagan* for the production. Although the music in *Barnam Van* is of *yakshagan* style because Karanth found the rhythm of the *kavitta* metre quite close to the beat of *chende*, Karanth makes certain alterations. As he explains in the 'Director's Note', '[S]ince pure *Yakshagana* music can prove to be obscure and incomprehensible, I have introduced other Asian musical instruments such as bells and gongs.' The beat of *chende* and *nakkara*[57] is used to emphasise the stylised movements of entry and exit of characters. Suresh Awasthi comments on Karanth's use of music in following words.

> The play begins with the music of *chenda* and *nakkara*, just like in the performance of *yakshagan* and *kathakali*. After that, the witches enter with a short sad alaap. Alaaps in male and female voices have been used quite effectively. When Macbeth decides to kill Duncan the *nakkara* underlines each line of his dialogue and the humming goes on in the background.... In the sleep-walking scene, Lady Macbeth's dialogues are supported by the beats of *nakkara* and *chende* coupled with the shrilling voices which gives the whole scene a ritualistic setting.[58]

Besides musical instruments, Karanth also creates music out of wood pieces as is done in Japanese *kabuki*. Costume too, is an elaborate affair in *yakshagan*. Characters in traditional *yakshagan* can be identified by the costumes typical to particular characters. Karanth does not entirely replicate *yakshagan* costumes for his characters but also borrows from diverse traditional theatres of Cambodia, Bali, Japan, Burma and Indonesia. With such strong similarity with *yakshagan* for the production, one may be tempted to think that it is *Macbeth* in *yakshagan* form. As Karanth himself clarifies, it is in fact the other way around. Karanth has not cast the play rigidly in a traditional form. A deliberate de-familiarisation with *yakshagan* is achieved by incorporating elements from other traditional forms and by modifying some of the conventions of *yakshagan*. Only those *yakshagan* elements have been incorporated which seem suitable for the visual presentation. Hence, as Karanth himself aptly observes, 'it is not *Macbeth* in *yakshagan*, but *yakshagan* in *Macbeth*.'[59]

Habib Tanvir's *Kamdev ka Apna Vasantritu ka Sapna*

> *I learnt from Shakespeare to always end with an anti-climax....*[60]
>
> Habib Tanvir

Habib Tanvir (1923–2009) belonged to the elder generation of theatre directors in post-Independence India. Tanvir's theatre drew a lot from folk forms of performance in India, especially the traditional performative styles of Chhattisgarh. There were several influences that brought Tanvir closer to the traditional forms of performance which he incorporated into his theatre. As a child, Tanvir was attracted towards folk songs and learnt some of them on his visits to his uncles in Raipur. The second important influence in Tanvir's initiation into folk forms was his brief involvement with IPTA in the 1940s. He himself acknowledges the inspiration that he got from IPTA,

> I worked in the Hindi group but we were also surrounded by the Gujarati, Marathi and Konkani groups. Each group had a music squad. These were strong music squads and some of the great figures in the world of music were associated with them. For example, the Marathi squad included stalwarts like Annabhau Sathe and Amar Sheikh. They drew upon the folk traditions like *burrakatha* and *pawara*.[61]

The third and probably the strongest influence on Tanvir that gave him the direction to work in theatre with a strong base in folk and traditional elements, was his travels across Europe, especially the eight months he spent in Berlin in 1956 watching Brecht's productions. It is interesting to note that Tanvir sustained himself in Europe by singing Chhattisgarhi folk songs in pubs and nightclubs.[62] Brecht had died the same year and his recent productions were being staged. Having seen Brecht's theatre which made use of various folk forms including Asian forms, Tanvir realised that

> ... it is only if one works with one's own cultural traditions and ethos that one can achieve something more durable, more innovative, and artistically more interesting.... The innovativeness of Brecht and his collaborators in music, Eisler and Kurt Weil, could only be achieved when one has a very very [sic.] established native tradition in music to draw upon. Likewise, in the matter of language, the innovations of Brecht were based on German colloquialisms, on his own creative adaptations of the local dialects and colloquial phrases to make new compounds out of them. So, these were the lessons I had learnt from my European travel. I thought you can do nothing worthwhile unless you went to your roots and tried to reinterpret traditions and used traditions as a vehicle for transmitting the most modern and contemporary messages.[63]

Once Tanvir returned to Delhi, he directed Sudraka's *Mricchkatika* (The Little Clay Cart) in 1958 in which he introduced some folk performers from Chhattisgarh. He left Delhi to form his own theatre group called *Naya* Theatre (New Theatre) in 1959. For Tanvir, *Naya* Theatre stood for, 'Indianness in theatre' and believed in 'an aesthetic blend of the folk and urban theatre techniques in order to interpret contemporary life in a manner at once Indian and universal'.[64] During his early career from 1958 to 1970 Tanvir directed plays like *Saat Paise* (Seven Pennies, 1959), *Jalidar Parde* (Perforated Curtains, 1959), *Phansi* (The Execution, 1960), *Rustam-o-Sohrab* (Rustam and Sohrab, 1961) and *Shatranj ke Mohre* (The Pawns of Chess, 1969). Later, Tanvir called these plays 'failures' and he said that it took him years to realise that,

> ... I was trying to apply my English training on the village actors—move diagonally, stand, speak, take this position. I had to unlearn

> it all. I saw that they couldn't even tell right from left on the stage and had no line sense. And I'd go on shouting: 'Don't you know the difference between the hand you eat with and the one you wash with?' ... I realized that those who were for years responding to an audience like this [without bothering about whether the audience was on one side, or three, or four, or whether some of them were sitting on the stage] could never try to unlearn all this and rigidly follow the rules of movement and that was one reason why Thakur Ram, a great actor ... wasn't able to be natural. Another reason was the *matrubhasha* [mother tongue]—he wasn't speaking his mother tongue, so it jarred on my ears, because he was speaking bad Hindi and not Chhattisgarhi, in which he was fluent, which was so sweet. This realization took me years—naïve of me, but still it took me years. Once I realized it I used Chhattisgarhi and I improvised, allowed them the freedom and then came pouncing down upon them to crystallize the movement—there you stay. And they began to learn. That quite simply was the method I learnt.[65]

With this realisation began the second phase (1970–1973) in Tanvir's career when he worked with folk performers and their repertoire in their dialects. His role was rather like editing and structuring their plays for the stage. Folk plays like *Arjun ka Sarthi* (Arjun's Charioteer) and *Gauri Gaura* were staged in 1972 as the Chhattisgarhi versions of the *Mahabharata*. The third and the most significant phase (1973–2008) in Tanvir's theatre career came after he held a month-long *nacha*[66] workshop with about a hundred participants in Raipur in 1973. Among the participants, 30 were folk actors and others were urban and rural artists and intellectuals as observers. The workshop became the turning point in Tanvir's theatre as it culminated in the much-acclaimed production titled *Gaon ka Naam Sasural Mor Naam Damaad* (The Village is in-Laws' House and I am the Son-in-Law). The play blended three folk comedies from the *nacha* repertoire. Thus, began the most productive phase of Tanvir's theatre during which he staged productions like Bhavabhuti's *Uttam Ramcharit* (Rama's Last Act, 1974–1975), *Charandas Chor* (Charandas the Thief, 1975–1976), *Mitti ki Gadi* (The Clay Cart, 1977–1978). Shakespeare's

A Midsummer Night's Dream adapted as *Kamdev ka Apna Vasantritu ka Sapna* (The Love God's Own, A Spring Time Dream, 1993) marked a high point of his achievement with this kind of theatre.

Kamdev ka Apna was Tanvir's first attempt at producing a Shakespearean play. In fact, Tanvir had always wanted to do a Shakespearean play but as he admits, 'I never liked the translations in Hindi, Urdu and Hindustani. I also did not fancy translating for I found it intimidating.'[67] It so happened that the English Shakespeare Company offered Tanvir a project to direct a Shakespearean play in collaboration with the English actors of the company and his own folk performers. Tanvir first thought of producing a Shakespearean tragedy but realised that a tragedy may not work in a bilingual production. He turned to comedies and found *A Midsummer Night's Dream* to be an apt play for a bilingual production. Tanvir saw the possibility of different languages being spoken by different characters in the play. The strategy that Tanvir devised was simple: the royalty would speak English, the inhabitants of the forest and fairies would speak Urdu, while the mechanicals would converse in their dialect. Once Tanvir was sure about the languages to be used, he started translating the play. Tanvir focused on only one plot and tried to be close to the original text. However, the translation posed several problems. The English title, for instance, was problematic for literal translation. As he comments,

> The title itself resists a literal translation—midsummer day and midsummer night being specific occasions for festivity for Britain and elsewhere in the West. Midsummer itself, particularly in tropical countries, does not exactly stand for convivial occasions. Even the meaning of autumn differs in East and West. Spring alone can perhaps be considered conducive to feelings of love all over the world. Hence, the change in the play's title.[68]

Similarly, *Kamdev*, the God of love and desire, in the Hindu mythology replaces the Western Cupid who may be unfamiliar to many Indians. Tanvir decided to retain the original names of the characters and places but changed the names of the flora and fauna, the fairies and the gods. The fairies are referred to as *pari*. The Indian substitutes for gods seem awkward sometimes. For instance, though the play is set in Athens, Bottom's lines, 'The raging rocks...The foolish Fates' in Act I, scene ii have been translated thus:

Parvat garjan laage
Dar ke sab jhan bhaage
Do peechhe dus aage
Aisi kala hu main,
Main Shankar ke pujari
Suraj meri savari
Thar thar sab nar naari
Kais bala hu main.[69]

The substitution for Phibbus (Phoebus) as *Shankar* (Lord Shiva) and his chariot as *suraj* (sun) is a little awkward. Tanvir's translation is among the very few versions of Shakespeare in Indian languages that translates blank verse into blank verse, rhymed verse into rhymed verse and prose into prose. Music has always played an important part in Tanvir's plays since most of them are rooted in folk stories and folk theatres. Even in *Kamdev ka Apna* though originally an English play, Tanvir has introduced songs based on *ghazals*, *thumris* and songs of the *nautanki* tradition. Theseus, for example, sings a *ghazal* in chaste Urdu towards the end:

Woh neem shab ki aahni
zabaan ki jumbishein suno-2
Jo baar baar de rahin hain-2
Aadhi raat ki khabar
Guzar gaya hai waqt sham
Is ajeeb khel mein
Hai raat jag der tak-2
Toh hogi jaldi hi sahar.[70]
(This is the difficulty of midnight
Listen to the movements of the tongue
which is repeatedly giving
the news of the midnight.

The evening has passed
in this strange play
It's night, sit up late
and it will be dawn soon; *translation mine*).

And,

Guzar gayi hai kisi tarah furqaton ki sham
Shab-e-firaaq ke haathon mein ab hai vasl ka jaam.[71]
(The evening of separation has passed somehow
The night of longing has the goblet of union in its hand; *translation mine*).

While Puck in Act II, scene i, depicts the situation 'The king doth keep his revels here tonight ...' in poetry following like a *chaubola* in *nautanki*:

Puck: *Ban ka raja ban ki rani se hai bahut naraaz,*
Kah de apni rani se, who idhar na phatke aaj
idhar na phatke aaj teri rani, ye tu bhi sun le
ban ka raja aata hai, lekar sab sevak apne ...[72]

Some modifications are necessary when translating a text from one culture to another, though Tanvir believes '[I]n spirit, however, the play in translation hopefully remains Shakespearean, if only because of the love of nature and life in general, including little creatures such as spiders, beetles, snails, blind-worms and snakes.'[73]

The project proposed by the English company got postponed due to financial constraints. Tanvir, however, decided to carry on with the play with some modifications. He now concentrated only on one of the plots—the rustic mechanicals planning to stage a play on the occasion of the royal wedding of Theseus, the Duke of Athens, with Hippolyta, the Queen of Amazons. The denizens of the fairy world were to be played by urban actors and the mechanicals by the folk artistes of Tanvir's group. Although Tanvir had already worked out the problem of language to be used by the two sets of actors, urban and the folk, he found it difficult, at least initially, to make the actors grasp the rhythm of dialogue delivery:

> The proper way to go about it is not to give in to the lilt of poetry; to keep the beat under and bring out the emotion, unlike in Parsi theatre. You have to know how to stretch a word so that the listener hears the beat but goes straight to the dramatic position.[74]

He further observes that the folk artistes had a better understanding of the song beats but found it difficult to manage the beat of the conversations. However, for the urban actors both were challenging, especially for the actors playing Puck, Oberon and Titania.[75]

Tanvir's theatre has always been one of austerity. Influenced by the folk forms, it is no surprise that Tanvir's theatre acquired the simplicity and lucidity of folk theatre. His much-acclaimed plays like *Charandas Chor*, *Gaon ka Naam Sasural* and *Mitti ki Gudi* are played on a bare stage with minimal props and sets. The same is true for *Kamdev ka Apna* where a hand-held half-curtain is the only element of the set. Referring to the simplicity that was the hallmark of Tanvir's theatre, Sudhanva Deshpande aptly remarks, '[W]ith its simplicity, its directness and minimalism, Habib Tanvir's theatre would have been considered avant-garde had it not been so popular, and so funny.'[76]

Lokendra Arambam's *Macbeth: Stage of Blood*

Manipur was a princely state under the British Raj. It was merged into the Indian nation-state in 1949 and this has become the source of contention among various groups in Manipur who want different political future for the state. As a result, the state has witnessed insurgency since the 1960s with groups like United National Liberation Front, Maoist Communist Party of Manipur and People's Revolutionary Party of Kangleipak trying to establish their stronghold. While some of these groups claim more political autonomy for Manipur a small section wants to establish Manipur as an independent nation-state. This has led to counter-insurgency by the government and enforcement of such draconian laws like The Armed Forces Special Powers Act (AFSPA) which grants special powers to the armed forces. Though useful in countering insurgency, the Act has been strongly criticised by human rights activists and Manipuri people who claim that the law is a violation of their right to live. There have been protests by the people of Manipur ever since the law has been enforced in the state. Twelve women from *Meira Paibi* (a women's social movement in Manipur), for instance, staged a protest against the excesses committed by the Indian Army by stripping themselves naked in front of the 17th Assam Rifles headquarters holding the banner 'Indian Army Rape Us'. However, the most sustained effort to get this law repealed has been made by Irom Chanu Sharmila, a civil rights and political activist from Manipur, who observed a hunger strike from 2 November 2000 to 9 August 2016. The law, however, has not been revoked. To add to the woes of Manipur, the state has also been witnessing ethnic clashes among the Meities, Nagas and Kukis all of whom claim their right over the land of Manipur. It is amidst this social and political turmoil that theatre directors like Ratan Thiyam, late H. Kanhailal and Lokendra Arambam among others have carried out their theatrical activities. Hence, it is no surprise that their theatre reflects the contemporary realities of Manipur.

Manipur has a rich performance tradition which includes *thang-ta*, *lai-haraoba*, *ras-lila*, *nat sankreetan* and *wari liba*.[77] Some of the Meitei ritualistic traditional performances date back to the 12th century and are generally associated with the fertility rituals and ancestral worship. *Lai-haraoba*, for instance, is a traditional fertility ritual. Manipur's history has played an important role in shaping its performance tradition. Till the 18th century, Manipur was an independent kingdom. Various performance forms like *lai-haraoba* and *wari liba* or the art of storytelling were patronised by the kings. With the coming of Vaishnavite Hinduism in Manipur in the 18th century, many natives converted into Hinduism. The performance traditions were also influenced by the newly introduced Hindu performance traditions. New forms like *raslila* emerged that assimilated the two cultures especially due to the efforts of the Vaishnava king Bhagyachandra (1763–1798) who 'effected a compromise between the dissenting faiths, manifested theatrically in the harmonious assimilation of both cultures in Manipuri *Ras Lila*.'[78] The 1891 defeat of Manipur in the Anglo-Manipuri war brought Manipur under the colonial control. The proscenium theatre made inroads into Manipur during this time via Bengal where 'modern' theatre had already begun to develop. The early plays staged in Manipur were mostly Bengali plays. Somorendra Arambam notes that it was only in 1925 that the first Manipuri drama *Narasingh* written by Lairenmayum Ibungohal Singh in 1922 was staged at the Palace compound of Maharaja Churchand Singh.[79] During the 1930s dramatic clubs like Meiti Dramatic Union (1931), Aryan Theatre (1935), Chitrangada Natya Mandir (1936), Society Theatre (1937), Rupmahal (1942) were established. The playwrights of the 1930s, who were influenced by Western models and Sanskrit drama, wrote plays that were filtered through their religious and moral fabric. For instance, in *Bhagyachandra* (1930), a Manipuri adaptation of *Macbeth* by Arambam Dorendrajit, it is the usurper and not the king who is killed thereby making the play 'a eulogy to good rule.'[80] One exception during this period was G.C. Tongbra who, influenced by G.B. Shaw, wrote social drama. Most of his plays mocked the hypocrisy of the society and social evils.

Theatre in Manipur has witnessed various experiments by young directors and actors. The 1960s and 1970s witnessed, as Arambam observes, 'a growth of youth power, youth influence, along with an increasing awareness by the people of their own identity, in the entire north-eastern region.'[81] It was the time when young directors like H. Kanhailal and Ratan Thiyam were trying to structure indigenous idioms to create a theatre that could express their distinct identity. Thiyam introduced ritualistic elements in his theatre while Kanhailal engaged himself with Badal Sircar's style of intimate theatre. Thiyam's theatre, which draws heavily upon the ritualistic traditions of Manipur, is less verbal and more spectacular because according to him 'the word cannot travel properly and reach the inner eye.'[82] His productions are fairly well-known as they travel across the world. Though Kanhailal too is inspired by Meitei ritualistic traditions his approach is different from Thiyam's. His theatre is not spectacular but psycho-physical. He was also a well-known figure in Manipuri theatre whose work has been well documented by Rustom Bharucha in *The Theatre of Kanhailal: Pebet and Memoirs of Africa*. A talented director who has somehow not figured prominently in the Manipuri theatre is Lokendra Arambam. Although he has committed himself to give expression to reflect upon the political and social situation of Manipur in his productions he never received much attention from the central funding agencies till 1997 when his *Macbeth: Stage of Blood* was sent to London to commemorate fifty years of the Indian Independence.

Arambam has deeply been involved in political theatre since the 1970s. Since then this quest has been dominated by the desire to express the pre-Vashnavaite Meitei culture and identity. The 1980s brought more political tension as a result of insurgency and counter-insurgency. Arambam under such circumstances had to tone down the political content of his theatre during the 1980s. His plays since then have been less overtly political. However, he has been exploring various ritual practices of Meitei culture as the mode of presentation and reflection upon the contemporary situation of Manipur. It is the continuation of his urge 'to do politically sensitive plays in which [I] reflect on [our] situation' coupled with his exploration into the Meitei ritual practices that finds manifestation in *Macbeth: Stage of Blood* in 1997.[83]

Macbeth: Stage of Blood premiered on the Loktak lake stage in 1995. It was performed again on the floating stage at the Ningthem Pukhri reservoir in 1997 and later that year in London to commemorate 50 years of Indian Independence. The play was directed by Arambam for his theatre group The Forum for the Laboratory Theatre of Manipur. The play situates the urtext amid the contemporary political and social milieu of Manipur. Arambam himself refers to his play as '*Macbeth* wrenched, twisted and subverted into a metaphor of the anarchy in Manipur'.[84] Along with the violence that Manipur has witnessed in the post-insurgency period of the 1990s, the issue of identity which has been so central to Arambam's expression gets reflected in the play. Arambam admits that he wanted to do *Macbeth* because it dealt with 'the issues of murder and violence' and that he had 'wanted to interpret Shakespeare from [my] own tribal tradition.'[85] He states that 'the symbology of *Macbeth* powerfully expresses the tragedy of Manipur and the crisis of identity in the Manipur psyche—at once gentle, dynamic and receptive but with a deeper inner turmoil which finds extreme expression in the conflicts of today.'[86] The play is quite complex for someone uninitiated into the Meitei culture because it incorporates various rituals and myths belonging to the pre-Vaishnavite Meitei culture. Also, the language used is the archaic Manipuri, parts of which are not comprehensible even by the young Manipuri speakers. The visual language, however, is powerful and communicates well with the audience. The environmental staging of the play on the floating stage, instead of the proscenium, serves a dual purpose. It enhances the ritualistic, symbolic and aesthetic dimensions of the production and second, it also demonstrates the postcolonial engagement with a Western playwright in indigenous performance idiom. The use of water for a stage serves as an important symbol. Water in many tribal cultures including the Meitei culture is significant as it symbolises purity, fertility and life. Meiteis believe in living in communion with nature, the failure of which causes suffering and disaster. Arambam himself explained that the stage was 'Mother Earth, isolated, naked, and a site of the relentless struggle for domination. The surrounding Water was not just the seed of life but also the tomb where the spirits of the dead were subsumed.'[87]

The play was translated by Somorendra Arambam, Lokendra's elder brother who inverted the sequential order of the play. The play opens with *Macbeth's* end with soldiers bringing the dead Macbeth to the stage. He wakes up to re-enact his story. The play ends where it had begun with Macbeth dead and soldiers taking him away for burial. The play moves backwards making the end both the beginning and the end. The end is significant in the context of post-insurgency Manipur where violence and killings have become the cyclic order. The structure of the play thus reflects the continuum of violence the state has been witnessing. Though the play more or less follows Shakespeare's plot, it does introduce some changes in the original. When the play was staged at the Thames in London, the drama critic of *The Independent* observed that the iambic pentameter has been 'abandoned in favour of the Manipuri martial art *Thang Ta* as Macbeth's inner turmoil is expressed purely through visual imagery and haunting live music'.[88] Another deviation from the urtext is the substitution of the three witches by seven in *Stage of Blood* which is in sync with the local Meitei mythology. The seven weird sisters derive from Meitei mythology and represent the seven 'virgin goddesses' known as *heloys* who have power to prophesy. They are both benevolent and malevolent forces of Nature which snatch Macbeth's soul and lead him towards his destruction. Yet another important change in Arambam's play is the melding of Lady Macbeth and Macbeth into one character. Arambam interprets Lady Macbeth as Macbeth's alter-ego. Both roles are played by a single actor who uses his body and a red shawl to demarcate the two aspects of the character. The decision to fuse both the characters does two things: it takes away the hatred and scorn traditionally conferred upon the 'fiend-like Queen' Lady Macbeth since the times of Shakespeare and second, with this 'unsexing' of Lady Macbeth Arambam makes the character of Macbeth more complex and pathetic as he is solely responsible for his actions and no one else.

As mentioned earlier, Arambam interprets the play according to the Meitei culture. According to the production's 'Programme Note' Macbeth 'is representative of a repressive state that has lost its soul … Malcolm and Macduff are not individual representatives of the righteous, but part of the unnamed unknown forces of the oppressed.'[89] Macbeth becomes evil not of his own will but because of the forces beyond his control. Arambam wanted to reflect upon the way

> … a murder is committed not because it becomes an obsession, but because one has to; one has to continue murdering one person after another; and it ends up in one being murdered. The tremendous political crisis in our state at present, where murder, violence and state terrorism are so widespread, finds an echo in my production.[90]

Macbeth then becomes a victim rather than a villain. This point becomes clearer when one locates Macbeth's claim to the land within the discourse on 'motherland' as against the state/nation in Manipur. Bipin Thongam observes that Macbeth,

> calls the land he overtook as his motherland despite being an illegal inheritor of the land and a traitor. He does not only worry about his kingship but also for the land which Duncan's son Malcolm will inherit eventually. Macbeth calls Malcolm an outsider. This is important because he is questioning the established rules. Malcolm even asks his mother if his father was a traitor. This subverts the idea of the inheritor or the rightful owner of a kingdom. It could be a direct representation of Manipur and the Naga dispute over the land as to who owns the state of Manipur? Is it the Manipuri-Nagas who want to join in the formation of greater 'Nagalim' or the Meiteis who object? At another level, the play deploys the political metaphors of Manipur vis-à-vis India.[91]

The play ends when Malcolm's army wrapped in reed-mats and giving the impression of the Birnam Wood advancing as if it were the elemental forces of nature, encircle Macbeth and finally kill him. The dead body is taken away for burial by the soldiers who had brought it on the stage in the beginning. The play thus ends where it had started.

Just like the use of Meitei rituals to express the distinct cultural identity, the costumes too are tribal as are the headgears and ornaments. The production uses live music using traditional musical instruments like bells, cymbals and drums which augment the creation of the much needed haunting and eerie atmosphere for a play like Macbeth. Arambam's theatre may seem coming closer to Ratan Thiyam's since both have appropriated various Manipuri traditions. However, there is an important difference between the two. While Thiyam's work can be seen as belonging to 'theatre of roots' looking towards 'Vaishnavite Hindu modes and conservative Sanskrit influences', Arambam's theatre looks to the pre-Vaishnavite Meitei culture.[92] The politicisation of Macbeth within the larger framework of Meitei identity, ethnicity and culture which has been haunting the people of Manipur in addition to the aesthetics evolved out of the traditional performance forms makes his production complex.

M.K. Raina's *Badshah Pather*

> *Who was Shakespeare but a bhand?*[93]
>
> Dipanita Nath

While Manipur in the north-east India has been embroiled in political turmoil yet another state from the northern-most part of India, Jammu and Kashmir, has been experiencing protracted insurgency since the late 1980s. As a result, like Manipur, Jammu and Kashmir is also reeling under the Armed Forces Special Powers Act since the 1990s. Militant groups such as Harkat-ul-Mujahideen, Lashkar-e-Taiba and Jammu and Kashmir Liberation Front (JKLF) have been operating in the valley and involved in terrorist activities. Their demand for a separate nation-state has been met with counter-insurgency by the Indian government. During the 1990s Hizbul Mujahideen, a pro-Pakistani and ultra-fundamentalist militant group had captured parts of the Valley. Following its extremely conservative ideology, Mujahideen imposed a strict and rigid interpretation of Islam in rural Kashmir. One such interpretation was to declare cultural expressions like folk forms of performance and other forms of entertainment as un-Islamic. Like other cultural forms *bhand pather*, an 11th century folk form of

Kashmir too was put under ban by these extremists. The traditional musical instruments of the *bhands* like *swarnai* (oboe), *dhol* (drum) and *nagara* (percussion) were destroyed and costumes torn away. M.K. Raina, a Kashmiri pandit, whose family had to flee from their hometown Srinagar in the 1990s during the peak of militancy, informs that Mohammad Subhan Bhagat, the guru of the folk form, was put under house arrest and later succumbed to the humiliation and shock.[94] This was a major loss for the folk theatre of Kashmir when the *bhands* stopped their practice. Though the folk form has seen revival due to efforts by theatre directors like Raina it is still an endangered form. Amidst the violence that the Valley has witnessed since the 1980s and which it still experiences as frequent encounters between the militants and the army Raina's decision to perform *Badshah Pather* (2009), an adaptation of Shakespeare's *King Lear*, merits mention. Raina states that when working with young boys at Akingham, a small village in Kashmir where *Badshah Pather* was rehearsed and performed, he found that

> … their bodies were not in the right proportion. There was stiffness, a distortion, a lack of grace. I started asking myself whether these problems were due to the stresses and tensions that their mothers had gone through before the children were born or if they were a result of the atmosphere they had grown up in.[95]

Raina worked constantly with the *bhands* and has been instrumental in its revival and in making this form known nationally.

The origins of *bhand pather* date back to the 11th century. The name is made up of two words: *bhand* means actor and *pather* is the play. As Raina says,

> The plays of the *bhands* are called *pather*, a word that seems to have derived from *patra*, dramatic character. *Bhand* comes from the *bhaana*, a satirical and realist drama, generally a monologue that is mentioned in Bharata's *Natya Shastra*. The *Bhand Pather* though is not a monologue but a social drama incorporating mythological legends and contemporary social satire.[96]

Balwant Gargi observes that *pather* seems to have come from *patra* meaning a scroll and *bhand* is a local variant of the classical *bhandika* or the clown.[97] *Bhand pather*, the indigenous theatre of Kashmir, includes all the components of folk theatre like dancing, singing, clowning, satire and humour. An important difference between *bhand pather* and other Indian folk forms like *jatra* is that the former is secular and does not have any religious framework primarily because, as Ghulam Bhagat, a *bhand*, explains, 'Islam does not associate with theatre.'[98] Even today, a ritual dance called *chhok* is performed at the temple of Goddess Shiva Bhagvati in Akingham by Muslim *bhands*. Traditionally, both Muslims and Hindus performed *bhand pather* in Kashmir. The secular character of the form has been well-observed by Javaid Iqbal Bhat in the following words:

> Bhand Pather lends itself for a study of the shifting landscape of the intercommunal relationships. *It is one of the unique sites on which the nuances and complexities of Kashmiriyat*[99] *can be easily worked out.* It has been nourished both by Hindu Shaivism and Sufi mysticism.... The most significant feature, in my opinion, of this art rich with the antique flavor is the way it presents us a non-idealized version of Kashmiriyat.[100]

Till the 1990s, there were Hindu *bhand* groups in Kashmir before they moved out of the Valley due to the communal violence.

Bhands tour the countryside and perform plays from their repertoire. A *bhand pather*, like other folk performances, is performed in the open air. The performance starts with the sound of *swarnai*, a wind instrument. The narrative is usually formulaic, consisting of a cruel king who is taught a lesson by the clown or the jester called *maskhara*. There can be any number of *maskharas* in a performance. The king usually is an outsider—the 'other'—suppressing the natives while the *maskhara* is the native 'self' who eventually wins over the king. In a traditional *pather*, the 'otherness' of the king is established through his speech. He usually speaks in a language not understood by the natives, like Persian, English, Punjabi or gibberish.[101] The 'self' in the form of *maskhara* speaks the native dialects. The most famous traditional *bhand pathers* are *Raze pather* (about kings) and *Gosain pather* (about ascetics and mendicants). Like other folk forms, *bhand pather* incorporates music using traditional instruments like *swarnai*, *dhol*, *nagara* or *thalej*. There are set musical compositions called *mukams* to which the *bhands* dance. As Kashmir has a strong tradition of *sufi* poetry, it is also incorporated into the *bhand pather*. As far as props are concerned, *bhand pather* uses very few, the mandatory props being a whip and a short bamboo stick. The whip is not simply a prop but represents authority as Raina observes,

> During the performance a character can be whipped a hundred times without being hurt because this property does not have the impact associated with a whip, it just looks deadly. It is used to transform all the elements that represent oppression into strong dramatic images. In sharp contrast the *bans* [the bamboo stick] are used by the jester or *maskhara*. These are split bamboo sticks that make a sharp sound. In his pantomime, the *maskhara* uses the *bans* emerges [sic] as the total opposite of the oppressor's whip.[102]

Bhands are trained by traditional *gurus* known as *maguns* who teach various skills like acting, dancing, music and acrobatics. Raina has held five workshops in Kashmir as part of NSD's extension programme since 2001 and mounted 14 productions mostly based on the works of Kashmiri writers. In 2009, with the help of traditional *ustads* of *bhand*, Raina organised a workshop at Akingham to train the local children and youth in this form. Raina chose Akingham because it is here that the Kashmir Bhagat Theatre, one of the oldest *bhand* companies, is based. The workshop culminated in the production of Shakespeare's *King Lear* adapted as *Badshah Pather*. Regarding the choice of the play, Raina explains,

> The number of plays in *bhand pather's* repertoire has diminished to just 7 or 8. We wanted to evolve a new play for performance. As *King Lear* is a play about a foolish king, it fits well in the schemata of *bhand pather*. Moreover, I knew that doing Shakespeare would be helpful in getting the marginalised form and performers recognition in urban centers.[103]

Doing a Shakespeare play with the *bhands* in a folk form was a challenging task for Raina, at least initially, due to several reasons. In the first place, a tragedy does not exist as a form in the *bhand pather* repertoire as in other folk and classical forms. The players agreed to enact the tragedy of Lear as it was the story of a foolish king. Another challenge for Raina was to work with a set of actors most of whom were illiterate and could not read the script. Lastly, Raina had to rework his formal training in theatre, as he says, '[Y]ou can't use techniques you have learnt. There are no auditoriums, you have to tell stories in an empty space.'[104] Also, performing in the open air in the broad daylight meant that Raina could not make use of lights and other technological paraphernalia. He had to depend upon his actors ultimately to tell the story.

The first problem was to get a performable translation. Initially, Raina had brought with him Harivansh Rai Bachhan's well-known Hindi translation of *King Lear* to be translated into Kashmiri. However, the Kashmiri translation could not make an impact on the actors as the language was quite literary. As Ghulam Bhagat, '[I]n the beginning we followed nothing but didn't have the courage to challenge our guru. Slowly the story, simple at heart, began to make sense to us.'[105] In fact, even Raina soon realised the futility of his efforts. He was trying to give these actors a pre-written text of Shakespeare which is not a convention in *bhand pather*. A traditional *bhand pather* does not have a written script but develops the plot through improvisations. Thus, Raina adopted the strategy of evolving a performance text of *King Lear* which would come from the actors themselves, rather than depending upon a ready-made script. The story of Lear was told to the actors and Raina worked in sequences with the actors. It was then through ensemble work that a performance script called *Badshah Pather* evolved. The scenes were formally 'blocked' by Raina which is not done in traditional *bhand pather*. The new performance text that evolved in the workshop concentrated on the main plot of the original play, that is, the story of an idiosyncratic king planning to divide his kingdom among his three daughters. *Badshah Pather* follows the main plot of the original play quite closely with slight change. The daughters become sons—Shamim (Goneril), Karim (Regan) and Rafiq (Cordelia)—primarily because women are not allowed to perform. Moreover, in most traditional Indian societies a woman is not entitled to a share in her parents' property. Having declared his intentions to divide his kingdom among his sons, the *Badshah* asks the sons to express their love for him. The two elder sons, like Goneril and Regan in the original, pass the love-test by replying in the superlatives. The youngest one replies like Cordelia that he loves the *Badshah* as much as a son should love his father. Hearing this, the *Badshah* banishes the youngest son and divides his kingdom between the elder sons. However, he soon realises his mistake when the elder sons throw him out and the youngest one comes for his rescue. The play ends with all three sons dying in the end. Finally, Lear too succumbs after the death of his youngest son. The parallel plot presents Bedar (Gloucester), Kehram (the illegitimate son, Edmund) and Sikander (the legitimate son, Edgar).

The play was performed at Akingham village in open air in broad daylight, surrounded by the audience on all sides like the traditional *bhand pather*. The staging of the performance was not an easy task. The Kashmiri separatists had called for a *bandh* on the day of performance and the director was cautioned against staging the play. The director, however, decided to proceed with the show as planned. What was heartening was the large number of spectators who turned up to watch the performance disregarding of the *bandh*. Since Sufism is deeply embedded in the culture of Kashmir, Raina let his version of *King Lear* be imbued with the age-old sufi philosophy of Kashmiri mystics. Raina interprets his Badshah as a sufi mystic who learns about the world and himself only after suffering. This is evident when the Badshah bursts into singing an old sufi song:

> Autumn will descend on youth
> Where does the youth disappear
> There only

Where your and my mother's house is
Sweep my ashes
from the funeral ground.[106]

Badshah's division of property also needs to be seen in the larger political context that has been haunting Kashmir and Kashmiris since the Indian independence. As Raina observes, 'Every family has a property dispute. In the larger picture, what is the tragedy of Kashmir but a conflict over land?'[107] This 'conflict over land' is manifested through the use of a life-size map of Kashmir brought onto the stage that the king wishes to divide among his sons. Although, Raina does not use the political map of Kashmir, yet it is evident from the graphical representation used in the scene, with all its mountains, valleys and rivers, that it is Kashmir. The king looks at the map as if looking in a mirror and then hugs it. This act is significant not just because it reflects the king's love for his kingdom but also for it foreshadows his future. As a political allegory, the play is symptomatic of Kashmir's political condition in the post-Partition times. In the events to come, as mentioned earlier, there seems to be an uncanny resemblance between the *badshah* and the state of Kashmir which has been left uncared for just like Lear. The *badshah*, thus, serves a metonymic function at this point in the play. He becomes the mirror-image of Kashmir which has been a source of political contention between the two 'sons'—India and Pakistan since their independence. Kashmir/*badshah*, just like Shakespeare's Lear, in Raina's production is definitely 'more sinned against than sinning.'

Notes

1. I borrow the phrase 'historicity of text and textuality of history' from Louis Montrose's essay 'Professing the Renaissance: The Poetics and Politics of Culture,' in *The New Historicism*, ed. H. Aram Veeser (New York and London: Routledge, 1989), 20.

2. Christy Desmet and Robert Sawyer, eds., *Shakespeare and Appropriation* (London: Routledge, 1999), 19.
3. Ngugi wa Thiong'O, *Decolonizing the Mind: The Politics of Language in African Literature* (London: Currey, 1986), 16.
4. P.V. Rajamannar, 'Welcome Address,' *Sangeet Natak* 38, no. 2 (2004): 5.
5. Quoted in 'Introduction', accessed 11 July 2019, https://sangeetnatak.gov.in/sna/introduction.php.
6. Aparna Bhargava Dharwadker, *Theatres of Independence: Drama, Theory, and Urban Performance in India since 1947* (New Delhi: Oxford University Press, 2006).
7. 'Recommendations of the Drama Seminar,' *Sangeet Natak* 38, no. 4 (2004): 128.
8. Mulk Raj Anand, 'Indian Theatre in the Context of World Theatre,' *Sangeet Natak* 38, no. 4 (2008): 16.
9. Ibid., 8.
10. Nandi Bhatia, ed. 'Introduction,' in *Modern Indian Theatre: A Reader* (New Delhi: Oxford University Press, 2009), xxi.
11. Suresh Awasthi, '"Theatre of Roots": Encounter with Tradition,' *The Drama Review* 33, no. 4 (1989): 48; italics mine.
12. Erin B. Mee, *Theatre of Roots: Redirecting the Modern Indian Stage* (Calcutta: Seagull Books, 2008), 200.
13. Quoted in ibid.
14. Arindam Dutta, 'The Politics of Display: India 1886 and 1986,' *Journal of Arts and Ideas*. Special Issue on *Sites of Art History: Canons and Expositions* 30/31 (1997): 122.
15. Ibid.
16. Rustom Bharucha, 'Anatomy of Official Cultural Discourse: A Non-Government Perspective,' *EPW* 37.31/32 (1992): 1676.
17. Nissar Allana, ed., *A Tribute to Bertolt Brecht* (New Delhi: Theatre and Television Associates, 1993), 2–3.
18. Vasudha Dalmia, *Poetics, Plays, and Performances: The Politics of Modern Indian Theatre* (New Delhi: Oxford University Press, 2006), 189.
19. Shanta Gandhi, 'An Approach to Our Traditional Theatre,' *Sangeet Natak* 77/78 (1985): 14.
20. G.P. Deshpande, 'History, Politics and the Modern Playwright,' *Theatre India* (May 1999): 96.

21. A.J. Gunawardana, 'Theatre as a Weapon: An Interview with Utpal Dutt,' *The Drama Review* 15, no. 2 (Spring 1971), 235.
22. Tapati Gupta, 'From Proscenium to Paddy Fields: Utpal Dutt's Shakespeare Jatra,' in *Re-playing Shakespeare in Asia*, eds. Poonam Trivedi and Minami Ryuta (NY: Routledge, 2010), 158.
23. Quoted in Rustom Bharucha, *Rehearsals of Revolution: The Political Theatre of Bengal* (Calcutta: Seagull, 1983), 242.
24. Utpal Dutt, 'Interview,' *Enact* (August–September 1972): 68–69.
25. Gunawardana, 'Theatre as a Weapon,' 235.
26. Himani Bannerji, 'Representation and Class Politics in the Theatre of Utpal Dutt,' Occasional Paper No. 106, Calcutta: Centre for Studies in Social Sciences (1988): 11.
27. Gunawardana, 'Theatre as a Weapon,' 235.
28. Utpal Dutt, 'Taking Shakespeare to the Common Man,' originally published in *Oxygen News, Shakespeare Quatercentenary Supplement* (1964); reprinted in *Epic Theatre*, Calcutta (March 1999): 19.
29. Gupta, 'From Proscenium to Paddy Fields,' 166.
30. Bharucha, *Rehearsals of Revolution*, 62.
31. Jyotsna Singh, 'Different Shakespeares: The Bard in Colonial/Postcolonial India,' *Theatre Journal* 41, no. 4 (1989): 454.
32. Gunawardana, 'Theatre as a Weapon,' 235.
33. Helen Gilbert and Joanne Tompkins, *Post-Colonial Drama: Theory, Practice, Politics* (London: Routledge, 1996), 21.
34. Gupta, 'From Proscenium to Paddy Fields,' 166.
35. Ibid., 177.
36. Quoted in Jyotsna Singh, 'The Postcolonial/Postmodern Shakespeare,' in *Shakespeare: Worldviews*, eds. Heather Kerr, Robin Eaden and Madge Mitton (Newark: University of Delware Press and London: Associated University Press, 1996), 38.
37. Bharucha, *Rehearsals of Revolution*, 62.
38. Gunawardana, 'Theatre as a Weapon,' 230.
39. Gupta, 'From Proscenium to Paddy Fields,' 165–166.
40. Ibid., 169.
41. Ibid.
42. B.V. Karanth, 'Director's Note,' *Barnam Van*, 1979.
43. B.V. Karanth, 'B.V. Karanth in Conversation with Jaidev Taneja.' Interview by Jaidev Taneja, Natrang Pratishthan, 14.

44. Quoted in Dalmia, *Poetics, Plays, and Performances*, 199.
45. Karanth, 'Director's Note.'
46. Raghuvir Sahay, 'A Word from the Translator,' *Barnam Van*, 1979.
47. Raghuvir Sahay, *Barnam Van* (New Delhi: Rajkamal Prakashan, 1980), 37.
48. Sahay, 'A Word from the Translator.'
49. Ibid.
50. Sahay, *Barnam Van*, 15.
51. Ibid.
52. Karanth, 'Director's Note.'
53. Ibid.
54. Ibid.
55. Suresh Awasthi, 'Shakespeare mein Yakshagan' [Yakshagan in Shakespeare], *Dinman* (December 1979): 41; translation mine.
56. *Maddale* and *chende* are both percussion instruments used in *yakshagan*. While *maddale* is played with fingers, *chende* is played with sticks.
57. *Nakkara:* Another percussion instrument played across India and especially in south Indian temples.
58. Awasthi, 'Shakespeare mein Yakshagan,' 41; translation mine.
59. Ibid., 40.
60. Habib Tanvir, 'It must Flow: A Life in Theatre,' in *Seagull Theatre Quarterly* 10 (June 1996): 28.
61. Habib Tanvir, 'In Conversation with Habib Tanvir,' in *Reflections and Reminiscences*, ed. Neeraj Malik and Javed Malick (New Delhi: Safdar Hashmi Memorial Trust, 2010), 103.
62. Ibid.
63. Ibid., 103–104.
64. Quoted in Mee, *Theatre of Roots*, 84.
65. Habib Tanvir, 'It Must Flow', 21–22.
66. Nacha: Folk theatre of Chhattisgarh which consists of short comic skits.
67. Quoted in Chitra Padmanabhan, 'The Playful Rites of Spring,' *The Economic Times*, 8 March 1994.
68. Habib Tanvir, 'Translating Spirit of a Poetic Comedy,' *The Economic Times*, 8 March 1994.
69. Habib Tanvir, *Kamdev ka Apna Vasantritu ka Sapna* (Delhi: Vani Prakashan, 2001), 8: translation mine.
70. Ibid., 62–63.
71. Ibid., 63.

72. Ibid., 13.
73. Tanvir, 'Translating Spirit of a Poetic Comedy.'
74. Quoted in Padmanabhan, 'The Playful Rites of Spring.'
75. Ibid.
76. Sudhanva Deshpande, 'Citizen of the World,' *Frontline* 26, no. 13 (2009): 112.
77. *Thang-ta* is an ancient Manipuri martial art form; *lai-haraoba* is a traditional dance form of Manipur performed on the festival by the same name to please traditional Meitei dieties; *ras-lila*: a Manipuri dance-drama form which celebrates Lord Krishna's seduction of *gopis* (cow herding girls) of Mathura; *nat sankreetan*: a ritualistic Manipuri form of performance which includes dancing, singing and drumming to celebrate the life and deeds of Lord Krishna; *wari liba*: a traditional Meitei story-telling form which narrates stories from the *Mahabharata* and *Ramayana*.
78. Lokendra Arambam, 'Manipuri Theatre,' in *The Oxford Companion to Indian Theatre*, ed. Ananda Lal (New Delhi: Oxford University Press, 2004), 252.
79. Somorendra Arambam, 'Manipuri Playwrights: An Overview,' *Seagull Theatre Quarterly*, 14–15 (June/September 1997): 178.
80. Poonam Trivedi, '"It is the Bloody Business Which Informs Thus …": Local Politics and Performative Praxis, Macbeth in India,' in *World-wide Shakespeares: Local Appropriations in Film and Performance*, ed. Sonia Massai (London: Routledge, 2005), 51.
81. Lokendra Arambam, 'Experimental Theatre in Manipur: At a Critical Juncture,' *Seagull Theatre Quarterly*, 14–15 (June/September 1997), 16.
82. Quoted in Dharwadker, *Theatres of Independence*, 105.
83. Lokendra Arambam, 'Working for Change,' *Seagull Theatre Quarterly*, 14–15 (June/September 1997): 36
84. Quoted in Trivedi, 'It is the Bloody Business Which Informs Thus …', 51.
85. Lokendra Arambam, 'Working for Change,' 36.
86. 'Manipuri Macbeth casts spell on London,' accessed 14 April 2019, http://www.rediff.com/news/aug/29mac.htm.
87. Quoted in Trivedi, 'It is the Bloody Business Which Informs Thus …,' 52.
88. 'Henious Macbeth,' accessed 14 April 2019, http://www.independent.co.uk/life-style/heinous-macbeth-1245618.html.
89. Quoted in Trivedi, 'It is the Bloody Business Which Informs Thus …,' 51.

90. Lokendra Arambam, 'Working for Change,' 36.
91. Bipin Singh Thongam, 'Narrativising Region through Manipuri Theatre: Identity Politics in the Plays of Heisnam Kanhailal, Ratan Thiyam and Lokendro Arambam,' M.Phil diss. (University of Hyderabad, 2009), 50.
92. Lokendra Arambam, 'Working for Change,' 31.
93. Dipanita Nath, 'Who was Shakespeare but a Bhand?', accessed 15 April 2019, http://indianexpress.com/article/lifestyle/art-and-culture/who-was-shakespeare-but-a-bhaand-2767150/.
94. Vikram Singh Thakur, interview with M.K. Raina, February 2011.
95. Quoted in Razdan, 'Bhand Pather,' accessed 10 April 2019, http://www.searchkashmir.org/2009/01/bhand-pather.html.
96. M.K. Raina, 'The Bhand Pather of Kashmir,' accessed 4 July 2019, http://www.koausa.org/BhandPather/index.html.
97. Balwant Gargi, *Folk Theater of India* (Seattle: University of Washington Press, 1966), 186.
98. Quoted in Pragya Tiwari, 'Drama in the Valley,' accessed 13 April 2019, https://www.deccanherald.com/content/28471/drama-valley.html.
99. *Kashmiriyat* is the general ethno-socio-cultural ethos of Kashmir based on the age-old communal harmony between Hindus and Muslims; italics mine.
100. Javaid Iqbal Bhat, 'Loss of a Syncretic Theatrical Form,' accessed 14 April 2019, https://www.folklore.ee/folklore/vol34/bhat.pdf.
101. Thakur, interview with M.K. Raina.
102. Raina, 'The Bhand Pather of Kashmir.'
103. Thakur, interview with M.K. Raina.
104. Quoted in P. Anima, 'Set to Stage,' *The Hindu*, 30 January 2010.
105. Quoted in Tiwari, 'Drama in the Valley.'
106. Quoted in Dipanita Nath, 'Who was Shakespeare but a Bhand?'
107. Ibid.

Conclusion

I have tried to identify varied responses to Shakespeare evoked by various Indian productions/translations/adaptations through two-and-a-half centuries. I have tried to contextualise these responses in the larger historical and cultural contexts of India. The work is a humble attempt to fill the lacuna in Shakespeare Studies by discussing Shakespeare's reception and production in India. As I have already mentioned in the 'Introduction', it is nearly impossible to include Shakespeare's reception in all Indian languages in a single work. Let me add another point of caution: Shakespeare has been produced in the post-Independence India in various interesting forms and styles. If the productions discussed in Chapter IV have received much attention in post-Independence India, there are other productions too, which are equally important for they provide a new interpretation to the Bard. However, such productions like Roysten Abel's much-acclaimed *Othello: A Play in Black and White* (1999) could not be included here. Abel's adaptation is completely rooted in urban India both in terms of content and form. In fact, a reviewer of *The Pioneer* went on to claim, 'If you thought Buz Luhrman's *Romeo and Juliet* was post-modern, you stand corrected. Roysten Abel's *Othello* goes a step forward.'[1] However, to engage with such productions is beyond the scope of this book. My focus here is to understand how Shakespeare productions, employing folk and traditional idioms in postcolonial India bring forth a kind of cultural alterity, thereby, distinguishing themselves from other Shakespeare productions across the world. Another significant point about these productions is that they reflect upon the larger discourse on postcolonial Indian theatrical cultures across languages as seen in Chapter IV. This is important since 'the most fundamental cultural history is always a history of forms.'[2]

My contention throughout the work has been that Shakespeare productions in India have largely been governed by their own aesthetics except for the very early school and college productions. When Shakespeare's plays moved out of schools and colleges in the 19th century, they were quickly adapted to suit the general Indian milieu and audience taste. Shakespeare may have served the British colonists' agenda academically but theatre in India took to Shakespeare on its own terms. The three prominent trends in Shakespeare productions in India can be identified as 'imitative', 'popular' and 'urban-folkish'. The earliest productions of Shakespeare in India by the educated elite tried to 'imitate' the way Shakespeare's plays were produced by the British colonists and followed the conventions of English theatre. There was also gradual and noticeable assimilation into the indigenous theatrical activities. By the 1870s, with the emergence of Parsi theatre, Shakespeare was out of the elite circle and was transformed into 'popular' modes. In the 1920s, with the growing momentum of nationalism, the once-revered Shakespeare was noticeable in its absence. Shakespeare's plays regained favour on the stage in the post-Independence decades. Utpal Dutt employed elements from *jatra* in producing Shakespeare; later theatre directors like Karanth, Tanvir, Arambam and Raina followed suit.

The study also proposes that categorising Indian productions of Shakespeare as 'colonial' and 'postcolonial' would not be appropriate, as all the productions of the colonial period cannot be called 'colonial' in an ideological sense. As has been explained, even during the colonial period, Shakespeare's plays were changed to suit the audience sensibility. Similarly, not every production in postcolonial India can be called 'postcolonial'. One may still find 'colonial' Shakespeare in the postcolonial India as is evident in the following account:

> *Twelfth Night*, first produced in 1928 by the Shakespeare Society of St. Stephen's, was the most frequently performed of all Shakespeare's plays, being revived in 1948, 1963, 1987, and 1993. When *As You Like It* was stage in modern English dress, a reviewer observed that the production demonstrated the truth of the assertion that Indians, and especially Stephanians, were 'the last Englishmen left on the earth.'[3]

Postcolonial appropriations of a canon are generally considered counter-discursive and resistant to canonical authority. I, however, contend that such a view would not explain the complexity of Shakespeare productions in India. Many of these productions do not necessarily subvert the canon by creating a counter-discourse. In fact, Shakespeare has evoked at least three kinds of responses in post-colonial societies: one, of rejection as a representative of colonialism; two, of value as a 'universal' writer and a 'touchstone' of greatness; and three, of appropriation to suit the local socio-political-cultural purposes. The last attitude has been the most productive in terms of Indian productions of Shakespeare. Productions like *Bhuli Nui Priya*, *Barnam Van*, *Kamdev ka Apna*, *Macbeth: Stage of Blood*, or *Badshah Pather* may not create a counter-discourse by subverting the English canon as Derek Walcott and Aimé Césaire have done with *The Tempest*, but they illustrate the appropriation of the master text in their own ways. This is particularly true of the productions which present a 'syncretic combination of indigenous and colonial forms in the post-colonial world.'[4] Arambam, for instance, has appropriated Shakespeare's *Macbeth* to express the social and political turmoil in present-day Manipur. Dutt, Karanth, Tanvir and Raina have appropriated Shakespeare to develop theatrical styles by blending elements of traditional and folk forms, Sanskrit theatre and 'modern' theatre. Thus, such productions go beyond the fixed categories of the colonial and the postcolonial and open up the possibility of a more nuanced discourse on theatrical expressivity. Once the boundary between the colonial and the postcolonial is blurred, one realises that these categories cannot be fixed, but, become hybrid conditions. Ania Loomba argues that 'every culture can be said to be hybrid—in fact, even "authentic" identities are the result of ongoing processes of selection, cutting and mixing of cultural vocabularies. In practice, hybridity and authenticity are rarely either/or positions.'[5] In such a hybrid world, it is difficult and pointless to identify 'authentic' Shakespeare. Loomba raises an important question:

> [...] does the idea of 'authentic' or 'inauthentic' Shakespeare have any meaning in a world where the entire Shakespeare trade is fueled by a frank acknowledgement of the legitimacy of inauthenticity? For even the New Globe is, as Dennis Kennedy has put it, 'a form of staged authenticity', combining aspects of the shrine with those of the amusement park. In this situation, the inauthenticity of the 'foreign' or indeed any other devotee should matter less than it once did, just as the authenticity of Shakespeare himself is less important to both audiences and vendors.[6]

The concept of 'authentic' itself, writes Richard Handler, is 'a cultural construct of the modern Western world.'[7] There cannot be an 'authentic' Shakespeare. How is one to believe that the Shakespeare text that has come down to the modern readers is 'authentic'? Shakespeare himself was a reviser of scripts. Moreover, Shakespeare texts have been mediated by numerous editors, compositors and scribes. Even the most trusted Quartos and Folios vary from each other. For instance, 'about 200 lines of *Hamlet* in the First Quarto version (Q1, 1603) do not appear in the First Folio version (F1, 1623), while about 85 lines found in F1 are not featured in Q1.'[8] Such multiplicity of Shakespeare texts makes it impossible to claim a version as the 'authentic' text of Shakespeare. Such views make efforts to discover 'authentic' Shakespeare a fruitless endeavour. Consequently, no production can claim to be an 'authentic' Shakespeare production. Apart from the text itself, present-day performance conditions are very different from the Elizabethan times. This is equally true for folk forms of performance which too have changed over time. Stuart Hall rightly theorises the past and its relation to us (although in the Caribbean context) which reflects the reality of Shakespeare productions in India:

> The past continues to speak to us. But it no longer addresses us as a simple, factual 'past', since our relation to it, like the child's relation to the mother, is always-already 'after the break'. It is always constructed through memory, fantasy, narrative and myth. Cultural identities are the points of identification, the unstable points of identification or suture, which are made, within the discourses of history and culture. Not an essence but a positioning. Hence, there is always a politics of identity, a politics of position, which has no absolute guarantee in an unproblematic, transcendental 'law of origin.'[9]

In this sense, any attempt at producing an 'authentic' Shakespeare play would invariably be 'inauthentic'. In fact, this 'inauthenticity' makes a Shakespeare production different from another and must be valourised. Thus, 'Indian Shakespeare' is as 'in/authentic' as any other Shakespeare production from Britain and needs more careful and nuanced academic engagement in the Shakespeare studies today.

Notes

1. Quoted in 'Othello: A Play in Black and White,' accessed 25 March 2018, http://www.roystenabel.com/othello.html.
2. Raymond Williams, *The Politics of Modernism: Against the New Conformists*, ed. Tony Pinkney (London: Verso, 1989), 84.
3. Quoted in Dennis Bartholomeusz, 'Shylock's Shoes: The Art of Localization,' in *India's Shakespeare: Translation, Interpretation, and Performance*, ed. Poonam Trivedi and Dennis Bartholomeusz (New Delhi: Pearson Longman, 2005), 213.
4. Helen Gilbert and Joanne Tompkins, *Post-Colonial Drama: Theory, Practice, Politics* (London: Routledge, 1996), 294.
5. Ania Loomba, '"Local-manufacture made-in-India Othello fellows": Issues of Race, Hybridity and Location in Post-colonial Shakespeare,' in *Post-Colonial Shakespeares*, ed. Ania Loomba and Martin Orkin (London: Routledge, 1998), 146–147.
6. Loomba, 'Shakespeare and the Possibilities of Postcolonial Performance,' in *A Companion to Shakespeare and Performance*, ed. Barbara Hodgdon and W.B. Worthen (USA: Blackwell Publishing, 2005), 123.
7. Richard Handler, 'Authenticity,' *Anthropology Today* 2, no. 1 (1986): 2.
8. Margarida Gandara Rauen, 'Moving Away from the "Centre": Theory, Drama and Performance,' in *Shakespeare without English: The Reception of Shakespeare in Non-Anglophone Countries*, ed. Sukanta Chaudhuri and Chee Seng Lim (New Delhi: Pearson Longman, 2006), 123.
9. Stuart Hall, 'Cultural Identity and Diaspora,' in *Postcolonial Theory: A Reader*, ed. Padmini Mongia (New Delhi: Oxford University Press, 2010), 113.

Appendix

Shakespeare Translations and Adaptations in Kannada

S. No.	Title	Translator's Title	Translator	Published
1.	*Othello*	*Raghavendrarao nataka*	Gundo Krishna Churamuri	1881
2.	*Othello*	*Surasena Charithre*	Basavappasastry	1895
3.	*Othello*	*Padmini*	Srikanthasastry	1911
4.	*Othello*	*Othello*	Krishnasastry	—
5.	*Othello*	*Othello*	Shanmukhayya	1954
6.	*Othello*	*Othello*	Huyilagola	1963
7.	*Othello*	*Othello*	—	1967
8.	*Othello*	*Othello*	Nissar Ahmed	1974
9.	*As You Like It*	*Sankalpa Siddhiyu*	KKR	1871
10.	*As You Like It*	*As You Like It*	Shastry	—
11.	*As You Like It*	*Kamalavat Parinaya*	Shamarya	—
12.	*As You Like It*	*Doremagalu*	Bharatisuta	1959
13.	*As You Like It*	*Nivu Bayasidamte*	Huyilagola	1963
14.	*All's Well That Ends Well*	*Satimani Vijaya*	Somanathayya	1897
15.	*Antony and Cleopatra*	*Antony and Cleopatra*	Mallaraje Arasu	—
16.	*The Comedy of Errors*	*Nagadavarannu Nagisuva Kathe*	Chennabasappa	1871
17.	*The Comedy of Errors*	*Bhrantivilasa*	Venkatacharya	1876
18.	*The Comedy of Errors*	*Viparyasa Jak Keddombi Damdhaleya*	Parvatavani	1947

S. No.	Title	Translator's Title	Translator	Published
19.	*King Henry VI*	*Prahasana*	Gundappa	1959
20.	*King Lear*	*Hemchandraraja Vilasa*	M.S. Puttanna	1889
21.	*King Lear*	*Liyar Maharaja*	Srinivasa	1959
22.	*King Lear*	*King Lear*	Huyilagola	1963
23.	*King Lear*	*King Lear*	H.S. Shivaprakasha	1988
24.	*Julius Caesar*	*Julius Caesar*	T.T. Sharma	1931
25.	*Julius Caesar*	*Savasamskara*	Channabasava	1939
26.	*Julius Caesar*	*Julius Caesar*	Inamdar	—
27.	*Julius Caesar*	*Julius Caesar*	Shanmukhayya	—
28.	*Julius Caesar*	*Julius Caesar*	Huyilagola	1963
29.	*Julius Caesar*	*Julius Caesar*	Shankar	1973
30.	*Julius Caesar*	*Julius Caesar*	K.S. Bhagvan	1975
31.	*Julius Caesar*	*Julius Caesar*	T. Niranjana	1977
32.	*The Two Gentlemen of Verona*	*Kusumkumara*	Annajirao	1897
33.	*The Tempest*	*Chandamaruta*	Subbarao	1893
34.	*The Tempest*	*Birugali*	Kuvempu	1930
35.	*The Tempest*	*Chandamaruta*	Masti Venkatesh Iyengar	1959
36.	*The Tempest*	*Mamtrikana magalu*	Mahalingabhatta	1963
37.	*The Tempest*	*Birugali*	Huyilagola	1963
38.	*The Tempest*	*Birugali*	Vi Vi	1967
39.	*The Tempest*	*Chandamaruta*	A.N. Murtyrao	1981
40.	*The Tempest*	*Dhum Dhum Suntaragali*	Vaidehi	1992
41.	*The Taming of the Shrew*	—	Vardachar	1881
42.	*The Taming of the Shrew*	*Gayyaliyannu Sadhumaduvike*	Narsimhachar	—
43.	*The Taming of the Shrew*	*Chandimardana*	Ramashastry	—

S. No.	Title	Translator's Title	Translator	Published
44.	*The Taming of the Shrew*	*Gayyaliyannu Sadhumaduvike*	Somanathayya	1897
45.	*The Taming of the Shrew*	*Chandimardana natakam*	Lakshman Rao	1910
46.	*The Taming of the Shrew*	*Tratikanataka*	Honnapuramath	1920
47.	*The Taming of the Shrew*	*Bahaddurganda*	Parvatavani	1947
48.	*The Taming of the Shrew*	*Gayyaligamda*	Murthy	1964
49.	*Twelfth Night*	*Dvadasa Ratri*	Masti Venkatesh Iyengar	1960
50.	*Twelfth Night*	*Hanneradaneya Ratri*	P.V. Narayan	1975
51.	*The Merchant of Venice*	*Panchali Parinaya*	Anadarao	1890
52.	*The Merchant of Venice*	*Venisu Nagarada Vanika*	Venkatacharya	1906
53.	*The Merchant of Venice*	*Venupuriya Vartaka*	Hanumanta Gowda	1928
54.	*The Merchant of Venice*	*Surtanagarada Sresthiyu*	Vasudevacharya Kerur	1929
55.	*The Merchant of Venice*	*Venis Vyapari*	Sukuma	1958
56.	*The Merchant of Venice*	*Venissina Vyapari*	Gundanna	1959
57.	*The Merchant of Venice*	*Venisina Vartaka*	Huyilagola	1962
58.	*The Merchant of Venice*	*The Merchant of Venice*	Jayarajacharya	—
59.	*The Merchant of Venice*	*The Merchant of Venice*	Sitaramayya	—
60.	*The Merchant of Venice*	*The Merchant of Venice*	Shanmukhayya	—
61.	*A Midsummer Night's Dream*	*Pramilarjuniya Vasantayamini*	Srikantesha Gowda	1890

S. No.	Title	Translator's Title	Translator	Published
62.	*A Midsummer Night's Dream*	*Swapanachamatkara Natakavu*	Vasudevacharya Kerur	1890
63.	*A Midsummer Night's Dream*	*Nadubesageya Iruluganasu*	Huyilagola	1963
64.	*A Midsummer Night's Dream*	*A Midsummer Night's Dream*	Nisar Ahmad	1974
65.	*Macbeth*	*Macbeth*	Channabasappa	1881
66.	*Macbeth*	*Prataprudra Deva*	Srikantesha Gowda	1895
67.	*Macbeth*	*Devesa Bhandara Natakavu*	Anantharya	1926
68.	*Macbeth*	*Rakatshi*	Kuvempu	1932
69.	*Macbeth*	*Macbeth*	Gundappa	1936
70.	*Macbeth*	*Macbeth*	Huyilagola	1963
71.	*Macbeth*	*Macbeth*	Ramachandra Deva	1976
72.	*Macbeth*	*Macbeth Maranayakana*	Parvatavani	1985
73.	*Macbeth*	*Drishtanta Maranayakana*	H.S. Shivaprakash	1990
74.	*Macbeth*	*Gombey Macbeth*	Vaidehi	1992
75.	*Romeo and Juliet*	*Kamalaksha Padmagandhiyarakathe*	Venkatesh B. Bhandiwad	1881
76.	*Romeo and Juliet*	*Ramavarma Lilavati*	Vardachar	1889
77.	*Romeo and Juliet*	*Ramavarma Lilavati Charitre*	Anandrao	1889
78.	*Romeo and Juliet*	*Ramavarma Lilavati Charitre*	Jayarajacharya	1889
79.	*Romeo and Juliet*	*Romeo and Juliet*	Basappa Shastri	—

S. No.	Title	Translator's Title	Translator	Published
80.	*Romeo and Juliet*	*Romeo and Juliet*	Srikantesha Gowda	—
81.	*Romeo and Juliet*	*Ramesh Lalitha*	Vasudevacharya Kerur	—
82.	*Romeo and Juliet*	*Asuya Parinama*	Amrutachari	1931
83.	*Romeo and Juliet*	*Romeo Mattu Juliet*	Shankaranarayana Rao	1949
84.	*Romeo and Juliet*	*Romeo and Juliet*	Y.M. Shanmukhayya	1952
85.	*Romeo and Juliet*	*Romeo Mattu Juliet*	Huyilagola	1963
86.	*The Winter's Tale*	*Manjughosha*	Rangacharya Mudgal	—
87.	*The Winter's Tale*	*Mahimamdana*	Annajirao	1900
88.	*The Winter's Tale*	*Manjuvani*	Srikanthasastry	1914
89.	*The Winter's Tale*	*Hemanta*	Shivarama Karantha	1982
90.	*Cymbeline*	*Jayasimharaja Charitre*	Puttanna	1881
91.	*Cymbeline*	*Jayasimharaja Charitram*	Naajappa M. Chakrapuri	1907
92.	*Cymbeline*	*Manjuvani*	Shrikantha Shastri Nanjanagud	1914
93.	*Hamlet*	*Hamlet*	Ananadarao	1905
94.	*Hamlet*	*Bhasamtaram*	A. Ananda Rao	1905
95.	*Hamlet*	*Hamlet*	Shivarama Karantha	1930
96.	*Hamlet*	*Samtapaka*	Amrutachari	1937
97.	*Hamlet*	*Hamlet*	Kulkarni	—
98.	*Hamlet*	*Hamlet*	Jayarajacharya	—
99.	*Hamlet*	*Hamlet*	Jivan Naryana	—
100.	*Hamlet*	*Hamlet*	Shivalingaswamy	—

S. No.	Title	Translator's Title	Translator	Published
101.	*Hamlet*	*Hamlet*	Hemantakumara	—
102.	*Hamlet*	*Hamlet*	Jivaji	—
103.	*Hamlet*	*Hamlet*	Savalgimatha	—
104.	*Hamlet*	*Hamlet*	Masti	1958
105.	*Hamlet*	*Hamlet*	Parvati	1960
106.	*Hamlet*	*Hamlet*	Kulkarni	1961
107.	*Hamlet*	*Hamlet*	Anadarao	1970
108.	*Hamlet*	*Hamlet*	Bhagwan	1973
109.	*Hamlet*	*Hamlet*	Ramchandra Dev	1978
110.	*Hamlet*	*Hamlet*	Parvatvani	1985
111.	*Coriolanus*	*Coriolanus*	K.V. Rajagopal	1981
112.	*Pericles*	*Parikalabhyu-daya*	Annajirao	1897
113.	*Timon of Athens*	*Athensina Arthavanta*	K.V. Subbanna	1994

Shakespeare Translations and Adaptations in Marathi

S. No.	Title	Translator's Title	Translator	Published
1.	*Henry VIII*	*Raja Raghanath Rao*	H.B. Atre	1904
2.	*All's Well That Ends Well*	*Vallabhanunaya*	V.M. Mahajani	1880
3.	*All's Well That Ends Well*	*Priyardhana*	V.S. Patvardhan	1912
4.	*As You Like It*	*Premagumpha*	V.S. Patvardhan	1908
5.	*As You Like It*	*Agadi Monasarakhel*	D.K. Bhat	1957
6.	*As You Like It*	*As You Like It*	Ajay Arosakar	1958
7.	*As You Like It*	*Jase Tumhamsa Avadela*	Shashikanta	—

S. No.	Title	Translator's Title	Translator	Published
8.	*Comedy of Errors*	*Mhatrya Vyaparyachi Goista*	R.V. Oka	1875
9.	*Comedy of Errors*	*Bhrantikrta Chamatkara*	R.B. Jathan and B.R. Pradhan	1877
10.	*Comedy of Errors*	*Gadya Apulagavbara*	S.M. Oak	1959
11.	*Comedy of Errors*	*Comedy of Errors*	D.K. Barve	1959
12.	*Comedy of Errors*	*Bhurala*	Ramachandra Mohani	1872
13.	*Comedy of Errors*	*Bhurala Athva Isvarkrita*	Vinayaka Patakar	1876
14.	*Comedy of Errors*	*Avalya Javalyanca Ghotala*	Vijaya Rasala	1949
15.	*Cymbeline*	*Tara*	V.M. Mahajani	1909
16.	*Cymbeline*	*Cymbeline*	B.D. Kher	1862
17.	*Hamlet*	*Hamlet*	Nanasaheb Phatak	—
18.	*Hamlet*	*Vikaravilasita*	G.G. Agarkar	1883
19.	*Hamlet*	*Himmata-Bahadura*	A.S. Barve	1890
20.	*Hamlet*	*Virasena*	G.V. Kanitkar	1883
21.	*Hamlet*	*Puspasena Rajaputra*	A.S. Barve	—
22.	*Hamlet*	*Teen-Anli Hamlet*	G.S. Jog	1959
23.	*Hamlet*	*Hamlet*	B.D. Kher	1958
24.	*Julius Caesar*	*Vijaya Sinha*	K.G. Natu	1872
25.	*Julius Caesar*	*Julius Caesar*	R.T. Pavanskar	1883
26.	*Julius Caesar*	*Julius Caesar*	K.B. Belsare	1912
27.	*Julius Caesar*	*Julius Caesar*	M.N. Kulkarni	1959
28.	*King Lear*	*Atipidacharita*	S.M. Ranade	1880
29.	*King Lear*	*Kanyapaariksana*	G.S. Gore	—
30.	*King Lear*	*Samrat Sinha*	P.K. Atre	1973

S. No.	Title	Translator's Title	Translator	Published
31.	*King Lear*	*Raja Lear*	G.V. Karandikar	1974
32.	*King Lear*	*King Lear*	D.M. Kher	1958
33.	*Macbeth*	*Manajirava*	S.M. Paranjpye	1896
34.	*Macbeth*	*Dakini Vilasa*	L.M. Joshi	1899
35.	*Macbeth*	*Rajmukut*	V.V. Shirvadkar	1954
36.	*Macbeth*	*Roopvidh*	Arun Naik	1988
37.	*Macbeth*	*Macbeth*	Ajay Arosakar	1958
38.	*Measure for Measure*	*Samana Sasana*	—	1909
39.	*Measure for Measure*	*Sumati-Vijaya*	H.M. Apte	1911
40.	*The Merchant of Venice*	*Strinaya-Chaturya*	A.V. Patkar	1871
41.	*The Merchant of Venice*	*Pranay Mudra*	V.S. Gurjar	1904
42.	*The Merchant of Venice*	*Mohanachi Anguthi*	D.G. Limaye	1909
43.	*The Merchant of Venice*	*Venice Nagarcha Vyapari*	K.B. Belsare	1910
44.	*The Merchant of Venice*	*Saudagar*	M. Agashe	—
45.	*The Merchant of Venice*	*Ek Paund Maans*	S.B. Gondhalekar	1944
46.	*The Merchant of Venice*	*Merchant of Venice*	Shankar Gopal Naravane	1921
47.	*The Merchant of Venice*	*Vilakshan Nyayachaturya*	Sakharam P. Pandit	1868
48.	*Othello*	*Othello*	M.G. Shastri	1867
49.	*Othello*	*Zunzarrao*	G.B. Deval	1890
50.	*Othello*	*Zunzarrao*	M.G. Kolhatkar	1890
51.	*Othello*	*Othellonamak Natak*	G.B. Deval	1890
52.	*Othello*	*Ajit Simha*	M.G. Kolhatkar	—
53.	*Othello*	*Othello*	V.V. Shirvadkar	1961
54.	*Othello*	*Nishpaap*	Dilip Pardesi	1984

S. No.	Title	Translator's Title	Translator	Published
55.	*Othello*	*Othello*	Arun Naik	1987
56.	*Othello*	*Othello*	Ajay Arosaskara	—
57.	*A Midsummer Night's Dream*	*Madhyamini Swapna*	K.N. Athale	—
58.	*A Midsummer Night's Dream*	*Veshaviparysa*	K.P. Gadgil	—
59.	*A Midsummer Night's Dream*	*Sita Sangeet*	C.G. Talvalkar	1889
60.	*A Midsummer Night's Dream*	*Madhu Yamini Swapan Darshan*	K.B. Belsare	1913
61.	*A Midsummer Night's Dream*	*A Midsummer Night's Dream*	B.D. Kher	1958
62.	*A Midsummer Night's Dream*	*Premamakrand Nataka*	A.N. Ukidave	1908
63.	*Romeo and Juliet*	*Prataparva Ane Manjula*	E.V. Musale	1882
64.	*Romeo and Juliet*	*Sasikala-Ratnapal*	Kanitkar	1882
65.	*Romeo and Juliet*	*Salini*	K.V. Karmakar	1901
66.	*Romeo and Juliet*	*Tara-Vilasa*	Dattaraya Mantakeskar	1908
67.	*Romeo and Juliet*	*Mohan-Tara*	K.R. Chapkhane	1908
68.	*Romeo and Juliet*	*Premcha Kalas*	K.B. Belsare	1908
69.	*Romeo and Juliet*	*Romeo and Juliet*	K.J. Purohit	1959
70.	*The Tempest*	*Tempest*	N.J. Kirtane	1875
71.	*The Tempest*	*Tuphan*	K.B. Belsare	1903
72.	*The Tempest*	*Tempest*	L.G. Deva	1958
73.	*The Tempest*	*Tuphan*	Ramvav B. Kirtikar	1893
74.	*Twelfth Night*	*Vesh Vibhram*	K.P. Gadgil	1891
75.	*Twelfth Night*	*Bhramvilas*	B.H. Pandit	1910
76.	*Twelfth Night*	*Priyardhana*	Navalkar	—

S. No.	Title	Translator's Title	Translator	Published
77.	*Twelfth Night*	*Prem Vinod*	A.V. Apte	1919
78.	*Twelfth Night*	*Vagvilas*	V.G. Joshi	1928
79.	*Twelfth Night*	*Madnachi Manjari*	Vidyadhar Gokhale	1967
80.	*Twelfth Night*	*Twelfth Night*	S. Behere	1958

Shakespeare Translations and Adaptations in Bengali

S. No.	Title	Translator's Title	Translator	Published
1.	*All's Well That Ends Well*	*Bhisak-Duhita*	Govindachandra Ray	1888
2.	*As You Like It*	*Ananga-Rangini*	Annada Prasad Basu	1897
3.	*As You Like It*	*As You Like It*	Sunil Kumar Chattopadhyay	1957
4.	*As You Like It*	*As You Like It*	Ashok Guha	1959
5.	*The Comedy of Errors*	*Bhram Kautuk*	Venimadhav Ghosh	1973
6.	*The Comedy of Errors*	*Bhrantivilas*	Ishwarchandra Vidyasagar	1884
7.	*The Comedy of Errors*	*Sarat Sashi Natak*	Nilratan Mukherjee	1882
8.	*Cymbeline*	*Susila Virsena*	Harimohan Mukhopadhyay	1868
9.	*Cymbeline*	*Kusumkumari*	Chandrakali Ghosh	1874
10.	*Hamlet*	*Amarsimha*	Paramath Natah Basu	1874
11.	*Hamlet*	*Chandranath*	Siddhesvara Gupta	1894
12.	*Hamlet*	*Hamlet*	Chandiprasad Ghosh	1894
13.	*Hamlet*	*Hamlet*	Manmohan Ray	

S. No.	Title	Translator's Title	Translator	Published
14.	*Hamlet*	*Hariraja*	Amrendranath Datta	1897
15.	*Hamlet*	*Hamlet*	Lalitmohan Adhikari	1893
16.	*Hamlet*	*Denmarker Raja Kumar*	Abu Shariyar	1976
17.	*Julius Caesar*	*Julius Caesar*	Jyotindranath Tagore	1907
18.	*Julius Caesar*	*Julius Caesar*	Sudhindranath Raha	1959
19.	*King Lear*	*Liyar*	Yatindra Mohan Ghosh	1902
20.	*King Lear*	*King Lear*	Kalyanvrat Datta	1957
21.	*King Lear*	*Dharma Va Ratnapuri*	Surendrachandra Basu	1921
22.	*Macbeth*	*Rudrapal*	Haralal Ray	1874
23.	*Macbeth*	*Macbeth*	Tarkanath Mukhopadhyay	1875
24.	*Macbeth*	*Karmvir*	Nagendranath Basu	1885
25.	*Macbeth*	*Bhramar*	Dhirendranath Paul	1891
26.	*Macbeth*	*Macbeth*	Girish Ghosh	1893
27.	*Macbeth*	*Macbeth*	Ashutosh Ghosh	1900
28.	*Macbeth*	*Macbeth*	Ashok Guha	1959
29.	*Macbeth*	*Macbeth*	Upendrakumar Kar	1923
30.	*Macbeth*	*Macbeth*	Sudhindranath Raha	1959
31.	*Macbeth*	*Macbeth*	Nirendranath Ray	1952
32.	*Measure for Measure*	*Vinimay*	Birendranath Ray	1909
33.	*The Merchant of Venice*	*Bhanumati-Chittavilas*	Harachandra Ghosh	1853
34.	*The Merchant of Venice*	*Sulata Natak*	Pyarelal Mukherjee	1877

S. No.	Title	Translator's Title	Translator	Published
35.	*The Merchant of Venice*	*Surlata*	Pyarelal Mukhopadhyay	1897
36.	*The Merchant of Venice*	*Saudagar*	Bhupendranath Bandopadhyay	1915
37.	*The Merchant of Venice*	*Merchant of Venice*	Manmohan Roy	1917
38.	*The Merchant of Venice*	*Merchant of Venice*	Pashupati Chattopadhyay	1920
39.	*The Merchant of Venice*	*The Merchant of Venice*	Sunilkumar Chattopadhyay	1956
40.	*The Merchant of Venice*	*Merchant of Venice*	Kalyanvrat Datta	1956
41.	*The Merchant of Venice*	*Bhinis Venik*	Mahadev De	1926
42.	*The Merchant of Venice*	*Merchant of Venice*	Ashutosh Ghosh	1925
43.	*The Merchant of Venice*	*Merchant of Venice*	Ashok Guha	1959
44.	*The Merchant of Venice*	*Sudkhor Saudagar*	Nagendranath Ray Chaudhuri	1915
45.	*A Midsummer Night's Dream*	*Jahanara*	Satishchandra Chattopadhyay	1903
46.	*A Midsummer Night's Dream*	*A Midsummer Night's Dream*	Manindra Datta	1956
47.	*A Midsummer Night's Dream*	*Kuhaki*	Devendranath Basu	1920
48.	*Othello*	*Bhimsimha*	Tarinicharan Pal	1882
49.	*Othello*	*Surasundari*	Surendranath Bhattacharya	1891
50.	*Othello*	*Othello*	Kaliprasanna Chattopadhyay	1894
51.	*Othello*	*Rudrasen*	Manilal Bandopadhyay	1906

S. No.	Title	Translator's Title	Translator	Published
52.	*Othello*	*Othello*	Devendranath Basu	1919
53.	*Othello*	*Othello*	Kaliprasanna Sharma	1893
54.	*Romeo and Juliet*	*Charumukh Chittahara*	Harachandra Ghosh	1864
55.	*Romeo and Juliet*	*Ajay Sinha-Vilasvati*	Yogendra Ghosh	1878
56.	*Romeo and Juliet*	*Romeo and Juliet*	Hemchandra Bandopadhyay	1895
57.	*Romeo and Juliet*	*Romeo Evam Julietera*	Gurudas Hajra	1848
58.	*Romeo and Juliet*	*Romeo-Juliet*	Sudhindranath Raha	1960
59.	*Romeo and Juliet*	*Romeo and Juliet*	Surendrachandra Basu	1892
60.	*The Taming of the Shrew*	*Chamundar Siksha*	Nagendranath Ray Chaudhuri	1915
61.	*The Tempest*	*Prakiti natak*	Charuchandra Mukherjee	1882
62.	*The Tempest*	*Nalini-Vasant*	Hemchandra Banopadhyay	1954
63.	*The Tempest*	*Jhanjha*	Nagendra Sarvadhikari	1913
64.	*The Tempest*	*Tempest*	Pashupati Chattopadhyay	1919
65.	*The Tempest*	*The Tempest*	Ashok Guha	1960
66.	*The Tempest*	*Tempest*	Nirmalkanti Mallick Chaudhuri	1956
67.	*Twelfth Night*	*Sushila-Chandraketu*	Kantichandra Mukhopadhyay	1872

Shakespeare Translations and Adaptations in Hindi

S. No.	Title	Translator's Title	Translator	Published
1.	*Love's Labour Lost*	*Nishphal Prem (story) in Hindi Shakespeare, Part VI*	Ganga Prasad	1914
2.	*Love's Labour Lost*	*Nishphal Prem*	Rangeya Raghav	1957
3.	*The Comedy of Errors*	*Bhramjhalak*	Munshi Ratnachanda Sahib	1882
4.	*The Comedy of Errors*	*Adbhut Bhram Jaal (story) in Shakepeare ke Manohar Natkon ke Ashaya ke Anuvad, Part II*	Kashinath Khattri	1884
5.	*The Comedy of Errors*	*Bhool Bhullaiyan (story) in Saraswati*	—	1906
6.	*The Comedy of Errors*	*Bhram Jaal (story) in Shakespeare Katha-gatha*	Jaivijay Narain Singh Sharma	1912
7.	*The Comedy of Errors*	*Bhool Bhullaiyan (story) in Hindi Shakespeare, Part III*	Ganga Prasad	1914
8.	*The Comedy of Errors*	*Bhool Bhullaiyan*	Lala Sitaram	1915
9.	*The Comedy of Errors*	*Gorakhdhandha*	B. Sinha	1917
10.	*The Comedy of Errors*	*Gorakhdhandha*	Ek Natak Premi	1917
11.	*The Comedy of Errors*	*Bhool Bhullaiyan*	Rangeya Raghav	1957
12.	*The Comedy of Errors*	*Bhul Chuk Maaf (story) in Shakespeare ki Kahaniyan*	Dharam Pal Shastri	1960

S. No.	Title	Translator's Title	Translator	Published
13.	*The Two Gentlemen of Verona*	*Verona Nagar ke Do Sajjan (story) in Shakepeare ke Manohar NAtkon ke Ashaya ke Anuvad, Part II*	Kashinath Khattri	1884
14.	*The Two Gentlemen of Verona*	*Varona ke Sajjan Yugal (story) in Shakespeare Katha-gatha*	Jaivijay Narain Singh Sharma	1912
15.	*The Two Gentlemen of Verona*	*Verona Nagar ke Do Bhadra Purush (story) in Hindi Shakespeare, Part III*	*Ganga Prasad*	1914
16.	*A Midsummer Night's Dream*	*Greeshma Ritu ki Raat ka Ek Swapna (story) in Shakespeare ke Manohar Natakon ke Ashaya ke Anuvad, Part II*	Kashinath Khattri	1884
17.	*A Midsummer Night's Dream*	*Garmion ki Raat ka Supna (story) in Shakespeare Katha-gatha*	Jaivijay Narain Singh Sharma	1912
18.	*A Midsummer Night's Dream*	*Greeshma Raat ke Swapna (story) in Hindi Shakespeare, Part II*	Ganga Prasad	1913
19.	*A Midsummer Night's Dream*	*Ek Sapna*	Rangeya Raghav	1958
20.	*The Merchant of Venice*	*Venice Nagar ka Vyapari*	Munshi Ratanchand Sahib	1879
21.	*The Merchant of Venice*	*Durlabh Bandhu*	Harishchandra	1881

S. No.	Title	Translator's Title	Translator	Published
22.	*The Merchant of Venice*	*Venice ka Saudagar*	Baleshwar Prasad	1885
23.	*The Merchant of Venice*	*Venice ka Saudagar*	Thakur Dayal Singh	1885
24.	*The Merchant of Venice*	*Venice ke Vyapari ka Vratant (story) in Shakespeare ke Manohar Natakon ke Ashaya ke Anuvad, Part I*	Kashinath Khattri	1882
25.	*The Merchant of Venice*	*Venice ka Banka*	Gokul Chand Sharma	1888
26.	*The Merchant of Venice*	*Venice Nagar ka Vyapari*	Arya	1888
27.	*The Merchant of Venice*	*Venice ka Vyapari*	Gopinath Purohit	1896
28.	*The Merchant of Venice*	*Venice ka Banka*	Ayodhya Singh Upadhyay 'Hariaudh'	1900
29.	*The Merchant of Venice*	*Venice ka Vyapari*	Ek Hindi Premi	1904
30.	*The Merchant of Venice*	*Ek Aurat ki Vakalat*	Shrikrishna Hasrat	1908
31.	*The Merchant of Venice*	*Venice ka Vyapari (story) in Shakespeare Granthavali*	Pandit Shivprasad Dubey	1912
32.	*The Merchant of Venice*	*Venice ka Saudagar (story) in Shakespeare Katha-gatha*	Jaivijay Narain Singh Sharma	1912
33.	*The Merchant of Venice*	*Venice ka Vyapari (story) in Hindi Shakespeare, Part II*	Ganga Prasad	1912
34.	*The Merchant of Venice*	*Dil Farosh*	Munshi Mehdi Hasan	1918

S. No.	Title	Translator's Title	Translator	Published
35.	*The Merchant of Venice*	*Venice ka Vyapari (story) in Shakespeare ke Natakon ki Kahaniyan*	Usha Khanna	1950
36.	*The Merchant of Venice*	*Venice ka Saudagar*	Rangeya Raghav	1957
37.	*The Merchant of Venice*	*Venice Nagar ka Vyapari (story) in Shakespeare ki Kahaniyan*	Dharam Pal Shastri	1960
38.	*The Taming of the Shrew*	*Karkash Stri ko Sudharne ki Vidhi (story) in Shakespeare ke Manohar Natakon ke Ashaya ke Anuvad, Part I*	Kashinath Khattri	1882
39.	*The Taming of the Shrew*	*Karkash Vashikaran*	Ishwar Chand Kundu	1911
40.	*The Taming of the Shrew*	*Karkash ka Seedha Karna (story) in Shakespeare Katha-gatha*	Jaivijay Narain Singh Sharma	1912
41.	*The Taming of the Shrew*	*Kutil Stree ko Vash mein Karna (story) in Hindi Shakespeare, Part I*	Ganga Prasad	1922
42.	*The Taming of the Shrew*	*Parivartan*	Rangeya Raghav	1957
43.	*The Taming of the Shrew*	*Karkash ka Sudhar*	Dharam Pal Shastri	1960
44.	*The Merry Wives of Windsor*	*Windsor ki Hansmukh Striyan (story) in Hindi Shakespeare, Part II*	Ganga Prasad	1914

S. No.	Title	Translator's Title	Translator	Published
45.	*Much Ado About Nothing*	*Vyartha Hora Machana Tha (story) in Shakespeare ke Manohar Natakon ke Ashaya ke Anuvad, Part II*	Kashinath Khattri	1884
46.	*Much Ado About Nothing*	*Man Mohan ka Jal*	Lala Sitaram	1912
47.	*Much Ado About Nothing*	*Baat na Kuchh Adambar Bhari (story) in Shakespeare Katha-gatha*	Jaivijay Narain Singh	1912
48.	*Much Ado About Nothing*	*Baat ka Batangarh (story) in Hindi Shakespeare, Part V*	Ganga Prasad	1914
49.	*Much Ado About Nothing*	*Til ka Taarh*	Rangeya Raghav	1957
50.	*As You Like It*	*Jaisa Tumhe Pasand Aave Karo (story) in Shakespeare ke Natakon ke Ashaya ke Anuvad, Part II*	Kashinath Khattri	1884
51.	*As You Like It*	*Manbhavan*	Gopinath Prohit	1887
52.	*As You Like It*	*Jaisi Jiski Bhavana (story) in Shakespeare Katha-gatha*	Jaivijay Narain Singh Sharma	1912
53.	*As You Like It*	*Krishna Kamini*	Seth Govind Das	1912
54.	*As You Like It*	*Apani Apani Ruchi*	Lala Sitaram	1915

S. No.	Title	Translator's Title	Translator	Published
55.	*As You Like It*	*Tumhari Ichcha (story) in Hindi Shakespeare, Part I*	Ganga Prasad	1922
56.	*As You Like It*	*Jaisi Aapki Ichcha (story) in Shakespeare ke Natakon ki Kahaniyan*	Usha Khanna	1950
57.	*As You Like It*	*Jaisa Tum Chaho*	Rangey Raghav	1957
58.	*As You Like It*	*Mano na Mano (story) in Shakespeare ki Kahaniyan*	Dharam Pal Shastri	1960
59.	*Twelfth Night*	*Do Bhin Bhai ke Rup Rang Mein Adbhut Prakar se Bhram Parh Jana (stiry) in Shakespeare ke Manohar Natakon ke Ashaya ke Anuvad, Part I*	Kashinath Khattri	1882
60.	*Twelfth Night*	*Bhool Bhullaiyan*	Munshi Mehdi Hasan	1905
61.	*Twelfth Night*	*Dwadashvin Ratri (story) Shakespeare Katha-gatha*	Jaivijay Narain Singh Sharma	1912
62.	*Twelfth Night*	*Barehvin Ratri (story) in Hindi Shakespeare, Part IV*	Ganga Prasad	1914
63.	*Twelfth Night*	*Barehvin Raat*	Rangeya Raghav	1957
64.	*Twelfth Night*	*Barehvin Raat*	Dharm Pal Shastri	1960
65.	*Twelfth Night*	*Barehvin Raat*	Kuldip Kapur	1961
66.	*Twelfth Night*	*Barehvin Raat*	Shyam Sunder Suman	1962

S. No.	Title	Translator's Title	Translator	Published
67.	*Twelfth Night*	*Piya Behrupiya/ Barvi Raat*	Amitosh Nagpal	2012
68.	*All's Well That Ends Well*	*Ant mein Jo Ho So Thik Hai (story) in Shakespeare ke Manohar Natakon ke Ashaya ke Anuvad, Part I*	*Kashinath Khattri*	1882
69.	*All's Well That Ends Well*	*Ant Bhale ka Bhala (story) in Shakespeare Katha-gatha*	*Jaivijay Narain Singh Sharma*	1912
70.	*All's Well That Ends Well*	*Vahi Bhala Jiska Ant Bhala (story) in Hindi Shakespeare, Part V*	*Ganga Prasad*	1914
71.	*Measure for Measure*	*Jaise ko Taisa (story) in Shakepeare ke Manohar Natkon ke Ashaya ke Anuvad, Part I*	Kashinath Khattri	1882
72.	*Measure for Measure*	*Jaise ko Taisa (story) in Shakespeare Katha-gatha*	Jaivijay Narain Singh Sharma	1912
73.	*Measure for Measure*	*Jaise ko Taisa (story) in Hindi Shakespeare, Part IV*	Ganga Prasad	1914
74.	*Measure for Measure*	*Bagula Bhagat*	Lala Sitaram	1915
75.	*Pericles*	*Raja Pericles ka Vratant (story) in Shakespeare ke Manohar Natakon ke Ashaya ke Anuvad, Part I*	Kashinath Khattri	1882

S. No.	Title	Translator's Title	Translator	Published
76.	*Pericles*	*Pericles (story) in Saraswati*	Radhakrishna Das	1900
77.	*Pericles*	*Bhagya ka Pher ya Pyare Krishna ki Kahani*	Purushottam Das Tandon	—
78.	*Pericles*	*Honhar*	Seth Govind Das	1912
79.	*Pericles*	*Pericles (story) in Shakespeare Katha-gatha*	Jaivijay Narain Singh Sharma	1912
80.	*Pericles*	*Pericles (story) in Hindi Shakespeare, Part I*	Ganga Prasad	1922
81.	*Cymbeline*	*Raja Cymbeline ka Vratant (story) in Shakepeare ke Manohar Natkon ke Ashaya ke Anuvad, Part I*	Kashinath Khattri	1882
82.	*Cymbeline*	*Cymbeline (story) in Saraswati*	Radhakrishna Das	1900
83.	*Cymbeline*	*Cymbeline (story) in Shakespeare Katha-gatha*	Jaivijay Narain Singh Sharma	1912
84.	*Cymbeline*	*Cymbeline (story) in Hindi Shakespeare, Part II*	Ganga Prasad	1913
85.	*Winter's Tale*	*Sharad Ritu ki Kahani*	Gokul Chand Sharma	1881
86.	*Winter's Tale*	*Sharad Ritu ki Kahani (story) in Shakepeare ke Manohar Natkon ke Ashaya ke Anuvad, Part I*	Kashinath Khattri	1882
87.	*Winter's Tale*	*Vyarth Sandesh*	Seth Govind Das	1912

S. No.	Title	Translator's Title	Translator	Published
88.	*Winter's Tale*	*Jadon ki Kahani (story) in Shakespeare Katha-gatha*	Jaivijay Narain Singh Sharma	1912
89.	*Winter's Tale*	*Sharad Ritu ki Kahani (story) in Hindi Shakespeare, Part I*	Ganga Prasad	1922
90.	*The Tempest*	*Prachand Pawan (story) in Shakespeare ke Manohar Natakon ke Ashaya ke Anuvad, Part II*	Kashinath Khattri	1884
91.	*The Tempest*	*Toofan*	Jagannath Prasad Chaturvedi	1897
92.	*The Tempest*	*Tempest*	Vindabanlal Varma	1908
93.	*The Tempest*	*Toofan (story) in Shakespeare Katha-gatha*	Jaivijay Narain Singh Sharma	1912
94.	*The Tempest*	*Toofan (story) in Shakespeare Granthavali*	Shiv Prasad Dubey	1912
95.	*The Tempest*	*Toofan (story)Hindi Shakespeare, Part II*	Ganga Prasad	1913
96.	*The Tempest*	*Jangal Mei Mangal*	Lala Sitaram	1915
97.	*The Tempest*	*Toofan*	Rangeya Raghav	1957
98.	*The Tempest*	*Toofan (story) in Shakespeare ki Kahaniyan*	Dharm Pal Shastri	1960
99.	*King John*	*Inglistan ka Raja John (story) in Hindi Shakespeare, Part III*	Ganga Prasad	1914

S. No.	Title	Translator's Title	Translator	Published
100.	*King John*	*Saide-Havas*	Avdeshpathi Varma	1923
101.	*Richard II*	*Dwitiya Richard (story) in Hindi Shakespeare, Part III*	Ganga Prasad	1914
102.	*Richard II*	*Raja Richard Dwitiya*	Lala Sitaram	1915
103.	*Henry IV, Part I*	*Chaturth Henry, Pratham Bhag (story) in Hindi Shakespeare*	Ganga Prasad	1914
104.	*Henry IV, Part II*	*Chaturth Henry, Dwitiya Bhag (story) in Hindi Shakespeare*	Ganga Prasad	1914
105.	*Henry V*	*Pancham Henry (story) in Hindi Shakespeare*	Ganga Prasad	1914
106.	*Henry V*	*Raja Henry Pancham*	Lala Sitaram	1916
107.	*Henry VI, Part I*	*Chhata Henry, Pahla Bhag (story) in Hindi Shakespeare*	Ganga Prasad	1914
108.	*Henry VI, Part II*	*Chhata Henry, Doosra Bhag (story) in Hindi Shakespeare*	Ganga Prasad	1914
109.	*Henry VI, Part III*	*Chhata Henry, Tisra Bhag (story) in Hindi Shakespeare*	Ganga Prasad	1914
110.	*Richard III*	*Tritiya Richard (story) in Hindi Shakespeare*	Ganga Prasad	1914
111.	*Henry VIII*	*Athwan Henry (story) in Hindi Shakespeare*	Ganga Prasad	1914

S. No.	Title	Translator's Title	Translator	Published
112.	*Titus Andronicus*	*Titus Andronicus (story) in Hindi Shakespeare*	Ganga Prasad	1914
113.	*Romeo and Juliet*	*Romeo aur Juliet-Do Mitra (story) in Shakespeare ke Manohar Natakon ke Ashaya ke Anuvad, Part II*	Kashinath Khattri	1884
114.	*Romeo and Juliet*	*Premlila*	Gopinath Purohit	1896
115.	*Romeo and Juliet*	*Romeo and Juliet*	Chaturbhuj Auditya	1911
116.	*Romeo and Juliet*	*Surendra Sundari*	Seth Govind Das	1912
117.	*Romeo and Juliet*	*Romeo Juliet (story) in Shakespeare Granthavali*	Shiv Prasad Dubey	1912
118.	*Romeo and Juliet*	*Romeo Juliet (story) in Shakespeare Katha-gatha*	Jaivijay Narain Singh Sharma	1912
119.	*Romeo and Juliet*	*Romeo Juliet*	Surya Prasad Mishra	—
120.	*Romeo and Juliet*	*Romeo Juliet (story) in Hindi Shakespeare, Part I*	Ganga Prasad	1922
121.	*Romeo and Juliet*	*Prem Kasauti*	Lala Sitaram	1931
122.	*Romeo and Juliet*	*Romeo Juliet*	Rangeya Raghav	1957
123.	*Romeo and Juliet*	*Romeo Juliet*	Shyam Sunder Suman	1961

S. No.	Title	Translator's Title	Translator	Published
124.	*Julius Caesar*	*Julius Caesar (story) in Hindi Shakespeare, Part II*	Ganga Prasad	1913
125.	*Julius Caesar*	*Julius Caesar*	Lala Sitaram	1915
126.	*Julius Caesar*	*Julius Caesar*	Rangeya Raghav	1957
127.	*Hamlet*	*Hamlet – Denmark ka Rajkumar (story) in Shakepeare ke Manohar Natkon ke Ashaya ke Anuvad, Part II*	Kashinath Khattri	1884
128.	*Hamlet*	*Hamlet (story) in Shakespeare Granthavali*	Shiv Prasad Dubey	1912
129.	*Hamlet*	*Hamlet (story) in Shakespeare Katha-gatha*	Jaivijay Narain Singh Sharma	1912
130.	*Hamlet*	*Jayant*	Ganpati Krishna Gurjar	1912
131.	*Hamlet*	*Hamlet (story) in Hindi Shakespeare, Part IV*	Ganga Prasad	1914
132.	*Hamlet*	*Hamlet ka Hindi Anuvad*	Nanak Chand Bhanot	—
133.	*Hamlet*	*Denmark ka Rajakumar Hamlet*	Lala Sitaram	1915
134.	*Hamlet*	*Hamlet (story) in Shakespeare ke Natakon ki Kahaniyan*	Usha Khanna	1950
135.	*Hamlet*	*Hamlet*	Rangeya Raghav	1957
136.	*Hamlet*	*Hamlet (story) in Shakespeare ki Kahaniyan*	Dharm Pal Shastri	1960

S. No.	Title	Translator's Title	Translator	Published
137.	*Hamlet*	*Hamlet*	Harivansh Rai Bachchan	1969
138.	*Troilus and Cressida*	*Troilus aur Cressida (story) in Hindi Shakespeare, Part VI*	Ganga Prasad	1914
139.	*Othello*	*Othello – Kapat ke Bure Parinam (story) in Shakepeare ke Manohar Natkon ke Ashaya ke Anuvad, Part II*	Kashinath Khattri	1884
140.	*Othello*	*Othello*	Gadadhar Sinha	1894
141.	*Othello*	*Othello*	Gopal Goil	1911
142.	*Othello*	*Othello (Story) in Shakespeare Katha-gatha*	Jaivijay Narayan Singh Sharma	1912
143.	*Othello*	*Othello (story) in Hindi Shakespeare, Part III*	Ganga Prasad	1914
144.	*Othello*	*Othello*	Lala Sitaram	1915
145.	*Othello*	*Othello*	Govindprasad Ghidiyal	1916
146.	*Othello*	*Uthello*	Usha Khanna	1950
147.	*Othello*	*Othello*	Vishnu Sharma	—
148.	*Othello*	*Othello*	Rangeya Raghav	1957
149.	*Othello*	*Othello*	Harivansh Rai Bachchan	1959
150.	*Othello*	*Othello*	Vidyarthi Diwakar Prasad	1962
151.	*King Lear*	*Raja Lear ka Vratanta (story) in Shakepeare ke Manohar Natkon ke Ashaya ke Anuvad, Part II*	Kashinath Khattri	1884

S. No.	Title	Translator's Title	Translator	Published
152.	*King Lear*	*Snehpariksha*	Badrinarain	1903
153.	*King Lear*	*Badshah Lear*	Chaturbhuj Audichya	1911
154.	*King Lear*	*Badshah Lear (story) in Shakespeare Katha-gatha*	Jaivijay Narain Singh Sharma	1912
155.	*King Lear*	*Raja Lear (story) in Shakespeare Granthavali*	Shiv Prasad Dubey	1912
156.	*King Lear*	*Raja Lear*	Lala Sitaram	1915
157.	*King Lear*	*Lear (story) in Hindi Shakespeare, Part I*	Ganga Prasad	1922
158.	*King Lear*	*Badshah Lear (story) in Shakespeare ke Natakon ki Kahaniyan*	Usha Khanna	1950
159.	*King Lear*	*Samrat Lear*	Rangeya Raghav	1957
160.	*King Lear*	*Raja Lear (story) in Shakespeare ki Kahaniyan*	Dharma Pal Shastri	1960
161.	*King Lear*	*King Lear*	Harivansh Rai Bachchan	1972
162.	*Macbeth*	*Macbeth – Kapati Badhik (story) in Shakepeare ke Manohar Natkon ke Ashaya ke Anuvad, Part II*	Kashinath Khattri	1884
163.	*Macbeth*	*Sahsendra Sahas*	M. P. Chaudhari	1893
164.	*Macbeth*	*Macbeth (story) in Shakespeare Granthavali*	Shiva Prasad Dubey	1912
165.	*Macbeth*	*Macbeth (story) in Shakespeare Katha-gatha*	Jaivijay Narayan Singh Sharma	1912

S. No.	Title	Translator's Title	Translator	Published
166.	*Macbeth*	*Macbeth (story) in Hindi Shakespeare, Part II*	Ganga Prasad	1913
167.	*Macbeth*	*Macbeth ka Bhashanuvad*	Lala Sitaram	1926
168.	*Macbeth*	*Macbeth*	Vishnu Sharma	—
169.	*Macbeth*	*Macbeth*	Rangeya Raghav	1957
170.	*Macbeth*	*Macbeth*	Harivansh Rai Bachchan	1957
171.	*Macbeth*	*Macbeth (story) in Shakespeare ki Kahaniyan*	Dharam Pal Shastri	1960
172.	*Macbeth*	*Barnam Van*	Raghuveer Sahay	1980
173.	*Antony and Cleopatra*	*Antony aur Cleopatra (story) in Hindi Shakespeare, Part V*	Ganga Prasad	1914
174.	*Coriolanus*	*Coriolanus (story) in Hindi Shakespeare, Part VI*	Ganga Prasad	1914
175.	*Timon of Athens*	*Athens Nagar ke Timon Nami Amir ka Vratanta (story) in Shakepeare ke Manohar Natkon ke Ashaya ke Anuvad, Part I*	Kashinath Khattri	1882
176.	*Timon of Athens*	*Athens ka Pradhan Timon (story) in Shakespeare Katha-gatha*	J.N. Singh Sharma	1912

S. No.	Title	Translator's Title	Translator	Published
177.	*Timon of Athens*	*Athens ka Timon (story) in Hindi Shakespeare, Part III*	Ganga Prasad	1914
178.	*Timon of Athens*	*Athens ka Raja Timon (story) in Shakespeare ki Kahaniyan*	Dharma Pal Shastri	1960

Shakespeare Translations and Adaptations in Urdu and Gujarati

S. No.	Title	Translator's Title	Translator	Published
1.	*As You Like It*	*Dilpazir*	Charandas Bakshi	1901
2.	*As You Like It*	*Kannan Kallol (GU)*	Apabhai Patel	—
3.	*As You Like It*	*Bage Behast (GU)*	K.N. Kabraji	—
4.	*Love's Labour Lost*	*Yaaron ki Mehnat Barbad*	Mohammad Sulaiman	1899
5.	*The Comedy of Errors*	*Jodiya Bhaiyo (GU)*	N.R. Ranina	1865
6.	*The Comedy of Errors*	*Bhram Jhalak*	Munshi Imdad Ali	1879
7.	*The Comedy of Errors*	*Ram Ratna (GU)*	N.K. Vaidya	1903
8.	*The Comedy of Errors*	*Bhool Bhullaiyan*	Munshi Mehdi Hasan	1905
9.	*The Comedy of Errors*	*Gorakhdhandha*	Narain Prasad 'Betab'	1912
10.	*The Comedy of Errors*	*Bhool Bhullaiyan*	Abdul Karim	1913
11.	*The Comedy of Errors*	*Parekha (GU)*	Maganlal Harilal	—
12.	*The Merchant of Venice*	*Strinyaykala (GU)*	Narsidas Vanamalidas	1893

S. No.	Title	Translator's Title	Translator	Published
13.	*The Merchant of Venice*	*Chand Shah-e-Sudkhor*	—	1895
14.	*The Merchant of Venice*	*Venice ka Saudagar*	Ashiq Hussain	1898
15.	*The Merchant of Venice*	*Tajir-e-Venice*	Muhammad Fateh Ali Nadhr	1884
16.	*The Merchant of Venice*	*Dil Farosh*	Agha Hashar Kashmiri	1900
17.	*The Merchant of Venice*	*Jagat Simha (GU)*	—	1904
18.	*The Merchant of Venice*	*Vibudh Vijay (GU)*	—	—
19.	*The Merchant of Venice*	*Venice no Veparai (GU)*	Nareabhesankara P. Dave	1911
20.	*The Merchant of Venice*	*Venice no Veparai (GU)*	Manacksha Kekobad	1920
21.	*The Taming of the Shrew*	*Nathari Firangiz Thekani Aavi (GU)*	Dinsha A. Tal Yarkhan	1852
22.	*The Taming of the Shrew*	*Karkash par Kaabu (GU)*	N.M. Shukla	1912
23.	*All's Well That Ends Well*	*Husnara (with scenes from Measure for Measure)*	—	1900
24.	*All's Well That Ends Well*	*Vaidya Kanya (GU)*	Narayan Hemchandra	1895
25.	*Measure for Measure*	*Shaheede Naaz*	Agha Hashar Kashmiri	1905
26.	*Cymbeline*	*Ramanasundari (GU)*	G.K. Delvadkar	1895
27.	*Cymbeline*	*Zulme narava*	—	1899
28.	*Cymbeline*	*Mitha Zahar*	Munshi Mustafa Saiyadalli	1900
29.	*Cymbeline*	*Champaraja Hando (GU)*	V.A. Oza	1900
30.	*Cymbeline*	*Cymbeline*	M. Abdul Aziz	1902

S. No.	Title	Translator's Title	Translator	Published
31.	*Winter's Tale*	*Chandrahasa (GU)*	V.A. Oza	1894
32.	*Winter's Tale*	*Mureede Shak*	Munshi Hasan	1898
33.	*King John*	*Said-e-havas*	Munshi Jalal	—
34.	*Richard III*	*Saide Havas*	Agha Hashar Kashmiri	1906
35.	*Titus Andronicus*	*Junun-e-vafa*	A.B. Latif Sad	1910
36.	*Romeo and Juliet*	*Romeo and Juliet (GU)*	Dosabhai Randeria	1876
37.	*Romeo and Juliet*	*Bazm-e-fani*	Mehar Hasan	1897
38.	*Romeo and Juliet*	*Gulnar Faroz*	Muhammad Shah	1900
39.	*Romeo and Juliet*	*Ishq-e-Firoz Gulnarsiyar*	Nazir Beg	1905
40.	*Romeo and Juliet*	*Gulzar-e-Firoz*	J.L. Seth	1908
41.	*Romeo and Juliet*	*Romeo Juliet*	Aziz Ahmed	—
42.	*Romeo and Juliet*	*Romeo Ane Julliet (GU)*	Kalyanray Desai	1913
43.	*Hamlet*	*Khun-e-nahaq*	Munshi Mehdi Hasan	1898
44.	*Hamlet*	*Khun-e-nahaq*	Munshi Arzu Sahib	—
45.	*Hamlet*	*Hamlet*	Muhammad Afza Khan	1902
46.	*Hamlet*	*Wagi'Ah-e-Jahangir-e-Nshd*	Nazir Beg	1904
47.	*Hamlet*	*Denmark ka Shehzadah*	Inayatullah Dehlvi	—
48.	*Hamlet*	*Denmark-no Rajkumar (GU)*	Nareabhesankara P. Dave	1917
49.	*Macbeth*	*Malavaketu (GU)*	N.V. Thakur	—
50.	*Macbeth*	*Macbeth (GU)*	Jaswant Thakur	—

S. No.	Title	Translator's Title	Translator	Published
51.	*Macbeth*	*Malavaketu Mayaprabhav (GU)*	Narayan Visnaji Thakur	—
52.	*Othello*	*Kashiraj na Karasthan (GU)*	N.R. Randeria	1866
53.	*Othello*	*Shaheed-e-vafa*	Munshi Mehdi Hasan	1898
54.	*Othello*	*Saubhagya Sundari (GU)*	—	1903
55.	*Othello*	*Venice no Habsi (GU)*	N.P. Dave	—
56.	*Othello*	*Othello*	Gopal Goil	1911
57.	*Othello*	*Sher-Dil*	Najar Dehlvi	1918
58.	*King Lear*	*Haar-Jeet*	Munshi Murad Ali	1905
59.	*King Lear*	*Safed Khun*	Agha Hashar Kashmiri	1906
60.	*King Lear*	*Mathnavi Shah Lear*	Barq Sitapuri	1921
61.	*Antony and Cleopatra*	*Kali Nagin*	—	1906
62.	*Antony and Cleopatra*	*Zan Mureed*	—	1909
63.	*Antony and Cleopatra*	Antuni aur Kalabatrah	Inayatullah Dehlvi	—

Shakespeare Translations and Adaptations in Malayalam

S. No.	Title	Translator's Title	Translator	Published/ Performed
1.	*Hamlet*	*Hamlet Natakam*	Kodgallur K. Tampuranun	1897
2.	*Hamlet*	*Hamlet*	A. Govinda Pillai	1902
3.	*Hamlet*	*Hamlet*	M.K. Kuriyan	1923
4.	*Hamlet*	*Hamlet*	A.J. Varky	1923

S. No.	Title	Translator's Title	Translator	Published/ Performed
5.	*Hamlet*	*Hamlet*	P.S. Venkatesvaran	1955
6.	*Julius Caesar*	*Julius Caesar*	P.S. Nair	1953
7.	*King Lear*	*Brittenile Rajavu Lear*	A. Govinda Pillai	1897
8.	*King Lear*	*Lear Rajavu/Lear Natakam*	K.M. Panikkar	1959
9.	*Macbeth*	*Macbeth*	Ramakrishna Pillai	1962
10.	*Macbeth*	*Macbeth*	Madhava Varier, Matasseri	1962
11.	*Macbeth*	*Macbeth*	Chandradasan	
12.	*Macbeth*	*Macbeth*	M.G. Jyothish	2009
13.	*Comedy of Errors*	*Almarattam*	Oomman Philipose	1866
14.	*Comedy of Errors*	*Vibhrama Vihasam*	Paramu Pillai, K.	1906
15.	*The Merchant of Venice*	*Venicile Vyapari*	A. Govinda Pillai	1902
16.	*The Merchant of Venice*	*Venicile Vyapari*	P.S. Venkitesavaran	1955
17.	*A Midsummer Night's Dream*	*Vasantikasvapnam*	C. Krishna Wariyar	1907
18.	*A Midsummer Night's Dream*	*Vichitravipinam*	Narayan Pillai, P.K.	1938
19.	*A Midsummer Night's Dream*	*Madhya Grishmakala Ratriyile oru Swapnam*	Madhava Varier, Matasseri	1966
20.	*A Midsummer Night's Dream*	*Oru Swapnam*	Paramu Pillai, K.	
21.	*Othello*	*Avivekattilundaya Appattu*	Pappu Pillai, K.	1903
22.	*Othello*	*Uddalacharitam*	Anujan Raja, P.C.	1922

S. No.	Title	Translator's Title	Translator	Published/ Performed
23.	*Othello*	*Duranat Dussanka*	Kainkkara M. Kumara Pillai	1931
24.	*Othello*	*Prema Homam*	M.R. Velu Pillai Shastri	1932
25.	*Othello*	*Othello*	M.R. Nair	1951
26.	*Othello*	*Othello*	Parmeswaran Pillai, V.N.	1966
27.	*Richard II*	*Richard Simham*	Varavur Narayan Menon	1938
28.	*The Taming of the Shrew*	*Kalahinida-manakam*	Kantattil Varghese Mapila	1893
29.	*Twelfth Night*	*Dvadasanisa Allenkil*	Koyathu Koccunni Menon	1954
30.	*Twelfth Night*	*Manampole Mangalyam*	C.P. Thomas	1919
31.	*The Tempest*	*Kodumkattu*	K.N. Panikkar	2000
32.	*The Tempest*	*Chathankattu*	Chandradasan	1995
33.	*Macbeth*	*Macbeth*	Chandradasan	2002

Works Consulted (Appendix)

Amur, G.S. 'Shakespeare in Kannada.' *Shakespeare in Indian Languages*, edited by D.A. Shankar. Shimla: Indian Institute of Advanced Study, 1999: 116–126.

Bhattacharya, S.K. 'Shakespeare and Bengali Theatre.' *Indian Literature* 7, no. 1 (1964): 27–40.

Guttal, Vijaya. 'Translation and Performance of Shakespeare in Kannada.' *India's Shakespeare: Translation, Interpretation, and Performance*, edited by Poonam Trivedi and Dennis Bartholomeusz. New Delhi: Pearson Longman, 2005: 95–107.

Mehta, C.C. 'Shakespeare and Gujarati Stage.' *Indian Literature* 7, no. 1 (1964): 41–50.

Mishra, Jagdish Prasad. *Shakespeare's Impact on Hindi Literature*. New Delhi: Munshiram Manoharlal, 1970.

Nair, Jayasree Ramakrishnan. 'Towards a Malayalee Shakespeare: The Search for an Ideal Form of Expression.' *Shakespeare in Indian Languages*, edited by D.A. Shankar. Shimla: Indian Institute of Advanced Study, 1999: 127–140.

Paul, Sunita, ed. *A Tribute to Shakespeare*. New Delhi: Theatre and Television Associates, 1989.

Rajadhyaksha, M.V. 'Shakespeare in Marathi.' *Indian Literature* 7, no. 1 (1964): 83–94.

Rao, A.N. Moorthy. 'Shakespeare in Kannada.' *Indian Literature* 7, no. 1 (1964): 63–72.

Satyanath, T.S. 'How Does Shakespeare Become Sekh Pir in Kannada?' *Translation Today* 1, no. 2 (October 2004): 44–102.

Trivedi, H.K. 'Hindi Translations of Shakespeare.' *Shakespeare Translation* 5 (1978): 79–91.

Yajnik, R.K. *The Indian Theatre: Its Origins and its Later Developments under European Influence*. London: George Allen & Unwin Ltd., 1933.

Bibliography

Aebischer, Pascale, Edward J. Esche and Nigel Wheale, eds. 2003. *Remaking Shakespeare: Performance across Media, Genres and Culture*. NY: Palgrave Macmillan.

Ashcroft, Bill. 2002. *Post-Colonial Transformation*. London and NY: Routledge.

Berry, Ralph. 1977. *On Directing Shakespeare: Interviews with Contemporary Directors*. NY: Harper & Row Publishers Inc.

Bhattacharya, Sankar. 1959. *Ardhendusekhar O' Bangla Theatre: A Biography*. Calcutta: Shankar Prakashan.

Bharucha, Rustom. 2004. 'Foreign Asia/Foreign Shakespeare: Dissenting Notes on New Asian Interculturality, Postcoloniality, and Recolonization.' *Theatre Journal* 56(1): 1–28.

Bishop, Tom and Alexander C.Y. Huang, eds. 2012. *The Shakespearean International Yearbook*, vol. 12. Special Section: 'Shakespeare in India.' Special Guest Editor, Sukanta Chaudhuri. Farnham: Ashgate.

Chopra, Vikram, ed. 1996. *Shakespeare; Varied Perspectives*. Delhi: B.R. Publishing Corporation.

Counsell, Colin and Laurie Wolf, eds. 2003. *Performance Analysis: An Introductory Coursebook*. London: Routledge.

Das, Veena, ed. 2003. *The Oxford India Companion to Sociology and Social Anthropology*. New Delhi: Oxford University Press.

Desmet, Christy and Robert Sawyer, eds. 1999. *Shakespeare and Appropriation*. London: Routledge.

Dionne, Craig and Parmita Kapadia. 2014. *Bollywood Shakespeares*. New York: Palgrave Macmillan.

Dollimore, Jonathan and Allan Sinfield, eds. 1995. *Political Shakespeare: New Essays in Cultural Materialism*. UK: Manchester University Press.

Gainor, J. Ellen, ed. 1995. *Imperialism and Theatre. Essays on World Theatre, Drama and Performance 1795–1995*. London: Routledge.

Gilbert, Helen and Joanne Tompkins, eds. 1996. *Post-Colonial Drama: Theory, Practice, Politics*. London: Routledge.

Greenblatt, Stephen. 1990. *Shakespeare Negotiations*. Oxford: Clarendon Press.

Gurr, Andrew and Mariko Ichikawa. 2000. *Staging in Shakespeare's Theatres*. Oxford: Oxford University Press.

Hansen, Kathryn. 1992. *Grounds for Play: The Nautanki Theatre of North India*. New Delhi: Manohar.

Harris, Jonathan Gil. 2018. *Masala Shakespeare: How a Firangi Writer Became Indian*. New Delhi: Aleph.

Hasan, Mohammad. 1964. 'Shakespeare in Urdu.' *Indian Literature* 7(1): 132–139.

Hutcheon, Linda. 2006. *A Theory of Adaptation*. London and NY: Routledge.

Jain, Nemi Chandra. 1995 (1971). *Indian Theatre: Tradition, Continuity and Change*. Delhi: Vikas Publishing House.

Kennedy, Dennis and Yong Li Lan, eds. 2010. *Shakespeare in Asia: Contemporary Performance*. Cambridge: Cambridge University Press.

Kott, Jan. 1974. *Shakespeare Our Contemporary*. New York: Norton.

Naikar, Basavaraj. 2002. *Indian Response to Shakespeare*. New Delhi: Atlantic Publishers and Distributors.

Panja, Shormishtha and Babli Moitra Saraf. 2016. *Performing Shakespeare in India: Exploring Indianness, Literature and Cultures*. New Delhi: Sage Publications.

Scolnicov, Hannah and Peter Holland, eds. 1989. *The Play Out of Context: Transferring Plays from Culture to Culture*. Cambridge: Cambridge University Press.

Sikdar, Lipika.1999. *Shakespeare in the Media*. Calcutta: Shakespeare Society of Eastern India.

Singh, Jyotsna G. 2019. *Shakespeare and Postcolonial Theory*. London and NY: Bloomsbury.

Trivedi, Poonam and Paromita Chakravarti, eds. 2019. *Shakespeare and Indian Cinemas: 'Local Habitations.'* New York: Routledge.

Wells, Stanley and Sarah Stanton, eds. 2002. *The Cambridge Companion to Shakespeare on Stage*. Cambridge: Cambridge University Press.

Index

K

S

About the Author

Vikram Singh Thakur teaches English Literature in the School of Letters at Ambedkar University Delhi, India. His research interests include postcolonial studies, Shakespeare studies, Indian literature and theatre. Besides being an academic he is also a theatre performer, dramaturg and an occasional poet. His most recent dramaturgical piece *Ba-Ismat* was based on the life and writings of Ismat Chughtai.